INTRODUCTION TO
ANIMAL RIGHTS

Other Temple University Press titles by Gary L. Francione:

Animals, Property, and the Law (1995), Foreword by William M. Kunstler

Rain Without Thunder: The Ideology of the Animal Rights Movement (1996)

Gary L. Francione is also Series Editor of *America in Transition: Radical Perspectives*, by Temple University Press.

INTRODUCTION TO

ANIMAL
RIGHTS

YOUR CHILD OR THE DOG?

Gary L. Francione

Foreword by Alan Watson

 Temple University Press   PHILADELPHIA

Temple University Press, Philadelphia 19122
Copyright © 2000 Temple University
All rights reserved
Published 2000
Reprinted 2007 with corrections
Printed in the United States of America

☉ The paper used in this publication meets the requirements of American National Standard for Information Sciences—Permanence of Paper for Printed Library Materials, ANSI Z39.48–1984

Library of Congress Cataloging-in-Publication Data

Francione, Gary L. (Gary Lawrence), 1954–
   Introduction to animal rights : your child or the dog? / Gary L. Francione ; foreword by Alan Watson.
       p.   cm.
   Includes bibliographical references (p.) and index.
   ISBN 1-56639-691-3 (cloth). —ISBN 1-56639-692-1 (paper)
   1. Animal rights—United States.   2. Animal welfare—United States.   I. Title.
   HV4764.F74   2000
   179′.3—dc21

00-52164
CIP

ISBN 13: 978-1-56639-691-2 (cloth: alk. paper)
ISBN 13: 978-1-56639-692-9 (paper: alk. paper)

Dedication

For Anna, my life partner and closest friend and ally, who, in addition to her other contributions to the quality of my life too numerous to mention, shamelessly manipulated me into rescuing a dog (my first ever) slated to be killed at a local shelter some twenty years ago and thereby started what has evolved into a considerable "pack." My debt to her on so many levels is inestimable.

For Eileen Chamberlain, Cheryl Byer, Gloria Binkowski, and Elisabeth Colville, who for years, quietly and without any expectation of or desire for recognition, have expended the larger share of their emotional and financial resources in caring for the animal refugees of this world, and who have saved so many lives.

For Patty Shenker, who has never stopped being there for us.

And for all of my animal companions, who have taught me so very much about the meaning of morality, and particularly for Bonnie Beale, a little shaggy white dog who was hit by a car that deliberately struck her as she tried to cross a busy street late at night in February 1998. She was dehydrated and starving when we found her. We made a midnight run to Dr. Bruce, who patched her up. She appears to be rather old; she has a crippled leg; she is deaf; she has bad eyesight; and she has a lung tumor that Dr. Ann has caused to go into remission. Bonnie loves to ride in the car, run around the yard, sit in our laps for endless periods of time, and sleep tucked under my chin or on Anna's shoulder. On her vegan diet, especially Amy's home-made biscuits, she has gone from less than nine pounds to over sixteen and she has more character per ounce than just about anyone I have ever met. Her picture is on the cover, and there is absolutely no doubt what-soever in my mind that she is a person, a member of the moral commu-nity who possesses the right not to be treated as a thing. She is a being with inherent value. I love her desperately.

Contents

Foreword by Alan Watson   ix

Acknowledgments   xv

Introduction   xix

1   The Diagnosis: Our Moral Schizophrenia about Animals   1

2   Vivisection: A Trickier Question   31

3   The Cause of Our Moral Schizophrenia: Animals as Property   50

4   The Cure for Our Moral Schizophrenia: The Principle of Equal Consideration   81

5   Robots, Religion, and Rationality   103

6   Having Our Cow and Eating Her Too: Bentham's Mistake   130

7   Animal Rights: Your Child or the Dog?   151

Appendix: Twenty Questions (and Answers)   167

Notes   189

Index   225

Photographs   following page 90

Foreword

OUR POLITICAL AND social history is studded with complacency: to human beings designated as slaves, to people of color, to gays, to women, and to animals. Social revulsion to oppression, when it comes, is often extreme and violent. Even when it is not, it may be swift and driven by an intellectual idea. The struggle has largely, but not finally or totally, been won against slavery; against racial and sexual prejudice; against homophobia. The controversy concerning the human/animal relationship has been ongoing for a good long time but with no resolution in sight. The outlook is, I suggest, about to change. I believe that this refreshingly courageous book by Professor Gary Francione will be a turning point in the way we, as humans, regard animals and how our attitudes translate into the way that we treat them.

Radical changes in human thinking and attitudes are always alarming and painful. Too many of us have a heavy investment in the status quo. We must remember that when the U.S. Declaration of Independence proclaimed that "We hold these truths to be self evident, that all men are created equal, that they are endowed by their Creator with certain inalienable rights, that among these are life, liberty, and the pursuit of happiness," millions of persons within the borders of the new United States were held in slavery. When the political and intellectual leaders gathered to set out the framework of the society that they wished to establish in their independent nation, slavery remained entrenched in the Constitution that they wrote. As the drafters chose the elements that they considered integral to the formation of a just and moral society, the morality of slavery was not seriously challenged. A society organized on the proclamation of the inherent dignity of each person countenanced and profited from a political system that was content to treat some human beings as *things* no different from inanimate objects. Men of high moral character, deep religious conviction, and considerable education and power of reflection were able to overlook this tragic dissonance and deny their fellow human beings standing within the moral community.

When slavery relegated some persons to the status of things, the law could not provide protection that would force a slave owner to respect any interest of his slave if it was in the owner's interest to exploit his slave property. Those who tried to make slavery more "humane" could not protect the slave against the decisions of the slave owner of how best to use his property. Incremental steps to freedom could not be made. We could not "reform" our way out of this situation. Giving slaves "rights" when they were still property was not the answer. Tactical and humanitarian reform was not enough. The situation was remedied by the abolition of slavery only after a bloody conflict.

Gary Francione now throws down the gauntlet concerning our use and treatment of animals. He challenges us to strip away the comfortable excuses provided by our apparent commitment to the "humane" treatment of animals and recognize that, underneath the laws and regulations concerning how we treat the animals with whom we share this planet, we in reality treat animals as things that possess no interests that we must take seriously.

How can this be? Is not the social norm that we must be "kind" to animals one of the few moral imperatives about which we all agree? Francione's book rips off the veil by which the humane ethic obscures how we view animals and deludes us into thinking that we take animal interests seriously. A society that took animal interests seriously would not kill billions of animals for the pleasure of the taste of their flesh when alternative foods are available; would not subject animals to the confinement and suffering inflicted by agribusiness or in scientific experiments; would not countenance the torment of animals in rodeos or circuses for our fleeting entertainment. Francione's trenchant indictment of our exploitation of the very animals we supposedly treat humanely reveals that we would tax our imagination to think of a means of exploiting animals that our humane society does not already permit.

Francione traces the failure of the humane treatment principle to a conceptual flaw in the moral theory that became incorporated into modern anticruelty laws. The humane treatment principle finds its origin in the theory of the nineteenth-century English philosopher and lawyer Jeremy Bentham. Bentham rejected the view that because animals supposedly lack rationality or the ability to communicate using language, humans could treat animals as things and had no moral obligations that they owed directly to them. Bentham maintained that *sentience*, or the ability to experience pain and suffering, was the only characteristic that was required to prove the moral status of animals. In a now famous passage, he wrote that "a full-grown horse or dog is beyond comparison a more rational, as well as a more conversable animal, than an infant of a day, or a week, or even a month, old. But suppose the case were otherwise, what would it avail? the question is not, Can they *reason?* nor, Can they *talk?* but, Can they *suffer?*"

The problem, according to Francione, is that although Bentham rejected human slavery, he never challenged the status of animals as the *property* of humans. As a result, the humane treatment principle, which requires that we "balance" human and animal interests and is thereby intended to treat animal interests as morally significant, was doomed to fail because even under Bentham's supposedly more enlightened view, animals still exist exclusively as the resources of humans. Even under the humane treatment principle, animals are nothing more than things.

Francione insists that we have learned at least one lesson from the abolition of slavery: if a human is to be included in the moral community, it cannot be permissible to treat that person exclusively as a means to the ends of another. One person cannot be the resource of another. If we also purport to take animal interests seriously, we cannot continue to consider animals as a resource to which we owe only humane treatment. Francione argues that there is no way that a "hybrid" system, one that purports to balance the interests of one group whose interests are protected by rights against the interests of another group whose interests are unprotected by rights, can serve to provide any significant protection to the interests of the latter.

The theory presented by Francione is original in that he does not rely on a traditional theory of liberal rights, as does Tom Regan in *The Case for Animal Rights*; nor does he rely on utilitarian theory, as does Peter Singer, who in *Animal Liberation* articulates a theory derived directly from Bentham. Francione demonstrates that the principle of equal consideration, which must be part of any moral theory, whether right-based or consequence-based, or based on the ecofeminist "ethic of care," requires that we reject the use and treatment of animals as resources. Such a requirement would have profound implications for our theory about our moral obligation to animals because *any* theory that rejects the status of animals as things must be committed to the abolition of animal exploitation and not merely to the regulation of animal use to ensure that it is more "humane."

Francione correctly observes, based on the history of property and the economic status of animals as having only that value that is accorded them by humans, that if animals are viewed only as commodities, it is unlikely that there will be significant changes in our treatment of them. But he makes the more profound observation that as long as animals are treated exclusively as means to human ends, their interests must always be dissimilar to human interests. Just as in the case of human slavery, the principle of equal consideration can never apply to animals, because their interests will always be systematically devalued. As a result, animals will, in Bentham's words, "stand degraded into the class of *things*."

According to Francione, the principle that we treat like cases alike prohibits us from treating any sentient being, whether a human or animal, exclusively as a resource. He argues that if animal interests are to have any moral significance, we must extend to them one basic right— the right not to be treated as a thing. We must abolish, and not merely regulate, our exploitation of animals. Francione maintains that our outright rejection of our treatment of animals as things is not quite as radical as it sounds when we consider that we already condemn the infliction of "unnecessary" suffering on animals and that the overwhelming portion of our animal use cannot be described as necessary in any sense. We may prefer human interests over animal interests in situations of genuine conflict or emergency, such as when we pass by a burning house occupied by a human and an animal and have time to save only one, but we must stop generating those conflicts by treating animals as things in the first instance.

The reader who digests the clearly articulated and compelling argument at the core of Francione's book must conclude that our treatment of animals negates our protests that we take their interests seriously. Francione insists that we must establish a new and completely different relationship with other animals, one that would transform our institutions, our industry, and our relationship with our environment.

Confronting uncomfortable truths is not easy. Francione puts the reality of our treatment of animals starkly before us. And he challenges us then to repeat our claim that we take animal interests seriously. When Francione peels back the obscuring comforts of our denial, our justifications for exploiting animals sound as hollow and hypocritical as did our defenses of human slavery. Francione's theory is radical, yet simple in the way that most revolutionary ideas are simple; it is reminiscent of the voice of the slave who proclaimed, "I am a man."

Francione's 1995 book, *Animals, Property, and the Law*, marked the beginning of the legal status of animals as a subject for serious academic study. In that book, Francione presented the definitive analysis of the status of animals as property and framed the discussion that continues to percolate both in classrooms and in the popular media. He followed in 1996 with *Rain Without Thunder: The Ideology of the Animal Rights Movement*, a study of the American animal rights movement in which he argued that the movement by and large rejected the animal rights position and embraced the regulation, and not the abolition, of animal exploitation.

In the present book, Francione provides a theory of animal rights that he derives from our conventional and widely shared moral views. Although he tackles some of the more difficult philosophical problems that inform animal ethics, his presentation is extraordinarily clear and accessible to any reader interested in the topic. It took someone of Francione's penetrating insight, keen intellect, and long practical experience as the nation's leading animal rights lawyer to produce an analysis that is bound to supplant earlier approaches to the human/animal relationship, and to provide a creative and rigorous theoretical basis for redefining that relationship.

There has been much recent attention to the increase in classes on animal rights offered at law schools. There can be no doubt that Francione's teaching, scholarship, and public interest litigation have been responsible for this trend. With his colleague Anna Charlton, Francione has taught animal rights law for over a decade at Rutgers Law School and conducted the only animal rights litigation clinic at any law school in the country. Before that, and while he and I were on the faculty of the University of Pennsylvania Law School, Francione taught animal rights as part of his jurisprudence course. Although others echo his views, Francione's work defines the standard in this area of inquiry.

Those who know me well may be puzzled by this foreword. For most of my adult life, I have been an avid bird hunter and angler. Even today, almost two decades after leaving Scotland, I count the members of my shooting group among my closest friends. I met Gary Francione through my friend, and his teacher, Professor David Yalden-Thomson, with whom I shot duck and geese three days a week in Virginia. But it is years since I have hunted with any seriousness. I go frequently to our farm in South Carolina, intending to fish. But I cannot remember when I actually put my rod into the boat. There was going to be a dove shoot on our farm, organized by a club, and I was asked to attend. I responded that I could not make up my mind. In the end, I did not attend. And I do not think that I will ever shoot birds again. I still eat meat, though less often. I will almost certainly fly-fish for trout again. So I have a conflict. I will not, and cannot, explain. But it is proper to record that I believe that if I had lived in 1850 in conditions similar to those in which I live now—in the South, with my family farm and many acres under cotton—I would not have opposed slavery, though possibly, I hope, I might have had qualms.

Alan Watson
Athens, Georgia
May 1, 2000

Acknowledgments

I OWE MY acknowledgment and gratitude first and foremost to my life partner and colleague at Rutgers Law School, Adjunct Professor Anna E. Charlton. In addition to being an excellent lawyer and teacher, Anna has been a constant part of the discussions that resulted in this book. She was the cofounder and codirector of the Rutgers Animal Rights Law Center. Many of the ideas presented here evolved from a seminar on animals and the law that she and I have taught at Rutgers Law School for the past decade. Indeed, I felt her to be so much a part of the project that I offered her coauthorship. She declined, but I regard this book as hers as much as mine.

I am deeply grateful for the many hours of discussion that I have had with Alan Watson and Drucilla Cornell, and I am honored that Alan Watson saw fit to write a foreword. I also appreciate my discussions with Peter Singer, with whom I generally disagree but who is a most generous and gracious colleague. My colleagues at Rutgers, Alfred Blumrosen, Alex Brooks, and Philip Shuchman, were always available to talk about jurisprudential issues, and I am grateful to them. The Dean of Rutgers Law School, Stuart Deutsch, Associate Dean Ronald K. Chen, Provost Norman Samuels, and former Dean Roger I. Abrams, did everything possible to facilitate my work.

I greatly benefited from discussions with Marc Bekoff, Ted Benton, Gloria Binkowski, Lesli Bisgould, Bill Bratton, Cheryl Byer, Eileen Chamberlain, Elisabeth Colville, Marly

Cornell, James Corrigan, David DeGrazia, Cora Diamond, Jane W. Evans, Ernie Feil, Priscilla Feral, the late José Ferrater Mora, Michael Allen Fox, Henry Furst, Deidre Gallagher, Jane Goldberg, Lori Gruen, Coral Hull, Terry Kay, Arthur Kinoy, the late William M. Kuntsler, Eileen Lanno, Sheldon Leder, Jeffrey Moussaieff Masson, Robert Orabona, Simon Oswitch, Maureen Plimmer, Jerry Silverman, Bonnie Sonder, and Shelton Walden. I presented outlines of the argument in this book at various places, including Rutgers, Brock University, Essex University, Harvard Law School, Manchester University, the University of Scranton, and at the American Philosophical Association, and received terrific feedback.

The students in our seminar at Rutgers on animals and the law have consistently stimulated my thinking about these issues, and I express my gratitude to all of them over the years. My research assistants, Daniel Agatino, Karen Bacon, Steven Flores, Michelle Lerner, Megan Metzelaar, and Lydia Zaidman did a marvelous job. Mr. Flores and Ms. Zaidman deserve special mention for the extraordinary effort they exerted. My secretary, Mary Ann Moore, Assistant Deans Marie Melito and Linda Garbaccio, and our Departmental Administrator, Roseann Raniere, did everything possible to be of assistance, as did our Librarian, Professor Carol Roehrenbeck, and her marvelous staff, including Marjorie Crawford, Dan Campbell, Susanna Camargo-Pohl, Helen Leskovac, Steven Perkins, Nina Ford, Evelyn Ramones, Brian Cudjoe, and Daniel Sanders. Kathleen Rehn and Bernadette Carter saved me from various computer disasters.

Very special thanks to Patty Shenker, Doug Stoll, Bill Crockett, Marly Cornell, Ernie Feil, Priscilla Feral and Robert Orabona of Friends of Animals, Henry Furst, Amy Sperling, Jane Rubin, my friends at the North American Vegetarian Society, and the Neuman-Publicker Foundation, who have all supported my work in various ways. Without Dr. John Kohler's acupuncture treatments, I never would have been able to sit in front of the computer for twelve hours a day. And I appreciate my parents' patience with my infrequent visits while I was writing this book.

Once again, the folks at Temple University Press—Doris Braendel, my editor and good friend, Press Director Lois Patton and her colleagues Charles Ault, David Wilson, Jenny French, Anne Marie Anderson, Gary Kramer, Tamika Hughes, Irene Imperio, Julie Luongo, and freelance copyeditors Keith Monley, Marly Cornell, Joan Vidal, and Megan Metzelaar—provided excellent professional support. I am proud to be an author for one of the few truly progressive and innovative university presses remaining in American academia. Many thanks to Friends of Animals, Animal Emancipation, Inc., Humane Farming Association and Gail A. Eisnitz, Joy Bush, The Fur-Bearers Association, and The American Anti-Vivisection Society for the excellent photographs.

Finally, my nonhuman family—Stratton, Emma, Chelsea, Robert, Stevie, Bonnie Beale, and Simon—have made it clear to me that wondering about whether animals can think, or whether they are self-conscious, or whether they have an emotional range very similar to ours, is on a level with wondering about whether other humans have these characteristics. We may not be able to prove with absolute certainty that animals have these characteristics, just as we cannot prove with certainty that human minds are all alike. But it may come as good news to those who seriously entertain doubts about either matter that the Flat Earth Society accepts new members.

Introduction

Animals: What We Say and What We Do

THERE IS A PROFOUND disparity between what we say we believe about animals, and how we actually treat them. On one hand, we claim to take animal interests seriously. Two-thirds of Americans polled by the Associated Press agree with the following statement: "An animal's right to live free of suffering should be just as important as a person's right to live free of suffering." More than 50 percent of Americans believe that it is wrong to kill animals to make fur coats or to hunt them for sport.[1] Almost 50 percent regard animals to be "just like humans in all important ways."[2] Over 50 percent live with cats or dogs, and approximately 90 percent of those people regard their pets as members of their families[3] and would risk injury or death to save the life of their pet.[4] Americans spend approximately $7 billion annually on veterinary care for dogs and cats[5] and over $20 billion on food and accessories for those and other pets.[6]

These attitudes are reflected in other nations as well. For example, 94 percent of Britons[7] and 88 percent of Spaniards[8] think that animals should be protected from acts of cruelty, and only 14 percent of Europeans support the use of genetic engineering that results in animal suffering, even if the purpose is to create drugs that would save human lives.[9] And every day we read news stories about remarkable efforts by humans to save animals. For example, in 1988, the rescue of three whales trapped under the ice in Alaska necessitated a significant volunteer effort, lasted several weeks, cost approximately $800,000, drew international media attention, and even brought the United States and the Soviet Union together in an effort to save the animals.[10]

On the other hand, our actual treatment of animals stands in stark contrast to our proclamations about our regard for their moral status. We subject billions of animals annually to enormous amounts of pain, suffering, and distress. According to the U.S. Department of Agriculture, we kill more than 8 billion animals a year for food, including approximately 37 million cows and calves, 102 million hogs, almost 4 million sheep and lambs, 7.9 billion chickens, 290 million turkeys, and 22 million ducks.[11] We slaughter more than 100,000 horses per year.[12] Every day, we slaughter approximately 23 million animals, or over 950,000 per hour, or almost 16,000 per minute, or over 260 every second. This is to say nothing of the billions more killed worldwide. These animals are raised under horrendous conditions, mutilated in various ways without pain relief, transported long distances in cramped, filthy containers, and finally slaughtered amid the stench, noise, and squalor of the abattoir. We kill billions of fish and other sea animals annually. We catch them with hooks and allow them to suffocate in nets. We buy lobsters at the supermarket, where they are kept for weeks in crowded tanks with their claws closed by rubber bands and without receiving any food, and we cook them alive in boiling water.

Hunters kill approximately 200 million animals in the United States annually; this figure includes 50 million mourning doves, 25 million squirrels and rabbits, 25 million quail, 20 million pheasants, 10 million ducks, 4 million deer, 2 million geese, 150,000 elk, and 21,000 bears.[13] In addition, hunters kill hundreds of thousands of antelope, swans, cougars, turkeys, raccoons, skunk, wolves, foxes, coyotes, bobcats, boars, and other animals. These numbers do not include animals killed on commercial game ranches or at events such as pigeon shoots. Moreover, hunters often cripple animals without killing or retrieving them. It is estimated, for example, that bow hunters do not retrieve 50 percent of the animals hit with their arrows.[14] This increases the true death toll from hunting by at least tens of millions of uncounted animals. The animals who are wounded often die slowly, over a period of hours or even days, from blood loss, punctured intestines and stomachs, and severe infections. Many animals have been hunted to the point of extinction.

In the United States alone, we use millions of animals annually for biomedical experiments, product testing, and education. These animals are used to measure the effects of toxins, diseases, drugs, radiation, bullets, and all forms of physical and psychological deprivations. Animals are burned, poisoned, irradiated, blinded, starved, given electric shocks and diseases (such as cancer) and infections (such as pneumonia), deprived of sleep, kept in solitary confinement, subjected to the removal of limbs and eyes, addicted to drugs, forced to withdraw from drug addiction, and caged for the duration of their lives. The animals who do not die during experimental procedures are almost always killed immediately afterward or are recycled for other experiments or tests until they are finally killed. And all of this, we are told, is for the purpose of improving human health and curing human disease.

Millions of animals are used for the sole purpose of providing entertainment. Animal "actors" are used in film and television. There are thousands of zoos, circuses, carnivals, horse and dog race tracks, marine-mammal shows, and rodeos in the United States, and these and similar activities, such as bullfighting, also take place in other countries. Animals used in entertainment are often forced to endure lifelong incarceration and confinement, poor living conditions, extreme physical danger and hardship, and brutal treatment. Most animals used for entertainment purposes are killed when no longer useful, or sold into research or as targets for shooting on commercial hunting preserves.

And we kill millions of animals annually simply for fashion. Approximately 40 million animals worldwide are trapped, snared, or raised in intensive confinement on fur farms, where they are electrocuted or gassed or have their necks broken. In the United States, 8 to 10 million mink, rabbits, foxes, coyotes, chinchillas, beavers, sables, racoons, and other animals are killed every year for fur.

In short, we may be said to suffer from a sort of "moral schizophrenia" when it comes to our thinking about animals. We claim to regard animals as having morally significant interests, but we treat them in ways that belie our claims.

Our Conventional Wisdom: We Can Prefer Humans But Only When "Necessary"

In this book, we are going to explore the matter of the moral status of animals in an effort to try to understand the disparity that exists between what we say about animals and how we actually treat them. A good starting point is to ask whether there is any conventional wisdom on the subject—any generally accepted intuitions or positions on the moral status of animals that can serve as a focus for our inquiry.

I think that most of us would agree that our moral thinking about animals is informed by two intuitions, both of which involve the concept of *necessity*.

Intuition 1: We Can Prefer Humans in Situations of "Necessity"

We do not think of animals as being "the same" as we are. Most of us share the view that in situations of true conflict between human and animal interests, or in some emergency that requires us to make a choice between a human and an animal—that is, when it is *necessary* to do so—we ought to prefer the interests of a human over the interests of an animal.

Imagine the following situation: you arrive home and find your house burning. There are two occupants alive inside the burning structure, your child and your dog. You are the only person in the vicinity of the burning house. The fire is burning so furiously that you have time to rescue either your child or your dog but not both. Which do you choose? The answer is simple. You save your child. But this is an unfair hypothetical. After all, most of us would save our own child even if the other being in the burning house were someone else's child, or Mother Teresa, or some other human whom we valued. Indeed, if we are willing to be honest about it, most of us would choose to save our own child over a dozen other people's children.

Let us vary the hypothetical somewhat. Imagine that the two occupants of the burning house are a dog and a human being, neither of whom is known to you. Which do you save? Again, the answer is simple: your moral intuition would tell you that you ought to prefer the human over the animal. If, however, the dog is a member of your family, a being with whom you have a relationship, and the human is unknown to you, the pull of this moral intuition may be weaker. And it may be weaker still, whether you know the dog or not, if the human in question is Adolf Hitler or Charles Manson. In any event, in most emergency situations—at least in the abstract—we regard it as morally preferable to choose the human over the animal.

Intuition 2: It Is Wrong to Inflict "Unnecessary" Suffering on Animals

Although we may prefer humans to animals in situations of true emergency or conflict, we also recognize that like us, and unlike plants and stones, animals (or at least many of them) are *sentient*—they are the sorts of beings who are conscious and can have subjective experiences of pain and suffering.[15] Like us, sentient nonhumans have an *interest* in not experiencing pain and suffering; that is, they are the sorts of beings who prefer, or desire, or want not to suffer pain. Animals may have other interests as well, but as long as they are sentient, we know that at the very least they have an interest in avoiding pain and suffering. We regard such an interest as morally significant and we accept that we ought not to inflict any *unnecessary* suffering on animals.

The Humane Treatment Principle: A Prohibition against "Unnecessary" Animal Suffering

These two intuitions that encompass our conventional wisdom about animals are represented in the *humane treatment principle*, which has been an entrenched and uncontroversial part of our culture since the nineteenth century. The humane treatment principle holds that we may prefer human interests over animal interests, but that we may do so only when it is necessary and that we therefore ought not to inflict unnecessary suffering on animals. The humane treatment principle is not only a moral rule but a legal rule as well: *animal welfare laws* purport to prohibit us from inflicting unnecessary suffering on animals. Moreover, our reason for prohibiting unnecessary animal suffering is not only that inflicting such suffering will make us act less kindly toward each other, but that we believe that it is a wrong to the animals themselves.

In order to determine whether a particular animal use or treatment is necessary under the humane treatment principle, we must balance animal interests and human interests. If the balance tips in favor of humans—if human interests in inflicting harm on an animal are stronger than the animal's interests in not being made to suffer—we consider that the use or treatment is morally justified because it is necessary. If the balance tips in favor of animals, then the infliction of harm is not morally justified because it is considered unnecessary. This balancing of interests is certainly not a precise operation, and we may very well disagree in our assessments of the relative weight of competing human and animal interests in particular cases, as well as about what constitutes necessary suffering. But whatever differences we may otherwise have, we *must* agree that if the prohibition against unnecessary suffering is to have any meaning at all, it is morally and legally wrong to inflict suffering on animals merely for our amusement or pleasure. We must agree that there are some meaningful limits on our use and treatment of animals.

The Problem: We Do Not Practice What We Preach

Although we claim that we may prefer humans to animals when necessary but that it is wrong to impose unnecessary suffering on them, the fact is that the overwhelming portion of our animal use can be justified *only* by habit, convention, amusement, convenience, or pleasure. To put the matter another way, most of the suffering that we impose on animals is completely unnecessary *however* we interpret that notion.

For example, the uses of animals in entertainment, such as in films, circuses, rodeos, and for sport hunting, cannot, by definition, be considered necessary. Nevertheless, these activities are all protected by laws that supposedly prohibit the infliction of unnecessary suffering on animals. It is certainly not necessary for us to wear fur coats, or to use animals to test duplicative household products, or to have yet another brand of lipstick or aftershave lotion. More important in terms of numbers of animals used, however, is the animal agriculture industry, in which more than 8 billion animals are killed for food annually in the United States alone. As we will see in Chapter 1, it is not necessary in any sense to eat meat or animal products: indeed, an increasing number of health care professionals maintain that animal products may be detrimental to human health. Moreover, respected environmental scientists have pointed out the tremendous costs to our planet of meat-based agriculture. In any event, our best justification for the enormous pain, suffering, and death inflicted on these billions of farm animals is that we enjoy the taste of their flesh. And although many of us regard the use of animals in experiments, product testing, and science education as presenting the classic "burning house" choice of us vs. them, the necessity of animal use for these purposes is open to serious question as well.

Animals as Property: An Unbalanced Balance

The reason for the profound inconsistency between what we say about animals and how we actually treat them is the status of animals as our *property*.[16] Animals are commodities that we own and that have no value other than that which we as property owners choose to give them. The property status of animals renders completely meaningless any balancing that is supposedly required under the humane treatment principle or animal welfare laws, because what we really balance are the interests of property owners against the interests of their animal property. It does not take much knowledge of property law or economics to recognize that such a balance will rarely, if ever, tip in the animal's favor. If someone suggested that you balance your interests against those of your automobile or your wristwatch, you would quite correctly regard the suggestion as absurd. Your automobile and your watch are your property. They have no morally significant interests; they are merely *things* that have no value except that which you, the owner, accord to them. Because animals are merely property, we are generally permitted to ignore their interests and to inflict the most horrendous pain and suffering or death on them when it is economically beneficial to us.

We say that we can prefer animal interests over human interests but only when necessary to do so, but it is *always* necessary to decide against animals in order to protect human property rights in animals. We are allowed to interpret necessary suffering as *any* suffering needed to use our animal property for a particular purpose—even if that purpose is our mere convenience or pleasure. We treat *every* human/animal interaction as analogous to the burning house conflict. The human property interest will almost always prevail. The animal in question is always a "pet" or a "laboratory" animal, or a "game" animal, or a "food" animal, or a "rodeo" animal, or some other form of animal property that exists solely for our use and has no value except as a means to *our* ends. There is really no choice to be made between the human and the animal interest because the choice has already been predetermined by the property status of the animal.

The Solution: Taking Animal Interests Seriously

If we want to take animal interests seriously and give content to our professed rejection of the infliction of unnecessary suffering on animals, we can do so in only one way: by applying *the principle of equal consideration*, or the rule that we must treat likes alike, to animals. There is nothing exotic or particularly complicated about the principle of equal consideration. Indeed, this principle is part of every moral theory and, like the humane treatment principle, is one that most of us already accept in our everyday thinking about moral issues. Applying the principle of equal consideration to animals does not mean that we are committed to the view that animals are the "same" as humans (whatever that means), or that animals are our "equals" in all respects. It means only that if humans and animals do have a similar interest, we must treat that interest in the same way unless there is a good reason for not doing so. Our conventional wisdom about animals is that they *are* similar to us in at least one way: they are sentient and they are the sorts of beings who, like us, have an interest in not suffering. In this sense, we are similar to each other and dissimilar to *everything* else in the universe that is not sentient.

We do not and cannot protect humans from all suffering, but we at least claim to protect all humans—whether young or old, brilliant or dull, rich or poor—from suffering *at all* as the result of being used exclusively as the resource of another. Although we may tolerate varying degrees and types of human exploitation, we draw a line. We do not regard it as morally permissible to treat any humans as the property of other humans; we do not regard it as morally permissible to treat any humans exclusively as means to the ends of other humans. Indeed, we protect the interest of humans in not being the property of others with a mechanism called a *right*. In particular, we regard every human as the holder of what we call a *basic right* not to be the property of another. Animals and humans are similar in that they are sentient. If animal interests in not suffering are to be morally significant, then we must apply the principle of equal consideration and extend to animals a basic right not to be treated as things, as our property, unless there is a morally sound reason to do otherwise. We must recognize that animals, like humans, have a morally significant interest in not suffering *at all* from being used as resources.

Since this is a book about animal rights, we may do well to take a brief digression at this point to explore the concept of rights as a general matter, the concept of a basic right, and what we mean by saying that the principle of equal consideration requires that we recognize that animals have a right not to be treated exclusively as human resources.

The Concept of Rights

There is a great deal of confusion surrounding the concept of rights. For our purposes, we need focus on only one aspect of the concept of a right that is common to virtually all theories about rights: a right is a particular way of protecting interests. To say that an interest is protected by a right is to say that the interest is protected against being ignored or violated simply because this will benefit someone else. We can think of a right of any sort as a fence or a wall that surrounds an interest and upon which hangs a "no trespass" sign that forbids entry, even if it would be beneficial to the person seeking that entry. As one writer describes it, rights are "moral notions that grow out of respect for the individual. They build protective fences around the individual. They establish areas where the individual is entitled to be protected against the state and the majority *even where a price is paid by the general welfare.*"[17]

For example, our right of free speech protects our interest in self-expression even if other people do not value that expression and would stifle our expression merely because it would benefit them. Rights, however, are not absolute in the sense that their protection has no exception. For example, my right of free speech does not protect my falsely shouting "fire" in a crowded movie theater or my making false and defamatory statements about another. In those cases, my interest in speech is not protected, but in neither case is any attempt made to censor the content of my speech merely because others disagree with me.

Just so, a right of liberty protects our interest in our freedom regardless of the value that others attach to that interest. If other people think I should be imprisoned for no other reason than that my imprisonment will benefit them, my right will prevent such treatment. Again, however, my right is not absolute. If I am convicted by a jury of my peers of committing a crime, then I can be made to forfeit my liberty. But my interest in my liberty will be protected against being taken away from me because other people value my interest in a different way.

Similarly, a right to own property protects our interest in owning things—our interest in using, selling, disposing of, and valuing those things—even if others would benefit from a disregard of that interest. Property rights, like other rights, again are not absolute; we cannot use our property in a way that injures or harms others. And sometimes the state may take property, though in such cases it is generally required to provide compensation to the owner.

The Basic Right Not to Be Treated as a Thing

We recognize that among humans there is a wide range of interests in that almost no two humans prefer or want or desire exactly the same things. Some humans prefer *La Bohème*; others prefer Pink Floyd. Some humans have an interest in obtaining a university education; others prefer to learn a trade; still others have no interest in either. But all humans who are not brain dead or otherwise nonsentient have an interest in avoiding pain and suffering.

Although we do not protect humans from all suffering, and although we may not even agree about which human interests should be pro tected by rights, we generally agree that *all* humans should be protected from suffering that results from being used as the property or commodity of another human. We do not regard it as legitimate to treat *any* humans, irrespective of their particular characteristics, as the property of other humans. Indeed, in a world deeply divided on many moral issues, one of the few norms endorsed by the international community is the prohibition of human slavery. Nor is it a matter of whether the particular form of slavery is "humane" or not; we condemn all human slavery. It would, of course, be incorrect to say that human slavery has been eliminated entirely from the planet, but the institution is universally regarded as morally odious and is legally prohibited. We protect the interest of a human in not being the property of others with a right, which is to say that we do not allow this interest to be ignored or abrogated simply because it will benefit someone else to do so. The right not to be treated as the property of others is *basic* in that it is different from any other rights we might have because it is the grounding for those other rights; it is a precondition for the possession of morally significant interests. If we do not recognize that a human has the right not to be treated exclusively as a means to the end of another, then any other right that we may grant her, such as a right of free speech, or of liberty, or to vote or own property, is completely meaningless.[18] To put the matter more simply, if I can enslave you and kill you at will, then any other right you may have will not be of much use to you. We may not agree about what other rights humans have, but in order for humans to have any rights at all, they must have the basic right not to be treated as things.

Animal Rights

The principle of equal consideration requires that we treat similar interests in a similar way unless there is a morally sound reason for not doing so. Is there a morally sound reason that justifies our giving all humans a basic right not to be the property of others while denying this same right to all animals and treating them merely as our resources?

The usual response is to claim that some empirical difference between humans and animals justifies this dissimilar treatment. For example, we maintain that animals cannot think rationally or abstractly, so it is acceptable for us to treat them as our property. In the first place, it is as difficult to deny that many animals are capable of rational or abstract thought as it is to deny that dogs have tails. But even if it were true that animals are not rational or cannot think in abstract ways, what possible difference could that make as a moral matter? Many humans, such as young children or severely retarded humans, cannot think rationally or in abstract terms, and we would never think of using such humans as subjects in painful biomedical experiments, or as sources of food or clothing. Despite what we say, we treat similar animal interests in a dissimilar way and thus deprive animal interests of moral significance.

There is no characteristic that serves to distinguish humans from all other animals. Whatever attribute we may think makes all humans "special" and thereby different from other animals is shared by some group of nonhumans. Whatever "defect" we may think makes animals inferior to us is shared by some group of us. In the end, the only difference between them and us is species, and species alone is not a morally relevant criterion for excluding animals from the moral community any more than is race a justification for human slavery or sex a justification for making women the property of their husbands. The use of species to justify the property status of animals is *speciesism* just as the use of race or sex to justify the property status of humans is racism or sexism.[19] If we want animal interests to have moral significance, then we have to treat like cases alike, and we cannot treat animals in ways in which we would not be willing to treat any human.

If we apply the principle of equal consideration to animals, then we must extend to animals the one basic right that we extend to all human beings: the right not to be treated as things. But just as our recognition that no humans should be the property of others required that we *abolish* slavery and not merely *regulate* it to be more "humane," our recognition that animals have this one basic right would mean that we could no longer justify our institutional exploitation of animals for food, clothing, amusement, or experiments. If we mean what we say and regard animals as having morally significant interests, then we really have no choice: we are similarly committed to the abolition of animal exploitation, and not merely to its regulation.

The position that I am proposing in this book is radical in the sense that it would force us to stop using animals in many of the ways that we now take for granted. In another sense, however, my argument is quite conservative in that it follows from a moral principle that we already claim to accept—that it is wrong to impose unnecessary suffering on animals. If the interest of animals in not suffering is truly a morally significant interest, and if animals are not merely things that are morally indistinguishable from inanimate objects, then we *must* interpret the prohibition against unnecessary animal suffering in a way similar to the way that we interpret the prohibition against unnecessary human suffering. In both cases, suffering cannot be justified because it facilitates the amusement, convenience, or pleasure of others. Humans and animals ought to be protected from suffering at all as the result of their use as the property or resources of others.

What about the Burning House?

Even if we would prefer the life of the human over the life of the animal in situations of true emergency or conflict, this tells us little about the majority of real-world situations in which we must assess our moral obligations to animals. In an overwhelming number of such instances, there is no true conflict or emergency. We manufacture those conflicts and emergencies by begging the question from the outset and treating animals as our property.

If we take animal interests seriously, this does not mean that we cannot prefer humans over animals in situations of true emergencies or conflicts. It does mean that we can no longer create those conflicts by ignoring the principle of equal consideration and by interpreting "unnecessary suffering" in a different way for animals than we do for humans. There may, of course, be situations in which we are confronted with a true emergency, such as the burning house that contains the dog and the child, where we have time to save only one. Even if we would always choose to save the human over the dog in such situations, that does not mean that animals are nothing but resources that we may use for our purposes. That would not be the conclusion we would draw if we made a choice between two humans. Imagine that two humans are in the burning house. One human is a young child; the other is a very old adult, who, barring the present conflagration, will soon die of natural causes anyway. You decide to save the young person for the simple reason that she has not yet lived her life. Would you then conclude that it is morally acceptable to enslave very old people? Or use them as forced organ donors or as unconsenting subjects in biomedical experiments? Surely not.

Similarly, assume that a wild animal is just about to attack my friend Fred. My choice to kill the animal in order to save Fred's life does not mean that it is morally acceptable to kill animals for food, any more than my moral justification in killing a deranged human who threatened to kill Fred would serve to justify my using deranged humans as unconsenting subjects in biomedical experiments.

In short, we may decide to choose the human over the animal in cases of true emergency—when it is necessary to do so—but that does not mean that we are justified in treating animals as resources for human use. And if the treatment of animals as resources cannot be justified, then the institutionalized exploitation of animals must be abolished.

Confusion about Animal Ethics

There is a great deal of confusion surrounding the public discourse on the moral status of animals. This confusion stems from two sources. First, it is thought by some that the animal rights position advocates that we accord to animals the same rights enjoyed by human beings. This is a misunderstanding of the animal rights position. I am not arguing that our recognition of the moral status of animals means that we are committed to treating animals and humans the same for all purposes, or that we must give animals a right to vote, or a right to own property, or a right to an education. My position is simple: we are obligated to extend to animals only *one* right—the right not to be treated as the property of humans.

Second, animal protection organizations, particularly in the United States, use the expression "animal rights" indiscriminately to describe any position, including purely regulatory or animal welfare measures, that is thought to reduce animal suffering. For example, a proposal to increase the size of cages used to hold laying hens assumes the legitimacy of treating animals as property; it is aimed at regulating our ownership of animals. A proposal that we abolish the egg industry altogether as a violation of the basic right of animals not to be used as our resources is an animal rights position. Yet animal protection organizations label both positions as advancing animal rights. Some animal advocates support such regulatory measures as means of eventually achieving the abolition of particular animal uses. There is, however, no empirical evidence that the regulation of animal exploitation leads to the abolition of exploitation.[20]

Earlier Approaches

In the past twenty-five years, much has been written about the moral status of nonhuman animals and the nature and extent of human obligations to animals.[21] There are, however, two approaches that have become prominent: the position advocated by Australian philosopher

Peter Singer in *Animal Liberation*[22] and that of American philosopher Tom Regan in *The Case for Animal Rights*.[23] The argument that I present in this book is significantly different from either of these earlier approaches.

In *Animal Liberation*, Singer rejects speciesism and purports to endorse the view that we ought to apply the principle of equal consideration to the interests of all sentient animals. But Singer does not believe that the moral significance of animal interests requires that we abolish the property status of animals or the institutions of animal exploitation that assume that animals are our resources. He maintains that we may continue to use animals for human purposes, but that we must give greater consideration to animal interests than is presently accorded to them. I will discuss Singer's views in greater detail in Chapter 6. For the moment, it is important to understand that the position argued for in this book is that applying the principle of equal consideration to animals (which is imperative if animal interests are to have moral significance) *requires* that we abolish the property status of animals. A fundamental tenet of the principle of equal consideration is "each to count for one and none for more than one." We have recognized that human slavery is morally impermissible precisely because it deprives humans of the benefit of the principle of equal consideration—the interests of slave owners will never be judged as similar to those of slaves. Slaves will always count for *less* than one. The same is true for animals: as long as animals are property, their interests will always count for *less* than one because the interests of property will never be judged as similar to the interests of property owners.

In *The Case for Animal Rights*, Tom Regan argues that animals have moral rights and that irrespective of consequences we ought to abolish and not merely regulate animal exploitation. Regan's theory does not extend to all sentient creatures but only to those he regards as being "subjects-of-a-life," who "have beliefs and desires; perception, memory, and a sense of the future, including their own future; an emotional life together with feelings of pleasure and pain; preference- and welfare-interests; the ability to initiate action in pursuit of their desires and goals; a psychophysical identity over time; and an individual welfare in the sense that their experiential life fares well or ill for them, logically independently of their utility for others and logically independently of their being the object of anyone else's interests."[24] Regan argues that all normal mammals, aged one year or more, qualify as subjects-of-a-life.[25]

Although I accept Regan's conclusion that animals possess rights and that our recognition of their status as right holders requires that we abolish and not merely regulate our institutional exploitation of them, the argument that I present differs from Regan's in at least four ways. First, I see no reason to restrict the class of protected animals to those that Regan describes as "subjects-of-a-life." Some animals and some humans may lack "the ability to initiate action in pursuit of their desires and goals" and they may have a most elementary "sense of the future" or "psychophysical identity over time," but if they are sentient, they nevertheless have an interest in not suffering or experiencing pain, and therefore they can be said to possesses an "experiential life [that] fares well or ill for them, logically independently of their utility for others and logically independently of their being the object of anyone else's interests." Although it is easier to identify the constellation of qualities that Regan describes as present in normally developed mammals of a particular age, there is no doubt that chickens and other birds are intelligent, sentient beings with an experiential life. And although most of us do not even think of fish as conscious of pain, researchers have concluded that fish "have subjective experiences and so are liable to suffer."[26]

Second, Regan argues that all "subjects-of-a-life" are equal in that they all have the same level of moral value despite any other characteristics they may have. So, for example, if a human and a dog both qualify as "subjects-of-a-life," it is morally impermissible to use either exclusively as a means to an end. However, Regan seems also to assume as a fact that animals are cognitively inferior to humans and that death is therefore a greater harm to humans than it is to animals. This leads Regan to the conclusion that in a situation involving true emergency, we are not only obligated to save the human over the animal but that we are obligated to choose to save one human over a million dogs.[27] In addition to my view that sentience alone and not the other qualities of a subject-of-a-life suffices for moral significance, I do not share Regan's position that it is some sort of empirical fact that death is a greater harm to humans than to animals, or that we are obligated to save one human over a million dogs. In situations of true emergency, we may be justified in saving the human over the animal, but we also may be justified in saving the animal over the human.[28]

Third, my argument, unlike Regan's, focuses on the legal status of animals as property. I argue that as long as animals are regarded as property, they will be treated as things without moral status and without morally significant interests. I argue that animals have only one right—a right not to be treated as property or resources.

Fourth, and most important, I argue that the basic right not to be treated as property may be derived directly from the principle of equal consideration and does not require the complicated rights theory upon which Regan relies. Indeed, it is my view that the requirement that we abolish animal exploitation must be part of *any* theory that purports to accord moral significance to animals. If we really believe that animals are not merely things and that they have morally significant interests, then whether we otherwise endorse rights theory or not, we are committed to the view that we can no longer treat animals as our resources. That does not mean that we cannot favor humans in situations of true emergency or conflict, but we cannot manufacture these situations of conflict through a moral structure that assumes that animals are nothing but resources for humans.

In sum, I argue that Regan and Singer ought to come to the same conclusion—that the moral status of animals necessarily precludes their use as human property—and that this conclusion relies only on our application of the principle of equal consideration to animal interests in avoiding pain and suffering.

A Word about "Proving" Moral Matters

Human treatment of animals is first and foremost a moral issue; it concerns how humans *ought* to behave toward animals. The relevant question is whether there are any moral limits on how we use and treat other animals and, if so, what those limits are and how we should ascertain them.

As a general matter, we cannot prove moral matters in the same way that we can, say, prove that two plus two equals four. The proposition "two plus two equals four" is self-evident—it is true by virtue of the very meaning of the terms that are used. Anyone who understands the meaning of the word "two" and the concept of addition must conclude that "two plus two equals four" is true and that "two plus two equals five" is false.

Most moral matters do not lend themselves to the certainty that we can have about mathematics. We cannot have mathematical certainty about our moral views—whatever they may be—concerning capital punishment, affirmative action, abortion, or animal rights. We may have compelling arguments that support our moral views, but we cannot say that those views are indisputably true and certain in the way that "two plus two equals four" is indisputably true and certain.

The fact that matters of morality are different from matters of mathematics leads some people to believe that moral views are no different from our opinions about what flowers or paintings, baseball team or musical group we like, and that no moral view can claim to be preferable to another. These beliefs are reflected by those who maintain that racist or sexist attitudes or language are simply matters of "political correctness." That is, they maintain that whether racism and sexism are morally wrong or right depends on shifting political and social conceptions and are ultimately subjective matters of convention, and that there is no absolute, objective moral "truth" about racism or sexism.

Such a view does not follow from the fact that we cannot achieve certainty in morality in the same way that we can in mathematics. Moral judgments may not be certain in the same way that mathematical statements are, but moral judgments do not require such certainty in order to be persuasive and compelling. If one moral view is supported by better reasons than others, then that moral view is presumably the one we should adopt—until some other moral position with even better reasons in its support comes along. If an argument in favor of a moral position is valid—that is, the conclusion of the argument follows from the premises in such a way that if the premises were true, the conclusion must also be true—then any such argument should be accepted over an argument in which there is no such relationship between the premises and conclusion. If a moral position "fits" more comfortably with other considered moral positions that we hold, then we ought to accept that moral position over another that does not so fit. For example, we may not be able to prove moral propositions in the way that we can prove that two plus two equals four, but we can offer many compelling reasons why we ought to condemn the Holocaust as a blatantly immoral event, and we can offer no reasons to regard such an event as morally justifiable. Moral condemnation of the Holocaust also fits with our considered judgment that intentionally killing innocent humans is morally wrong. But could we "prove" that the Holocaust was immoral to, say, a Nazi or some other brand of white supremacist who believes that Jews (or any other group) are inferior and may be treated solely as means to the end of whatever group serves as the "master" class? No, we could not. That does not mean, however, that the immorality of the Holocaust is a matter of opinion.

In this book, I will argue that the animal rights position, which maintains that we ought to abolish and not merely regulate animal use, is supported by sound reasons and valid arguments. And although I do not purport to be able to prove that the animal rights position is true in the same way that a mathematical proposition is true, I will argue that the position I defend fits comfortably with the two intuitions that reflect our conventional wisdom about the moral status of animals: that we may prefer humans over animals in situations of true emergency or necessity and that we ought not to inflict unnecessary suffering on animals. That is, the animal rights position can explain both of those intuitions and can unify them, thus achieving a "reflective equilibrium" between a theory about the moral status of animals and our common sense or conventional wisdom about the moral status of animals.[29] That is the best that we can hope to achieve when we are talking about moral matters and not mathematics.

Animal Minds

One issue that I am not going to explore in detail in this book is whether animals possess minds or are capable of cognitive activity. For many years now, philosophers have been debating whether animals have minds at all and, if so, whether we can know anything about what goes in their minds. Although this theoretical debate may be of interest to some, we will not dwell on it to any considerable degree except when we come to consider the view, held by some in the seventeenth century and retained by a few diehards today, that animals have no minds or interests at all. We must consider this position because if it is true, then animals would be no different from stones or car engines and we would not need to be concerned, as a moral matter, about their use and treatment. We will also consider differences between human and animal minds that have been offered as justifications for excluding animals from the moral community. But apart from these inquiries, I will assume that all sentient animals, all animals that are conscious of pain, have minds and are capable of cognitive activity.

To deny that animals are conscious of pain, or to assert that we cannot know whether animals feel pain, is as absurd as to deny that other humans are conscious of pain or to assert that we cannot know whether other humans feel pain. The neurological and physiological similarities between humans and nonhumans render the fact of animal sentience noncontroversial. Even mainstream science accepts that animals are sentient. For example, the U.S. Public Health Service states that "[u]nless the contrary is established, investigators should consider that procedures that cause pain or distress in human beings may cause pain or distress in other animals."[30] And scientists use animals in pain experiments, which would, of course, be useless if animals did not experience pain, and in a way that is substantially similar to the way that we feel pain. Indeed, in 1992, the National Research Council published a book entitled *Recognition and Alleviation of Pain and Distress in Laboratory Animals*, in which it acknowledged that animals used in experiments "will be subjected to conditions that cause them pain and distress."[31] In short, virtually *no one* any longer questions whether animals feel pain and distress.[32]

Although the matter may befuddle some academic philosophers, the rest of us accept that many animals, such as dogs, cats, primates, cows, pigs, rodents, chickens, fish, and so forth are sentient; that is precisely why we all accept a moral rule that it is wrong to impose unnecessary suffering on animals. If animals were indifferent to pain, we would not have a humane treatment principle in the first place. To be sentient *means* to be the sort of being who has subjective experiences of pain (and pleasure) and to have interests in not experiencing that pain (or in experiencing pleasure). Most of the animals that we use for food, experiments, entertainment, and clothing unquestionably have such subjective experiences. And it is those subjective experiences that distinguish animals—human and nonhuman—from rocks and plants, and that make nonhuman animals a subject of our moral concern in the first place.

But then the observation that animals possess minds is not exactly new. For example, the French essayist Michel E. de Montaigne wrote in 1592 "that there is no reason to image that the beasts do, through a natural and enforced instinct, the same things that we do by choice and skill. From like results we must infer like faculties (and from more abundant results, more abundant faculties); and we must consequently confess that the same reason, the same methods, that we employ in working are also employed by the animals (if not some other and better ones)."[33] The existence of animal minds is recognized explicitly in the evolutionary theory of Charles Darwin and in the writings of particular scientists and philosophers stretching back to ancient Greece.[34]

An Outline of the Book

In Chapters 1 and 2, we will explore what I call our "moral schizophrenia" about animals. We all claim to accept the humane treatment principle and to agree that inflicting unnecessary suffering on animals is morally wrong. Nevertheless, the overwhelming portion of our animal use cannot be described as necessary in any coherent or meaningful sense.

In Chapter 3, we will see that the reason for our schizophrenia is related to the status of animals as property. As long as we regard animals as things that we own and they have only that value which we accord them, animal suffering will almost always be considered necessary as long as it provides some benefit for us as property owners.

In Chapter 4, we will explore the cure for our moral schizophrenia: the application of the principle of equal consideration, which requires that we extend to animals the basic right not to be treated as human property and that we abolish animal exploitation. In Chapter 5, we will consider whether there are any sound moral reasons that would justify our not extending this basic right to animals.

In Chapter 6, we will consider as a historical matter how the humane treatment principle went wrong and why we thought that we could treat animals as having moral status while at the same time we continued to use them as our resources.

In Chapter 7, we will discuss whether we can preserve our intuition that we may prefer humans in situations of true emergency or conflict while at the same time we accept the position that all sentient nonhumans possess a basic right not to be treated as things and that we may not use animals as our resources.

In the Appendix, I will discuss twenty commonly asked questions about animal rights, and I will endeavor to provide answers to those questions.

1

The Diagnosis: Our Moral Schizophrenia about Animals

OUR MORAL ATTITUDES about animals are, to say the very least, schizophrenic. On the one hand, we all agree that it is morally wrong to impose unnecessary suffering on animals. On the other hand, the overwhelming amount of suffering that we do impose on animals cannot be regarded as analogous to our choice to save the human being in the burning house or, indeed, as necessary in any meaningful sense of the word.

In this chapter, we will explore the disparity between what we say about animals and how we actually treat them. First, we will examine the moral status of animals before the nineteenth century. Second, we will see how the status of animals supposedly changed with the moral and legal acceptance of the humane treatment principle, that is, the notion that we have a moral obligation not to impose "unnecessary" suffering on animals. Third, we will see that there is a very great disparity between what we say we believe about the moral status of animals and how we actually treat them.

Animals as Things

Before the nineteenth century, Western culture did not as a general matter recognize that human beings had any moral obligations to animals. Animals did not matter morally at all and were considered to be completely outside the moral community. We could have moral obligations that concerned

1

animals, but these obligations were really owed to other humans and not to animals at all. Animals were regarded as *things*, as having a moral status no different from that of inanimate objects such as stones or clocks.

As late as the seventeenth century, the view was advanced that animals are nothing more than robots, with no ability to think or feel. For example, René Descartes (1596–1650), considered the founder of modern philosophy, maintained that animals are not conscious—they have no mind whatsoever—because they do not possess a soul, which God invested only in human beings. In support of the idea that animals lack consciousness, Descartes argued that they do not use verbal or sign language—something that every human being does but that no animal does. Descartes certainly recognized that animals act in what appear to be purposive and intelligent ways and that they seem to be conscious, but he claimed that they are really no different from machines made by God. Indeed, he referred to animals as "automatons, or moving machines."[1] Moreover, just as a clock can tell time better than human beings can, so some animal machines can perform some tasks better than humans can.

An obvious implication of Descartes's position—and one that he readily accepted—was that animals are not sentient; they are not conscious of pain, pleasure, or anything else.[2] Descartes and his followers performed experiments in which they nailed animals by their paws onto boards and cut them open to reveal their beating hearts. They burned, scalded, and mutilated animals in every conceivable manner. When the animals reacted as though they were suffering pain, Descartes dismissed the reaction as no different from the sound of a machine that was functioning improperly. A crying dog, Descartes maintained, is no different from a whining gear that needs oil.

In Descartes's view, it is as senseless to talk about our moral obligations to animals, machines created by God, as it is to talk about our moral obligations to clocks, machines created by humans. We can have moral obligations that *concern* the clock, but any such obligations are really owed to other humans and not to the clock itself. If I smash the clock with a hammer, you may object because the clock belongs to you, or because I injure you when a piece of the smashed clock accidentally strikes you, or because it is wasteful to smash a perfectly good clock that could be used by someone else. I may be similarly obligated not to damage your dog, but the obligation is owed to you, not to the dog. The dog, like the clock, according to Descartes, is nothing more than a machine and possesses no interests in the first place.[3]

There were others who did not share Descartes's view that animals are merely machines but who still denied that we can owe any moral obligations to animals. For example, the eighteenth-century German philosopher Immanuel Kant (1724–1804) recognized that animals are sentient and can suffer, but he denied that we can have any direct moral obligations to them because they are neither rational nor self-aware. According to Kant, animals are merely a means to human ends; they are "man's instruments"; they exist only for our use and have no value in themselves. To the extent that our treatment of animals matters at all for Kant, it does so only because of its impact on other humans: "he who is cruel to animals becomes hard also in his dealings with men."[4] Kant argued that if we shoot and kill a faithful and obedient dog because the dog has grown old and is no longer capable of serving us, our act violates no obligation that we owe to the dog. The act is wrong only because of our moral obligation to reward the faithful service of other human beings; killing the dog tends to make us less inclined to fulfill these human obligations. "[S]o far as animals are concerned, we have no direct duties." Animals exist "merely as a means to an end. That end is man."[5]

The view that we have no direct moral obligations to animals was also reflected in the law.[6] Before the nineteenth century, the law did not recognize any legal obligations to animals. To the extent that the law provided them any protection, it was again couched solely in terms of human concerns, primarily property interests. If Simon injured Jane's cow, Simon's act might violate a "malicious mischief" statute if Jane could prove that the act manifested malice toward Jane. If Simon had malice toward the cow but not toward Jane, then he could not be held to have violated these malicious mischief laws. The law protected Jane's property interest in her cow, but it did not recognize or protect any interest of the cow. It was irrelevant whether Simon's malice was directed toward Jane's cow or toward any other property that she owned.

To the extent that the law condemned cruelty to animals, that condemnation with very rare exceptions was expressed as a concern that such conduct would translate into cruelty to other humans, or concern that acts of cruelty to animals might threaten public morals. That is, the law reflected the notion expressed by Kant that if there were any reason for us to be kind to animals, it had nothing to do with any obligation that we owed to animals, but only with our moral obligations to other humans.

Simon the Sadist

Consider the following example. Simon proposes to torture a dog by burning the dog with a blowtorch. Simon's only reason for torturing the dog is that he derives pleasure from this sort of activity. Does Simon's proposal raise any moral concern? Is Simon violating some moral obligation not to use the animal in this way for his amusement? Or is Simon's action morally no different from crushing and eating a walnut?

I think that most of us would not hesitate to maintain that blowtorching the dog simply for fun is not a morally justifiable act under any circumstances. What is the basis of our moral judgment? Is it merely that we are concerned about the effect of Simon's action on other humans? Do we object to the torture of the dog merely because it might upset other humans who like dogs? Do we object because by torturing the dog Simon may become a more callous or unkind person in his dealings with other humans? We may very well rest our moral objection to Simon's action in part on our concern for the effect of his action on other humans, but that is not our primary reason for objecting. After all, we condemn the act even if Simon tortures the animal in secret. We object to Simon's action even if, apart from his appetite for torturing dogs, Simon is a charming human being who shows only kindness to other human beings.

Suppose that the dog is the companion animal of Simon's neighbor, Jane. Do we object to the torture because the dog is Jane's property? We may very well object to Simon's action because the dog belongs to Jane, but, again, that is not our first concern. We would find Simon's action objectionable even if the dog were a stray.

The primary reason why we find Simon's action morally objectionable is its direct effect on the dog. The dog is sentient; like us, the dog is the sort of being who is conscious of pain and has an interest in not being blowtorched. We have an obligation—one owed directly to the dog and not merely one that concerns the dog—not to torture the dog. The sole ground for this obligation is that the dog is sentient; no other characteristic, such as rationality, self-consciousness, or the ability to communicate in a human language, is necessary. Simply because the dog can experience pain and suffering, we regard it as morally necessary to justify our infliction of harm on the dog. We may disagree about whether a particular justification suffices, but we all agree that some justification is required, and Simon's pleasure simply cannot constitute such a justification. An integral part of our moral thinking is the idea that, other things being equal, the fact that an action causes pain counts as a reason against that action—not merely because imposing harm on another sentient being somehow diminishes us, but because imposing harm on another sentient being is wrong in itself. And it does not matter whether Simon proposes to blowtorch for pleasure the dog or another animal, such as a cow. We object to his conduct in either case.

In short, most of us reject the characterization of animals as things that has dominated Western thinking for many centuries.

The Humane Treatment Principle: A Revolution in Moral Thought about Animals

For the better part of two hundred years, Anglo-American moral and legal culture has made a distinction between sentient creatures and inanimate objects. Although we believe that we ought to prefer humans over animals in situations of true conflict or emergency, most of us accept as completely uncontroversial that our use and treatment of animals are guided by the humane treatment principle, or the view that because animals can suffer, we have a moral obligation that we owe directly to animals not to impose unnecessary suffering on them.

The humane treatment principle finds its origins in the theories of English lawyer and utilitarian philosopher Jeremy Bentham (1748–1832). Bentham argued that although there are differences between humans and animals, there is an important similarity. Both humans and animals can suffer and the capacity for suffering—not the capacity for speech or reason or anything else—is all that is required for animals to matter morally and for humans to have direct moral obligations to them. Bentham argued that animals had been "degraded into the class of *things*," with the result that their interest in not suffering had been ignored.[7] In a statement as profound as it was simple, Bentham asserted: "the question is not, Can they *reason?* nor, Can they *talk?* but, Can they *suffer?*"[8]

Bentham's principle represented nothing less than a revolution in our moral thinking about animals in that it rejected the views of those, like Descartes, who maintained that animals were not sentient and had no interests, as well as of those, like Kant, who maintained that animals had interests but that those interests were not morally significant because we could have no direct obligations to animals, only to other humans. Bentham argued that our duty not to inflict unnecessary suffering on animals was owed directly to them and was based solely on their sentience and on no other characteristic. This marked a sharp departure from a cultural tradition that had never before regarded animals as anything other than things devoid of morally significant interests.

Who Is Sentient?: Insects and Plants

Not all animals may be sentient, and it may be difficult to draw the line separating those who are capable of consciously experiencing pain and suffering from those who are not. There is, however, no doubt that most of the animals we exploit are sentient. Although we may not know whether insects are capable of consciously experiencing pain, we know that primates, cows, pigs, chickens, and rodents are sentient and capable of subjective mental experiences. Indeed, it is widely accepted by scientists that many fish and other sea animals are sentient. I may not know whether a dog feels pain in exactly the same way that I do, but then I cannot really know whether another human being feels pain in exactly the same way that I do. If you tell me that you are in pain in a language that I understand, I assume that you mean the same thing that I mean when I say I am in pain. But I do not know. I have no access to your mind that allows me to prove that our experiences are identical. Unless I have some reason to believe that you are lying or otherwise deceiving me, I assume that you are in pain because you and I share certain neurological and physiological similarities that make it likely that your sensation of pain is similar to mine. Likewise, I may not know whether my dog experiences pain in exactly the same way I do, but I have no doubt that dogs and cows and pigs and chickens are the types of beings who are neurologically and physiologically able to experience pain and to suffer. In this sense, all sentient beings, despite any differences, are similar to each other and dissimilar to everything else in the world that is not sentient.

It is important to recognize that the observation that animals are sentient is different from saying that they are merely alive. To be sentient means to be the sort of being who is conscious of pain and pleasure; there is an "I" who has subjective experiences. Not everything that is alive is necessarily sentient; for example, as far as we know, plants, which are alive, do not feel pain. Plants do not behave in ways that indicate that they feel pain, and they lack the neurological and physiological structures that we associate with sentience in human and nonhuman animals. Moreover, pain in humans and nonhumans serves a very practical function. It is a signal to the human or animal to escape from the source of pain in order to avoid damage or death. Sentient beings use pain as a means to the end of survival. Plants cannot use pain as a signal in this way—flowers do not and cannot try to run away when we pick them—and it is therefore difficult to explain why plants would evolve mechanisms for sentience if such mechanisms were utterly useless.

The Humane Treatment Principle as Law

The humane treatment principle is so entrenched in our moral culture that the legal systems of the United States and other nations purport to establish the principle as a legal standard in animal welfare laws. These laws are of two kinds. General animal welfare laws, such as anticruelty laws, supposedly prohibit cruelty or the infliction of suffering on animals without distinguishing between various uses of animals. For example, New York law imposes a criminal sanction on any person who "over-drives, overloads, tortures or cruelly beats or unjustifiably injures, maims, mutilates or kills any animal."[9] Delaware law prohibits cruelty and defines as "cruel" "every act or omission to act whereby unnecessary or unjustifiable physical pain or suffering is caused or permitted," and includes "mistreatment of any animal or neglect of any animal under the care and control of the neglector, whereby unnecessary or unjustifiable physical pain or suffering is caused."[10] In Britain, the Protection of Animals Act of 1911 makes it a criminal offense to "cruelly beat, kick, ill-treat, over-ride, over-drive, over-load, torture, infuriate, or terrify any animal" or to impose "unnecessary suffering" on animals.[11] Specific animal welfare laws purport to apply the humane treatment principle to a particular animal use. For example, the American Animal Welfare Act, enacted in 1966 and amended on numerous occasions,[12] the British Cruelty to Animals Act, enacted in 1876,[13] and the British Animals (Scientific Procedures) Act of 1986,[14] concern the treatment of animals used in experiments. The American Humane Slaughter Act, originally enacted in 1958, regulates the killing of animals used for food.[15]

Animal welfare laws replaced malicious mischief laws and emerged in the nineteenth century as a direct application of the humane treatment principle. As we saw earlier, if Simon injured Jane's cow, prior law generally required a showing that Simon bore malice toward Jane. And to the extent that courts had any concern about cruelty to animals, this concern was limited to the effect that cruelty might have on public sensibilities or to the tendency of cruelty to animals to encourage cruelty to other humans. Anticruelty laws allowed for Simon's prosecution even if he bore Jane no ill will and instead had malice only toward her cow. Moreover, these laws were explicitly based on the moral significance of animal interests themselves, in addition to the detrimental repercussions of cruelty to animals for other humans or property interests.[16] Malicious mischief statutes were "intended to protect the beasts as property instead of as creatures susceptible of suffering." Anticruelty statutes were "designed for the protection of animals."[17] These new laws were intended "for the benefit of animals, as creatures capable of feeling and suffering, and [were] intended to protect them from cruelty, without reference to their being property."[18] Anticruelty laws were often explicit in applying to all animals, whether owned or unowned. These laws were intended to instill in humans "a humane regard for the rights and feelings of the brute creation by reproving evil and indifferent tendencies in human nature in its intercourse with animals."[19] They were said to "recognize and attempt to protect some abstract rights in all that animate creation, made subject to man by the creation, from the largest and noblest to the smallest and most insignificant."[20] Anticruelty laws recognize, at least in part, that because animals are sentient, humans have legal obligations that they owe directly to animals to refrain from imposing unnecessary pain and suffering on them. These laws are intended to provide what courts describe as "protection of the animals themselves" rather than protection of human interests alone, because "[p]ain is an evil" and because "[i]t is impossible for a right minded man . . . to say that unjustifiable cruelty [to animals] is not a wrong."[21]

Many animal welfare laws are criminal laws. For the most part, only those moral rules that are widely accepted, such as prohibitions against killing other humans or inflicting physical harm on them, or taking or destroying their property, are enshrined in criminal laws. That many animal welfare laws are criminal laws suggests that we take animal interests seriously enough to punish violations of the humane treatment principle with the social stigma of a criminal penalty.

The humane treatment principle and the animal welfare laws that reflect it require that we balance the interests of animals against our interests when we use animals for a particular purpose. To balance interests means to assess the relative strengths of conflicting interests. If our interests in inflicting suffering outweigh the animals' interests, then our interests prevail and the animal suffering is regarded as necessary. If no justifiable human interests are at stake, then the infliction of suffering on animals must be regarded as unnecessary. For example, the British law regulating the use of animals in experiments requires that before any experiment is approved, it is necessary to "weigh the likely adverse effects on the animals concerned against the [human] benefit likely to accrue."[22] The humane treatment principle seems to say that we may use animals, but only when it is necessary to do so—only when we are faced with a true emergency analogous to the burning house scenario that requires us to make a choice—and that we should impose only the minimum amount of pain and suffering necessary for our purpose. If a prohibition against unnecessary suffering of animals is to have any meaningful content, we must not inflict suffering on animals merely for our pleasure, amusement, or convenience. If there is a feasible alternative to our use of animals in a particular situation, then the principle would seem to proscribe such use.

Our Uses of Animals: We Are All Simon

Our actual use and treatment of animals differ greatly from the moral and legal norms enshrined in the humane treatment principle. We treat virtually *every* human/animal interaction as involving a burning house that requires us to make a choice between humans and animals. But the overwhelming portion of our animal uses cannot be described as necessary in any meaningful sense of the word; rather, they merely further the satisfaction of human pleasure, amusement, or convenience. This wholly unnecessary animal use results in an enormous amount of animal pain, suffering, and death. In short, we are no different from Simon the sadist, whose infliction of suffering on the dog cannot be considered necessary.

Let us briefly review our use of animals for food, hunting, entertainment, and fur, as these account for most of our use. In the next chapter we will explore the use of animals in science, product testing, and education, areas in which animal use cannot be dismissed in quite the same way, but in which there are still serious questions about the necessity of animal use.

Animal Agriculture: Pain and Suffering Because We Like the Taste of Meat

The most numerically significant use of animals by Americans—more than 8 billion of them annually—is for food. Most animals used for food are bred, raised, and killed on enormous mechanized farms that specialize in one species and house hundreds of thousands of animals at a time. This practice is known as "factory farming" and is defined by *The Agricultural Dictionary* as a "type of farming which is usually operated on a large scale according to modern business efficiency standards, solely for monetary profit, as contrasted to a so-called family farm, or farming as a way of life."[23] Factory farms are usually owned by large corporations and are operated on economies of scale. They are highly automated and fully enclosed, and the concepts of profit and efficiency that drive them require that animals be viewed as nothing more than economic commodities. The goal of the factory farm is to produce the maximum amount of meat, dairy products, or eggs with the least amount of human labor and financial outlay.

In practice, factory farming means that animals are raised in the smallest possible spaces and the cheapest facilities, and that they receive the least expensive food in a manner that requires the minimum of human labor. For example, beef cattle are squeezed shoulder to shoulder in large dirt corrals called feedlots. Other animals, including pigs and chickens, are housed in massive confinement buildings that resemble factory warehouses, and most of these animals never see the outdoors until they are sent to slaughter.

In factory farms, animals do not even have enough space to move their limbs or turn around. Broiler chickens are crammed into buildings holding thousands of birds, while chickens used in egg production are confined four to a wire "battery cage" that usually measures 192 square inches, often with cages stacked three to five layers high. These animals have no place to nest or to exercise for their entire lives, and they often injure their feet and break their bones by catching their necks, wings, and toes on the cramped wire cages. Female pigs used for breeding are kept in metal farrowing stalls two feet wide. These stalls keep the sows completely immobile so that they do not crush the piglets in the confined space or stop the piglets from nursing continually. Most pigs not used for breeding live in small indoor "grower-finisher" cages, usually made of metal and often stacked two or three levels high with several pigs in each cage. Many dairy cows are raised indoors in "tie stalls" set up in long rows for easy inspection and handling. These tie stalls prevent cows from turning around, exercising in any way, or grooming themselves. Other dairy cows are kept in crowded dirt feedlots like cows intended for beef production. Because animals are raised and transported in confined conditions, they are susceptible to injury and disease, and factory farmers regularly add antibiotics and other drugs to their feed. For example, more than 80 percent of pigs have pneumonia at the time of slaughter.[24]

In addition, factory farmers often mutilate animals in order to decrease injuries from close confinement and to make the animals more docile. For example, chickens used in both egg and broiler production have their beaks burned or chopped off to prevent the cannibalism and feather pecking that develop from close confinement. Farmers cut off the ends of the birds' toes—a process called "toe trimming"—in order to prevent clawing and entanglement in wire-mesh cages. Cattle raised for beef are usually dehorned to minimize damage in crowded feedlots and trucks. The dehorning, a very painful process, is done with caustic paste, hot irons, saws, or "dehorning spoons" used to gouge the horns from the skull. Bulls are castrated for the dual purpose of ensuring docility and making their meat more tender. Most castration is performed with a knife, but is also done with pincers or pliers that sever the spermatic cord or with "elastrator" rubber rings that shut off the blood supply to the testicles. Pigs are also castrated and have their tails cut off and their teeth clipped in order to prevent tail biting and other stress-induced behavior that can lead to infections. For the most part, these mutilations are performed without pain relief.

The treatment of female animals as nothing more than reproductive machines is another salient characteristic of modern animal agriculture. They are pushed into faster hormonal cycles, artificially inseminated, kept constantly pregnant, separated from their babies as early as one day after birth, and slaughtered as soon as their reproductive capacities diminish. Male animals also fall prey to "assembly-line" reproductive processes. For example, bulls used to identify cows in heat and ready for artificial insemination have their penises redirected sideways, amputated, or surgically attached to their lower abdominal walls to ensure that they will not attempt to have intercourse with the cow. The male calves of dairy cows are either sold immediately for slaughter as low-grade veal or slaughtered after several months as high-quality "white" veal (that is, veal with undeveloped muscle). In order to prevent the development of muscle, these calves are confined in crates so small that they are unable to perform basic grooming or even to turn around. These crates are contained in large buildings that are kept darkened to encourage the calves to be as inactive as possible. They are fed a liquid diet that completely lacks roughage and induces anemia to ensure the whiteness of their meat. They are given no bedding material in their crates, so they have nothing to satisfy their urge to ruminate. Egg farmers discard male chicks as soon as their sex is determined because the males cannot lay eggs and are not needed for broiler production. The chicks are suffocated in plastic bags, decapitated, gassed, or crushed.

As technology becomes more sophisticated, the practices of intensive agriculture follow without any regard for the suffering, distress, or discomfort of animals. Using selective breeding, growth hormones, feed additives, and genetic engineering, farmers force animals to grow faster and larger. Biogenetic research has produced pigs with human growth genes, turkeys that are twice the size of normal birds, and "double-muscled" calves. The animals created thus far have had trouble standing and moving, have contracted multiple stress-related diseases, and have developed lung problems and other internal disorders. The newest high-tech form of exploitation—cloning—often produces deformed animals.

Finally, the slaughter of farm animals, like the production of them, has been made as economically efficient as possible—from mass transportation to assembly-line slaughter. Hens are pulled from their battery cages or from the floor of the broiler house and transported to the slaughterhouse packed in crates stacked ten or more deep. Many chickens arrive at the slaughterhouse with broken bones from the crating and transportation process. They are then hung upside down, their feet in clips, and are moved along a conveyor to an electrified bath that supposedly stuns them before a large rotating blade decapitates them, after which they are submerged in boiling water to facilitate feather removal. Many chickens are not stunned sufficiently, and sometimes the blade removes only part of the animal's head. The result is that many chickens are immersed alive in the scalding water.

Cows and pigs are shipped standing in trucks or railroad cars, with large numbers of them packed together for long periods of time, often without rest, food, or water. For cows, the rate of death and severe injury during transportation is as high as 25 percent. Those cows and pigs who fall in the trucks or rail cars are often trampled and later are unable to stand. When these "downed" or non-ambulatory animals arrive at the slaughterhouse, they are often dragged by their legs with chains or are merely left to languish until dead. Once at the slaughterhouse, animals are led to the killing floor, where they are stunned by electric shock, shackled, hoisted upside down, and butchered. Delivering a potent shock is often difficult or too much trouble for the slaughterhouse workers, and the result is that some animals regain consciousness while hanging and waiting for slaughter or during the slaughtering process itself. At slaughterhouses that produce kosher or *halal* meat, the animals are not stunned before having their carotid arteries severed.

Animals used in the dairy industry end up in the slaughterhouse eventually. They are, however, kept alive and exploited longer than are their "meat" counterparts. Dairy cows are repeatedly impregnated—usually on a device called a "rape rack," where they are inseminated by a bull or by a human who manually inserts the bull semen—in order to keep them lactating. Their calves are taken from them shortly after birth, usually within a day or two. In any event, the life of a dairy cow is certainly no better than that of a "meat" animal, and more animal suffering is probably caused by the production of dairy products than of meat simply because dairy cows are generally used for a longer period of time and treated more brutally before they are slaughtered.

This has been a mere survey of some of the more salient aspects of modern intensive agriculture in America. Most other industrialized nations practice factory farming with only minor differences from ours. Britain, for example, requires that calves be raised in small pens where the animals have at least some ability to move and some social interaction with other calves. Switzerland requires more room, perches, and nesting boxes for battery hens. But these differences are meager comfort for the animals to whom they apply and no comfort at all for the billions of others. Although some people hopefully believe that conditions on factory farms are improving, it remains to be seen whether this belief is justified. In July 1999, for example, the European Union issued a council directive that will supposedly require an "enriched" system of egg production in place of the traditional battery, to be phased in beginning in 2002 and completed by 2012. This enriched system will provide more room and roosting structures for the birds. There is, however, serious doubt about whether this directive will be implemented because directives generally require domestic implementing legislation, and opposition to this one is already building in several European nations. Indeed, past efforts by the European Community to modify the egg battery have met with little success. Even when countries pass legislation that modifies intensive agriculture, it has been ignored for economic reasons. Moreover, intensive agriculture is now coming into use in third world nations as well.

It is in no way necessary for human beings to eat meat or other animal products. Indeed, voices as mainstream as the U.S. Department of Agriculture and the American Dietetic Association have now recognized that a completely plant-based diet, supplemented by vitamin B-12, can provide the human body with sufficient protein, vitamins, minerals, and other nutrients to maintain excellent health. For health-related reasons, animal foods have been coming under greater suspicion within the mainstream scientific community. Even the most traditional health care professionals are urging a reduction in our consumption of meat and other animal products; others are calling for the elimination of such products from our diet. It is an uncontested fact that vegetarians have lower rates of many forms of cancer, heart disease, diabetes, hypertension, gallstones and kidney stones, and other diseases. And we seem to hear on an almost daily basis of illnesses—ranging from simple food poisoning to more exotic maladies such as Creutzfeldt-Jakob ("mad cow") disease—connected with eating meat. Countries that have shifted from plant-based diets to meat-based diets have experienced increased rates of obesity, heart disease, and cancer. So not only are animal foods unnecessary for our health; they may very well be detrimental to it.[25]

Moreover—and again, the evidence is uncontested—animal agriculture has serious environmental consequences.[26] Animals consume more protein than they produce. For every kilogram (2.2 pounds) of animal protein produced, animals consume almost six kilograms, or over thirteen pounds, of plant protein from grains and forage.[27] More than 50 percent of U.S. grain and 40 percent of world grain is fed to animals to produce meat, rather than consumed directly by people. Animals in the United States consume about five times as much grain as is consumed directly by our entire human population. In addition to forage and grasses, 236 million tons of grain—or 1,978 pounds per person—are fed annually to animals to produce meat products. Because we need so many crops to feed the billions of animals we consume, we use an enormous amount of land to grow those crops. Estimates vary, but a conservative assessment is that approximately one-third of the land area in the United States is devoted to the production of livestock. Our unlimited need for land to produce crops for animals has resulted in the devastation of topsoil. Approximately 90 percent of cropland in the United States is losing topsoil at a rate thirteen times above the sustainable rate. Erosion may exceed one hundred times the sustainable rate on severely overgrazed pastures, and approximately 54 percent of our pasture land is overgrazed. Moreover, the need for land to produce grain and forage for animals has resulted in forest destruction throughout the world; as older pastures are destroyed through overgrazing, new land is cleared to replace them. It takes only one-sixth of an acre to supply a vegetarian with food for one year; it takes three and one-quarter acres to supply a meat eater with food for a year. This means that an acre of land can feed twenty times more vegetarians than it can meat eaters. Every day we feed enough grain to American livestock to provide two loaves of bread to every human being on earth.

Animal agriculture also consumes enormous amounts of other resources, such as water and energy. Almost 90 percent of the fresh water consumed after withdrawal is for agricultural production, including livestock production. The production of animal protein requires much more water than is required to produce plant protein. For example, it takes more than 100,000 liters of water to produce one kilogram of beef, and approximately 900 liters of water to produce one kilogram of wheat. On rangeland, it takes more than 200,000 liters of water to produce one kilogram of beef. It takes approximately 3,500 liters of water to produce one kilogram of chicken, and 500 liters of water to produce one kilogram of potatoes.[28]

The average amount of fossil energy used for animal-protein production is more than eight times the average for grain-protein production.[29] Given that the United States imports over half of its oil already and will probably be importing most or all of it by the end of the first quarter of this century, the extraordinarily inefficient use of fossil energy to support animal agriculture should call into serious question whether human beings, who claim to be rational, are thinking rationally.

In addition to the consumption of huge amounts of water and energy, animal agriculture results in serious water pollution because animals produce about 1.4 billion tons of waste per year—130 times more than the human population produces. Much of this waste is not recycled but is dumped into our waters, with the result that the nitrogen in the waste reduces the amount of dissolved oxygen in the water and causes levels of ammonia, nitrates, phosphates, and bacteria to increase. One hog farm in Utah produces as much waste as does the city of Los Angeles, and water pollution from hog farms has become a serious problem in states such as North Carolina. The processing of animal foods also contributes significantly to water pollution. For example, although some whey, a waste product generated in making cheese, is used as a food additive (it takes about ten pounds of milk to produce one pound of cheese), much of it is dumped into the sewage system and results in river pollution.

Animal agriculture also contributes significantly to global warming because cattle, sheep, and goats, in their flatulence and waste, emit 70 to 80 million tons of methane—one of the greenhouse gases—every year, accounting for as much as 30 percent of the methane released into the atmosphere. Deforestation to produce more land for crops and grazing also results in the release of large amounts of carbon dioxide, another greenhouse gas.

Some defenders of meat eating claim that in certain parts of the world eating animal products is necessary because no other sources of food are feasible. Assuming that such claims about the nonavailability of alternative food sources are accurate, any such reliance on animal foods must constitute a minuscule portion of the total consumption of animal foods. There may be situations in which a person is truly confronted with the choice of killing and eating an animal or starving to death. But then there have been instances in which humans have eaten humans in situations of true emergency. Fortunately, most of us do not find ourselves in such situations, and most of us have a wide variety of nonanimal foods available to us.

Other defenders of meat eating claim that even if the practice is unnecessary, in that we could survive well (if not better) on a vegetarian diet, humans have been eating meat for centuries and the practice is justified by "tradition." There are, however, at least two problems with such an argument. First, there are and have been historically a number of cultures that do not eat animal foods, so if there is a tradition, it cannot be described as one that we share as a species. Indeed, until the modern era—and especially until the rise of agribusiness—most people of the world ate far, far less meat than they do today. Second, and more important, even if there were a tradition shared by all humans, or some humans, what moral difference would it make? If animal use is not necessary in the particular case, how can any tradition override the animal interests at stake if these interests are morally significant, as we claim that they are? The argument for tradition in moral justifications is always at least suspect. Tradition, after all, has often been offered as a justification for sexism, racism, and other conduct that we now acknowledge as morally unjustifiable. Were we slaves to tradition, Rosa Parks would still be riding in the back of the bus.

Finally, some who support eating animals agree that factory farms are morally unacceptable but argue that eating animals would be all right if they were raised on family farms. We should not be misled into thinking that the issue is whether animal agriculture can be made more "humane." People raised and killed animals for food before the advent of factory farming. The practices on the nineteenth-century or early-twentieth-century family farm may have afforded animals more time outdoors, or allowed animal mothers to spend at least some time with their babies, but they still endured plenty of pain and suffering. If we take the humane treatment principle seriously, we must conclude that none of the suffering involved in the production of meat, whether on the factory farm or the family farm, is any more necessary than the suffering of the dog that Simon blowtorches.

Right from the outset, then, our most numerically significant use of animals—for food—runs afoul of the moral principle that we all claim to accept: that we should not impose harm on animals if there is a feasible alternative, and certainly never merely because we derive pleasure or amusement from animal suffering. There is a feasible alternative to our use of animals for food that is every bit as good, if not better, for our health and the health of the planet—the use of plants. As Albert Einstein noted, "Nothing will benefit human health and increase the chances for survival of life on Earth as much as the evolution [to] a vegetarian diet."[30] Yet we choose to eat meat and animal products—we choose animal pain, suffering, and death—and our only justification is human pleasure. But if we take animal interests seriously at all, how can we possibly justify inflicting pain, suffering, and death on animals simply because we like the taste of their flesh?

The suggestion that our taking animal interests seriously requires that we become vegetarians may seem radical. But as philosopher James Rachels has observed, "the opposite is true: the rule against causing unnecessary pain is the least eccentric of all moral principles, and that rule leads straight to the conclusion that we should abandon the business of meat production and adopt alternative diets. Considered in this light, vegetarianism may be thought of as a severely conservative moral stance."[31]

Hunting: Pain and Suffering for Sport

The second largest use of animals in the United States is sport hunting, which involves our killing at least 200 million animals per year, not counting the tens of millions that are wounded and not retrieved and those killed on game farms or in similar contexts. Let us debunk the myth that those who hunt do so primarily for economic reasons. Hunting is a middle-class activity. According to one defender of hunting, "[t]he average hunter in the United States today is white, male, forty-two years old . . . has a professional/managerial or services/labor job, and earns $43,120 per year . . . [and] spends about a thousand dollars a year on hunting licenses, equipment, travel, food, lodging, and so on."[32]

Hunters use rifles, pistols, bows and arrows, primitive firearms like muzzle-loaders, and high-powered semiautomatic and automatic weapons. They hunt wild animals whose habitats have been maintained for hunting purposes, animals who have been raised and released to be hunted, and even captive exotic animals sold to hunting preserves by zoos and circuses. Hunters commonly lie in wait in tree stands to ambush animals with their guns; bait animals with salt licks and other foods to the animals' liking and then ambush them at close range; attract the animals with mechanical instruments that imitate the sounds of other animals, including distress calls and mating calls; use dogs with or without radio collars; and "jacklight" at night by immobilizing the animals with spotlights and then shooting them. Hunters and their public relations organizations, such as the Wildlife Conservation Fund of America, try to convince the public that hunters perform some sort of "service" for animals by killing those who would be doomed to a slower death by starvation because of animal overpopulation. Let us assume for the purposes of argument that overpopulation of some animals does sometimes occur "naturally," that is, without human intervention. The question remains whether hunting is the necessary or appropriate corrective, a question I will take up later. The truth is that most game animals are managed through artificial habitat manipulation whose objective is higher reproductive rates and greater population precisely so that hunters will have animals to kill. Whether on public or private land, the overwhelming majority of animals hunters pursue are purposefully nourished, sheltered, and restocked to ensure that their populations remain high enough to meet hunter demand.

Because hunters spend large amounts of money buying licenses, permits, and equipment, and because in the United States the federal government dispenses funds to state wildlife agencies based on the number of licenses they sell, state and local wildlife agencies view game animals as economic resources to be maintained for "maximum harvest."[33] As one wildlife biologist has written, "Most state wildlife agencies have developed along a business model, with hunters and fishers their primary 'clients,' . . . [w]ildlife agencies provide a product for which hunters pay."[34] To induce higher rates of reproduction and denser populations of game animals, federal and state wildlife agencies manipulate populations and ecosystems through a variety of techniques, including the clear-cutting and burning of wooded areas to provide grazing ground for deer and other game animals; destroying predator populations; digging and diverting waterways and damming streams and rivers to provide lakes and marshes for ducks; planting berry bushes and fruit trees to attract deer and bear; winter-feeding; providing roost structures and nesting grounds to attract popular species; restocking areas when populations get low; and fencing in tracts of land to increase population density. Even whitetail deer—the animals most often claimed by hunters to be overpopulated and in need of "thinning out"—are managed and manipulated by wildlife agencies to maintain dense populations for hunters. Wildlife agencies often limit hunting to bucks so as to ensure that the does remain to reproduce and thus increase population size. Some wildlife agencies also employ management techniques for the purpose of producing "trophy deer," or large, heavy stags with giant antlers prized by hunters. As a general matter, wildlife agencies are hostile to nonlethal alternatives to hunting, such as contraception, which has proven effective in controlling the size of deer herds but decreases the availability of animals for hunters to kill.[35]

Wildlife agencies also breed certain animals for hunters to shoot on public land. For example, ring-necked pheasants, brought to the United States during the nineteenth century for hunters who wanted more exotic targets, are actually raised by some state wildlife agencies on pheasant farms resembling poultry factory farms and are used to stock public hunting areas. The Wildlife Board of the Department of Environmental Protection of Connecticut purchases and releases approximately twenty-five thousand pheasants annually so that hunters can kill them.[36] Other states engage in this practice as well. Because these pheasants are raised in cages and pens and do not know how to live in the wild, those who survive the hunting season are doomed to die from starvation, exposure to the elements, and predators.

In recent years, private game preserves in which hunters shoot confined animals have proliferated. Often the animals involved are exotics who have been purchased by the landowner from a circus or zoo, or have been specially raised by the landowner for these "canned hunts" and are quite tame. Many of these preserves stock their ranches with trophy-size animals and advertise "guaranteed kills," locked gates, short-range shooting, and the ability to custom-order animals of species not already in stock at the preserve. Canned hunts have been banned in several states and restricted by species in some others, but the majority of states allow this activity, and it is estimated that there are currently over a thousand of these commercial preserves in the United States.[37]

Similar to "canned hunts" are live-bird shoots. Every year, thousands of captive pigeon shoots take place across the United States. Some of these shoots are sponsored by private clubs and some by charitable organizations or municipalities in order to raise money for local causes. One event attracting international attention has been the annual Labor Day pigeon shoot in Hegins, Pennsylvania, involving the shooting at close range of thousands of birds in one day by shooters who paid a fee to participate in the event. The organizers of this event have claimed that it raised funds for local schools and municipal projects. The birds, many of whom were emaciated and dehydrated, were released from boxes several yards in front of the shooters. Most of the birds were not killed outright by the often unskilled and drunken shooters, but were left to die slowly or were killed by local children employed to smash the wounded pigeons on the pavement or against a wall.[38]

Again, I have focused primarily on hunting in America, but many of the same observations could be made about Canada, Great Britain, and other Western nations that purport to embrace the humane treatment principle. Great Britain, for example, has a number of game estates that offer guided hunts for British and foreign hunters. Wild-hare hunting is quite popular among British hunters, as is the hunting of pen-raised pheasants on artificially stocked preserves. Fox hunting has historically been a popular activity for the upper classes in Britain and claims the lives of twenty to twenty-five thousand foxes annually. Habitats are maintained on popular hunting grounds to foster larger fox populations.[39] "Carted-deer" hunting is another popular pastime among British hunters. Because wild deer are scarce in many parts of Britain, they are raised in enclosed pastures and then carted to hunts in trailers. Stags are castrated with knives or elastrators, and their antlers are sawed off to make them more manageable. The hunters do not kill these animals during the actual hunt but instead chase them with hounds, corner them, and then release them for other hunts. The deer are used for up to ten of these sessions, although some animals die from the stress or are killed by the hounds. There is increasing pressure in Britain to ban the hunting of mammals with dogs, but a core minority still strongly supports it.

There can be no doubt that hunted animals suffer considerably. Indeed, a 1997 study by Professor Patrick Bateson of Cambridge University found that objective physiological measurements obtained from deer hunted with hounds made it "clear that lengthy chases in the course of hunting with hounds impose on red deer stresses that are likely to cause great suffering" and that hunting causes the "deer to experience conditions that lie far outside those conditions that would normally be experienced by the species living in a natural environment."[40] Bateson concluded that "[o]n measures that are commonly used as indicators of poor welfare, hunted deer are in very poor condition by the time they are killed. Indeed, they are no better off than injured animals which both sides in the hunting dispute believe should be put down because of the suffering that they are thought to endure."[41]

As in the case of animal agriculture, hunting involves the infliction of an enormous amount of pain and suffering on animals, and the overwhelming amount of that pain and suffering simply cannot be characterized as necessary. Hunting is a sport. Its defenders often argue that even if unnecessary, hunting is justified as a human "tradition." Just as in the case of animal agriculture, an argument based on tradition begs the question whether such practices should be morally sanctioned.

Fishing: Pain and Suffering That We Do Not Even Recognize

We kill billions of fish and other sea animals every year. For the most part, we do not even think of fish as sentient creatures, probably because they are cold-blooded and lack facial expressions that we can understand. Indeed, even many people who for moral reasons do not eat meat or chicken continue to eat fish. They do not think of fish as suffering when they are hooked or when they suffocate in the air. As I have already mentioned, however, scientists recognize that fish are, indeed, sentient.[42] Moreover, bony fish, like other vertebrates, such as mammals, reptiles, birds, and amphibians, have brain receptors for benzodiazepines, which indicates that these fish can experience states of anxiety.[43] Indeed, some researchers claim that fish suffer at least as much from fear as they do from the hook.[44]

Many people eat fish because they believe it to be a healthier alternative to beef, pork, or chicken. This, however, is a myth. Many fish contain as much saturated fat and cholesterol as does beef, if not more.

Moreover, fish become repositories for industrial and chemical pollutants that are dumped into the world's waters, and fish can accumulate levels of toxins in their bodies that are much higher than that of the water in which they live. These toxins include PCBs and dioxin, which are carcinogens, mercury, which can cause damage to the brain and nervous system, lead, which can cause brain and developmental damage in young children, and pesticides such as DDT. The most significant source of PCBs in the human diet is fish, and PCBs accumulate in our body tissues and remain there for decades. Many fish are also contaminated by bacteria from human or animal feces.

Our consumption of fish and other sea animals also has a profound environmental impact. Chronic overfishing threatens the ecological viability of ocean systems worldwide with fish populations declining at alarming rates.[45] Most fish are caught by large commercial fishing operations that use huge nets or hook lines that can stretch for miles. These commercial operations are indiscriminate in their methods, and an estimated 18 to 40 million tons of usually fatally injured fish are thrown back annually by commercial fishers. Some shrimp trawlers discard 15 tons of fish for every ton of shrimp that they catch. In addition, thousands of marine mammals (such as dolphins), sea turtles, and diving seabirds become entangled in fishing equipment. In the 1980s, fish farms, similar to the factory farms that raise cows, pigs, chickens, and other animals under intensive conditions, began to provide a larger share of the fish supply, and, like their meat counterparts, fish farms raise a range of problems. The fish are raised in crowded pens and fish farms create significant water pollution. The fish are subject to various diseases, infections, and parasites, and they are fed antibiotics that are passed on to humans. Fish who escape from fish farms can carry disease into surrounding waters. Moreover, fish farms are generally situated on coastal lands, and essential coastal habitats such as mangrove forests and wetlands are destroyed by these farms.[46] Birds and other animals are also injured or killed by local, non-commercial "sport" fishing as a result of swallowing or becoming entangled in discarded fishing hooks or line, or ingesting lead weights or plastic lures.

Animals in Entertainment: Pain and Suffering for Sheer Amusement

In thousands of zoos, circuses, carnivals, race tracks, and rodeos, we use animals every day for our own amusement.[47] The very terms in which we conceive of these activities—"entertainment," "diversion," "amusement," "sport," and so forth—belie any claim to their "necessity." If entertainment could be considered a necessity, then any barbarity perpetrated in its name could conceivably slip through the humane treatment principle, which itself would be meaningless. Nevertheless, let us consider some of the ways in which we use animals for our entertainment.[48]

Circuses and traveling animal acts. Animals used in circuses are usually confined in small, barren cages that provide them with only enough room to stand up and lie down. Large animals such as elephants are kept chained whenever they are not performing and whenever they are transported, often inside railroad cars, over long distances, and in extreme heat. In order to persuade circus animals to perform acts that are not physically or psychologically normal for them, and amid screaming humans, bright lights, and other loud noises, trainers often assert their dominance over the animals through fear. Whips, chains, electric prods, metal hooks, and ropes are all regularly used for training. Animal trainers sometimes burn the front paws of "dancing" bears to make them stand upright on their hind legs and routinely beat and choke animals as standard "animal-handling procedures." Traveling animal acts and roadside exhibitions, which often treat animals even worse than do larger circuses, feature mules or horses who dive off high platforms into water, or acts in which humans wrestle with bears who are usually declawed, defanged, and drugged.

Circuses, especially those that travel, often do not provide particularly good veterinary care for animals, since most veterinarians, trained only to deal with dogs, cats, other small animals, and farm animals, have no expertise in treating exotic animals. As a result of untreated or improperly treated disease and stress, the animals often perish at an early age. Asian elephants, to give just one example, live to be about sixty years in the wild; in circuses, they rarely live past thirty.

Zoos. Zoos are a popular form of entertainment in the United States.[49] Over one thousand species of animals are kept in large zoos and in smaller roadside zoos across the country. These animals are captured from their natural habitats, bred in zoos' captive-breeding programs, or purchased or borrowed from other zoos. They are often forced to travel long distances in cramped containers, and many animals arrive ill, injured, or dead.

The conditions of many American zoos can only be described as deplorable. Animals are kept in barren cages that provide no physical or mental stimulation whatsoever. When zoos advertise "natural habitats," this usually means concrete banks and "trees" made of plastic resin with metal "leaves"; electric fencing surrounds any real vegetation. Off-exhibit areas, which are hidden from public view but in which animals spend most of their lives, remain unchanged by such upgrades and are nothing more than cages. Animals in zoos—even "good" zoos, or those with "natural habitats"—often exhibit neurotic, stress-induced behaviors, such as pacing, head bobbing, weaving back and forth, and throwing feces at humans. Some animals develop ulcers, others infections in their feet from standing in urine and excrement. The stress of confinement prevents some animals from engaging in normal behaviors like sex and childbearing, as evidenced by the difficulties that zoos have had in getting certain species to reproduce in captive-breeding programs.

Zoo employees who have little or no training in dealing with exotic animals commonly subject zoo animals to rough handling and improper care. For example, employees at a midwestern zoo severely beat an elephant with a metal hook because she would not walk onto a shipping truck. An elephant at the El Paso zoo was chained and beaten severely with an ax handle to "assert dominance" over her. Veterinary care is often inadequate at zoos for the same reason it is inadequate in circuses—veterinarians are simply not trained to deal with the broad range of species confined in zoos. The problem is even worse at roadside zoos, which are often located in remote places where the closest veterinarian has little experience with anything but small domestic or farm animals.

Some defenders of zoos argue that they are necessary because they preserve endangered species through their captive-breeding programs. This claim is nonsense. Of the more than one thousand species housed at zoos that have breeding programs, only about fifty species have been involved in programs intended to increase populations for release into the wild, and very few animals have actually been released successfully. Dollar for dollar, captive-breeding programs in zoos must be *the* most inefficient way to protect endangered or threatened species. The overwhelming majority of animals born at zoos are not intended for release but are instead the result of unplanned procreation or breeding designed to provide continuous "animal baby" tourist attractions. Often zoos have no room to house these surplus animals, particularly through adulthood, and so they frequently sell them to other, smaller zoos, foreign zoos, circuses, traveling animal acts, laboratories, private exotic-animal collectors, and ranches where "canned" hunts occur. From 50 to 80 percent of all large animals found in roadside zoos originate in the breeding programs of large zoos. Some zoos even breed animals for the sole purpose of gaining additional income by selling these animals to high-paying commercial game ranches.

Older animals, or animals no longer popular for exhibition, are also sold. The American Association of Zoological Parks and Aquariums, an association of more than 170 of America's supposedly "better" zoos, lists more than a thousand surplus animals for sale. Even major zoos sell older animals or the products of captive-breeding programs to hunting ranches or to dealers who sell the animals to hunting ranches. Several of the board members of a San Antonio zoo have owned hunting ranches and bought animals directly from the zoo for their canned hunts.

Finally, zoos are often defended on the ground that they provide education about animals to the public. But the average zoo visitor spends little time in reading whatever information may accompany an animal display, and many zoos provide very little educational information in the first place. Animals confined in zoos teach us little about what they are really like; indeed, it is difficult to argue that observing lions in a zoo display is a better educational device than watching a film taken of lions in the wild in which the animals have not been harmed or their natural behaviors altered.

Rodeos. Rodeos are a popular form of entertainment across the United States.[50] Approximately eight hundred professional rodeos and an unknown number of smaller events are held in this country annually. There are also "specialty" rodeos, such as all-women rodeos, all-gay rodeos, all-black rodeos, military rodeos, police rodeos, and children's rodeos. Fundamental to the entertainment value of rodeos are the fear and desperation of the animals involved, as it is only such fear and desperation that cause these animals to run about and to provide rodeo contestants with an opportunity to demonstrate their skills.

The events sanctioned by professional rodeo associations include bronco riding and bull riding, in which horses and bulls are fitted with "bucking straps" that irritate their abdominal areas and cause them to buck; calf or steer roping, in which a calf or steer running at a speed of up to thirty miles an hour is roped, jerked to a sudden stop, and flipped over and tied; team roping, in which one contestant ropes a running animal around the head and horns while another lassoes and ties the hind feet; and steer wrestling, in which a mounted contestant jumps from a horse onto the back of a steer and twists the animal's neck until he falls to the ground.

Animals used in rodeos are often confined in chutes adjacent to the show rings and tormented with electric prods until they become frantic, at which time the chute is opened. The calf or steer then bolts from the chute to escape the pain of the electric prod. Animals used in rodeos are frequently injured in these events. Horses break legs; calves and steers break bones, break their necks, sever their windpipes, and become paralyzed after running into fences and being flipped by ropes. Contestants in rodeos wear metal spurs that they dig into the necks and shoulders of the horses they ride. Although professional rodeo associations require that veterinarians be present or on call, about half of these rodeos do not have any veterinarian present, and amateur rodeos often do not even have a veterinarian on call.

Horse racing and dog racing. Millions of Americans attend the more than sixty thousand horse races that take place in the United States each year, and even more watch these events on television. Wagering on horse races exceeds $13 billion annually. Many horses are subject to fatal and near-fatal injuries every year from broken bones, as well as severely ruptured ligaments and other impairments. According to a 1993 University of Minnesota study, in one year 840 horses suffered fatal injuries while racing, and an even larger number were killed by injuries sustained during workouts. Approximately 3,500 horses suffered nonfatal injuries that were serious enough to prevent the horses from completing the races.[51]

When horses are no longer useful for racing, they are used for breeding or, as is usually the case, sold at auction for slaughter. Approximately 75 percent of all racehorses end up at the slaughterhouse; according to the Food and Agricultural Organization of the United Nations, the United States slaughters approximately one hundred thousand horses per year.

In addition to horse racing, the United States has a large dog-racing business. Approximately forty thousand racing greyhounds are born annually and shipped to training farms around the country. Although the greyhound-racing industry appears to be in decline, approximately forty-eight racing tracks still operate in fifteen states, handling over $2 billion annually in wagering. The dogs at greyhound tracks are often housed in small individual cages that are stacked one upon another in kennel facilities that hold up to a thousand dogs. They are kept in their cages for eighteen to twenty-two hours a day. Older dogs and those who are less competitive are killed, sold to laboratories, sold to racetracks in

Latin America, or given to adoption groups. The Greyhound Protection League, which coordinates the rescue and adoption of greyhounds used for racing, estimates that between twenty and twenty-five thousand dogs are killed every year as a direct result of the racing industry, and that about ten thousand are adopted.[52]

Marine-mammal shows. A number of amusement parks contain marine-mammal shows in which dolphins, orcas, seals, sea lions, and other animals perform "tricks" for the public. These animals are, for the most part, captured from the wild and trained with methods that include physical intimidation and deprivation. In the wild many marine mammals live with families in pods or other social groupings for the whole of their lives, and the conditions of confinement are highly stressful for these animals under the best of circumstances. Moreover, animals such as dolphins and killer whales navigate and communicate through echolocation, a process by which the animals send out sounds at different frequencies. When these animals are confined in tanks, pools, and other spaces, their sounds bounce back at them, causing them severe distress. In the words of animal trainer Richard O'Barry, who trained the dolphins used in the *Flipper* television series, "To imprison [these animals] in small concrete pens is the same as sentencing sight-oriented creatures like ourselves to live in enclosed spaces surrounded by mirrors. It would be disturbing—maddening."[53]

Most captive marine mammals live only a fraction of their normal life spans; they die from stress or from ulcers or other stress-induced diseases. Eighty percent of all the orcas who have been captured in the last thirty years have died, usually before the age of eight; in the wild they can live to be eighty years old. Besides dying prematurely, marine mammals often engage in stress-induced aberrant behaviors, such as aggression and fighting, that do not occur in the wild.

Animal "actors." Over three hundred movies and television shows using animals are made annually in the United States. Although the American Humane Association (AHA) supposedly supervises the production of these movies and shows, this organization has no significant legal authority over animal use. Indeed, the AHA receives funding from and has a very close relationship with the movie industry it is supposed to regulate. As Jill Donner, a television writer-producer, has noted, "AHA has done nothing to change the fact that when an animal is used for entertainment, abuse is almost always an unseen part of the performance."[54] Not only are animals abused, injured, and killed during the making of films and television shows, they are also abused and injured during their training and confinement off the set. Animals are often trained with violent methods, and they spend most of their lives in small cages or other small enclosures. American television personality Bob Barker has been instrumental in exposing the abuse of animals used in films.

All of these uses of animals for entertainment purposes have one thing in common: they are wholly unnecessary. And if a prohibition against unnecessary suffering means *anything*, it should mean a prohibition of these uses. Again, I have focused primarily upon uses of animals in the United States, but Americans certainly hold no monopoly on animal use for entertainment purposes. Such "spectator sports" as bullfighting are popular in Spain and France, and many European zoos are as bad as or worse than zoos in the United States. Many uses of animals for entertainment purposes, such as rodeos or bullfights, are thought to be justified by cultural tradition. Such an argument is no more valid in this context than it is in the context of animal agriculture or hunting.

Fur: Pain and Suffering for Fashion[55]

Approximately 40 million animals are killed annually worldwide so that we can make their pelts into coats and other articles of clothing. About 30 million of these animals, including mink, foxes, chinchillas, and raccoon dogs are raised and killed on "fur farms" that involve conditions similar to those seen in factory farming. The animals are kept in small wire cages in large sheds, and this extreme confinement of animals that would normally range over a large territory causes many of them to develop behavioral disorders such as stereotypical pattern pacing, infanticide, and self-mutilation. Confinement-induced stress also causes ulcers and other physical disorders. Inbreeding and efforts to develop new fur colors have resulted in deformities such as twisted necks and hearing loss, as well as in weakened immune systems. Ranch-raised fur animals are killed by gassing, neck breaking, poison injection, and anal or genital electrocution. Some European nations are phasing out fur farming for some or all species, although fur farming is increasing in Asia.

Another 10 million animals are trapped for their fur. This figure does not include those non-target or "trash" animals, such as squirrels, opossums, dogs, cats, and birds, that are inadvertently caught in these traps and that make the true number of animal deaths much higher. The primary device for trapping furbearing animals is the leghold trap, which is composed of two metal jaws that slam shut on the animal's paw. Although these traps are sometimes lined with a strip of synthetic material, such "padded" traps are every bit as painful and traumatic for the animal as the unpadded variety. Trappers also use body-grip traps in which two rectangular frames slam shut on the full body of the animal, as well as snares, which are cables shaped like a noose that catch the animal's paw and become tighter as the animal struggles to become free. Animals are often left in these traps for days at a time. They suffer dehydration, blood loss, predation, limb swelling, torn ligaments, and self-mutilation, such as chewing off their limbs in order to escape and the loss of teeth as the animal bites at the metal trap. If the animal is still alive when the trap is checked, the trapper will shoot, stomp, or club the trapped animal. The leghold trap has been banned in a number of countries, and some countries have banned the use of body-grip traps and snares as well.

In the United States estimates vary, but approximately 8 to 10 million animals are killed for fur each year, and the number of animals trapped is estimated to be between 4 and 5 million. Again, this number does not include non-target animals that are trapped and either killed or released in an injured state. The leghold trap is the most common device used to capture furbearing animals in the United States. Although 80 percent of Americans are in favor of banning the trap, only five states have done so, and efforts to obtain a ban at the federal level have thus far been unsuccessful. State laws vary on the required times to check traps. Some states have no time limits while others require trap checks on a periodic basis (for example, twenty-four hours), but these time limits are rarely enforced even where they exist, and an animal caught in a leghold trap, body-grip trap, or snare can remain there for long periods of time. Approximately 3 million mink are produced on American fur farms, and other species, such as fox, rabbit, and chinchilla, are farmed as well. It can take anywhere from ten to twenty pelts to make one fox coat; thirty to seventy pelts to make one mink coat; thirty to forty pelts to make one raccoon or rabbit coat, and thirty to two hundred pelts to make one chinchilla coat.

No one can seriously maintain that the use of animals for fur is necessary. Not only do trapped or farmed animals suffer considerably, but the environmental effects of the fur industry are devastating. Fur farms, like factory farms used for animal agriculture, produce enormous amounts of waste that pollute soil, ground water, and air, and increase algae growth that affects fish. As a part of fur production, various animals have been introduced into foreign habitats with often unfortunate results, and trapping causes the immediate destruction of predator populations that then rebound to even higher levels because of increased food sources and habitat.

We should not forget that other animal products, such as leather and wool, are also used for clothing, though they are more a byproduct of animal use for food than is fur. In any event, there are many alternatives, such as cotton and synthetics, that render wholly unnecessary the use of any animals for clothing.

We accept as an uncontroversial matter that merely because animals are sentient—that they are capable of suffering—we have a direct moral and legal obligation not to inflict unnecessary suffering on them. Although we may not always agree as to what constitutes necessary suffering, it is clear that if the humane treatment principle is to be meaningful, it must preclude the infliction of suffering for purposes of our amusement, pleasure, or convenience. Nevertheless, the most significant number of animals that we use—for food—are raised and killed merely because we derive pleasure from eating them. Other significant animal use—for sport hunting, fishing, entertainment, and fashion—also runs afoul of the prohibition against unnecessary suffering. Although we may prefer humans over animals in situations of true emergency or conflict, our decision to eat meat, attend a rodeo, go hunting, or buy a fur coat, is simply not comparable to a situation in which we are confronted with the decision to save the human or the animal in a burning house.

In the next chapter, we will explore the question of necessity in a different context—the use of animals for biomedical experiments, testing, and education. Although such uses may arguably not be unnecessary in the same way, we will see that there are, nevertheless, important questions about the necessity of animal use in that context as well.

2

Vivisection: A Trickier Question

IN CHAPTER 1, we encountered the humane treatment principle, which holds that we may prefer humans to animals in situations of true emergency or conflict, but also holds that we have an obligation that we owe directly to animals not to inflict unnecessary suffering on them. We also saw that animal agriculture, which accounts for the largest number of animals by far that we use annually, as well as hunting, fishing, the use of animals in entertainment, and the use of animals for fur, cannot be regarded as necessary in any sense. If the humane treatment principle means anything, it means that we cannot justify animal suffering merely because it facilitates our pleasure, amusement, or convenience, or because it represents some "tradition."

In this chapter, we will consider animal use in a context that many of us think presents a true conflict or emergency that requires us to choose human interests over animal interests: vivisection, or the use of animals in experiments, testing, and education. Later in the book, I will argue that if we want to accord moral significance to animal interests, then we ought not to use animals even for these purposes any more than we ought to use homeless or retarded humans to provide benefits for the rest of us. For the present, I will assume simply that we cannot analyze vivisection in the same way that we did the uses discussed in Chapter 1, in that we cannot characterize the use of animals to find cures for human diseases as transparently frivolous. I will, however, argue that the alleged necessity of vivisection raises very serious questions, even if we assume that experiments on animals are apparently analogous to the situation of the burning house. Although vivisection technically covers any use of live animals for experiments, testing, or science education, I will consider these topics separately.

As a prelude to this discussion, it is interesting to note that the use of animals for scientific purposes was a primary focus of both the British animal advocates in the nineteenth century and the American animal rights movement in the twentieth.[1] This is not to say that animal advocates have not promoted vegetarianism, or opposed hunting or the use of animals in entertainment or for fur. It is only to observe that vivisection has been a major concern of animal advocates, even though it at least appears to present more difficult necessity issues than do these other uses of animals and involves fewer animals than does the use of animals for food or hunting. As a result, there are more laws in both the United States and Great Britain that purport to regulate vivisection than any other animal use. Whether these laws are effective is a separate matter that will be addressed in Chapter 3. The emphasis by animal advocates on vivisection may have to do with the fact that this use of animals involves a relatively small and specialized portion of the population, and therefore the criticism of vivisection is less threatening to the general public than is advocacy of vegetarianism. Indeed, there have been many animal advocates who opposed vivisection but who continued to eat meat and engage in other forms of animal exploitation, or who have taken positions against vivisection but not against other forms of animal exploitation.[2]

The Use of Animals in Experiments

Those who support the use of animals in experiments argue that animal use is morally acceptable when it is necessary for human health, where there are no feasible alternatives, and as long as the researcher acts to minimize any pain and discomfort the animals experience. The Foundation for Biomedical Research claims that animals are used only for important purposes, such as finding cures for cancer, diabetes, hypertension, Alzheimer's disease, infectious diseases, AIDS, and cystic fibrosis, and that "research institutions make every effort to eliminate or minimize any possible pain and distress to laboratory animals." The

Foundation claims that "[w]hile researchers place a higher value on human life than animal life, they recognize their special obligation to safeguard the welfare of laboratory animals . . . [and to] [u]se animal models only when nonanimal models are inadequate or inappropriate . . . [and to] [u]se as few animals as possible."[3] According to the Foundation, only a small number of animals used in experiments in American laboratories experience any pain or distress. As a general matter, the research community purports to accept the "three R's": *reduction*, or the use of fewer animals to obtain the required information; *refinement*, or the alteration of existing procedures to minimize pain, suffering, distress, or discomfort; and *replacement*, or the use of research models, such as computer modeling, that do not involve animals.[4] The "three R's" represent an explicit recognition that if there are alternatives to using animals, then using animals at all is wrong, and that when researchers do determine that they need to use animals for a particular experimental purpose, they are morally obligated to impose only that amount of pain and suffering necessary for the purpose. These views are reflected in laws such as the federal Animal Welfare Act and its implementing regulations, which require those who use animals in experiments to demonstrate that they have considered alternatives to animal use and that they have consulted with a veterinarian for the planning of any painful procedures.

In other words, those who support vivisection claim in effect that their use of animals, unlike that for food or hunting, entertainment, or fur, is truly necessary: they claim to use animals only when there is no feasible alternative, whereas there is virtually always a feasible alternative to our other animal uses. They portray our use of animals in experiments as involving a choice similar to that we face when we encounter the burning house and argue that we must choose between saving the human with the dreaded disease or the animals we are going to use in the experiment. And they claim that they impose only that amount of suffering on the animals that is necessary for the purpose.

Despite these claims, the reality of animal use in this context is a far cry from the picture of researchers in spotless labs using a small number of animals to find cures for cancer or AIDS and inflicting little or no pain or distress. To the contrary, the use of animals in biomedical research is no less callous or exploitive, no less an industry, than is factory farming or wildlife management. Animal experimenters use animals for all sorts of trivial purposes that cannot be considered necessary in any coherent sense. Moreover, the empirical data suggest that experimenters are not particularly conscientious about minimizing pain and distress in animals, in part because they are reluctant even to recognize the existence of that pain and distress. In a very real sense, many in the research community still cling to the idea that animals are Cartesian automatons that do not even experience pain and suffering.[5]

In the United States millions of animals are used annually for the development and testing of surgical procedures, devices, pharmaceutical drugs, and consumer products, as well as for various kinds of experiments involving the creation of models of diseases that are supposed to mimic conditions found in humans. Vivisectors view laboratory animals as "research tools" that are similar enough to humans to be of use in understanding human physical and psychological problems but dissimilar enough to render them disposable in a way that humans are not. According to the Office of Technology Assessment of the U.S. Congress (OTA), "[e]stimates of the animals used in the United States each year range from 10 million to upwards of 100 million." OTA concluded that "[a]ll these data are unreliable" because "every estimate of animal use stands as a rough approximation."[6] The federal government regulates animal experimentation through the federal Animal Welfare Act, which is enforced and administered by the U.S. Department of Agriculture (USDA).[7] The USDA requires that research facilities report numbers of animals used, but the Animal Welfare Act does not cover rats and mice, and therefore reporting requirements do not apply to these animals, which, according to the federal government, account for approximately 90 percent of the animals used. Federal reporting requirements also exclude birds, reptiles, and amphibians, as well as horses and other farm animals used in agricultural research. Moreover, many animals are produced for experiments but are ultimately not used because they do not meet certain specifications, such as age, sex, or general health. Federal estimates of animals that are discarded for these reasons are as high as 50 percent. As a result, although the USDA reports that approximately 1.5 to 2 million animals are used annually in experiments, this number, when adjusted to include rats, mice, and other laboratory animals, and those animals that are not actually used in experiments, is probably well in excess of 20 million annually, and this is a *most* conservative estimate.[8]

Most of the animals used in laboratory experiments are bred and sold by large corporations, such as Charles River Laboratories, which describes itself as "the largest laboratory animal production company in the world. We currently produce highly defined purpose-bred laboratory animals in 14 countries, including the United States, Canada, Japan, and throughout Europe."[9] Charles River advertises its own patent-protected strains of animals and even offers animals that are genetically altered to meet researcher desires. Animals may be bred to have certain sorts of seizures, to be susceptible to particular cancers, to have muscular dystrophy or diabetes, to have no immune response, or to be anemic. As one Charles River representative stated, "If you read the papers, everything seems to have carcinogenic effects, but that means more animal testing, which means growth for Charles River. So you can see why we continue to be enthused and excited."[10] Because corporations like Charles River charge hundreds or thousands of dollars for larger animals, such as dogs or cats, laboratories that use these animals often acquire them directly from animal shelters or pounds for a nominal fee, or from animal dealers who collect dogs and cats from shelters, race tracks, and private homes (in response to "free to good home" ads), and then sell them to laboratories for large sums but for less than what is charged by commercial animal producers. A significant number of animals who are used in laboratories are stolen pets who end up in the hands of animal dealers.[11] In addition to the revenues generated by the sale of animals to laboratories, rivers of capital flow into industries that manufacture cages and other supplies necessary to house the millions of animals involved, and hundreds of millions of federal tax dollars are provided annually as grants to vivisectors. Animal research is big business.

Animals used in laboratories are kept in small cages, usually made of metal or plastic, for the duration of their lives.[12] For example, federal regulations require that a guinea pig weighing less than 350 grams be provided sixty square inches of living space. For the most part, animals are kept isolated from other animals, and few animals receive any opportunity for exercise.

Although supporters of vivisection would have the public believe that the use of animals in experiments is necessary, this position is open to question on a number of levels.

First, animals are routinely used to develop medical procedures or therapies; therefore, it is difficult to make any accurate factual representation about the actual causal role that animal use has played in any particular medical discoveries. Since animals are always used as models of disease or to test procedures or drugs, how can we know whether the procedures or discoveries that are attributed to animal use would not have occurred in its absence? In order to understand this point more clearly, consider the following example. Jane, a car mechanic, wears special gloves when she is working on car engines. Every time Jane successfully solves an engine problem, she attributes her success to these special gloves. Jane's attribution of a causal relationship between her wearing the gloves and her particular success may indeed be accurate. But then again, it may not be accurate, and if Jane is to know for certain what effect the gloves have, she will need to do the same job without the gloves. Only then will Jane be able to say with confidence that the gloves are responsible for her successes. Similarly, researchers always use animals to test or develop procedures or drugs and, like Jane, they cannot prove that the animal use is causally responsible for any successes they achieve.

Even if there is a causal link between animal use and benefits for human health, that link is usually very attenuated. We are all used to hearing from the media about supposed scientific discoveries involving animals and the story almost always ends with a caveat about whether the results will ever be applicable to humans, or that any application to human health problems is years away. Animal use is often portrayed as involving applied research, or research that is directly applicable to human problems, when it in fact involves basic research, which employs scientific method to investigate the processes of natural phenomena, most of which will never lead to any application for humans. Moreover, because of the biological differences between humans and other animals, there is always a problem extrapolating the results of animal experiments to humans.

Second, to say that animal use is necessary for human health is to say that there is no way to solve human health problems in the absence of animal use. But even if animal experiments produce information that is beneficial to human health, it does not follow that animal experiments are the only or the most efficient way to solve human health problems. Animal experiments cost billions of dollars annually. If those dollars were spent in other ways, the end result might very well be better. The billions of dollars that have been spent on AIDS research using animals, for example, have produced very little of use to humans suffering from AIDS. AIDS researcher Dr. Dani Bolognesi has stated that "[n]o animal models faithfully reproduce . . . HIV-1 infection and disease in humans, and the studies of experimental vaccines in animal models . . . have yielded disparate results."[13] If those same dollars were spent on public safe-sex education campaigns, needle exchanges, and condom distribution, the rate of new HIV cases would drop dramatically. In many ways, the choice to use animal experiments to solve a problem is as much a political as a scientific decision. Animal experiments are considered an acceptable way of solving the AIDS problem; needle exchanges, condom distribution, and education about safe sex are much more controversial. But that does not mean that animal experiments are any more effective in solving the problem; indeed, they may be less effective.

Third, there is considerable empirical evidence that challenges the notion that animal experiments are necessary for human health purposes and that indicates that in many instances animal use has actually been counterproductive. For example, by 1963 various studies had demonstrated a strong correlation between cigarette smoking and lung cancer, but virtually all attempts to create an animal model of lung cancer through smoking had failed. As a result, leading cancer researchers, such as Dr. Clarence Little, proclaimed that the failure to induce experimental cancers in animals "casts serious doubt on the validity of the cigarette-lung cancer theory."[14] Because the animal experiments did not agree with the human data, the cigarette industry was able to delay health warnings about cigarettes for years, and many humans died as a result. Again, animal research served a political and economic goal, not a scientific one. Similarly, it was clear by the early 1940s that asbestos caused cancer in humans, but since animal experiments did not confirm the dangers of asbestos, this substance went unregulated in the United States for decades.[15]

Although the United States launched a "War on Cancer" in 1971 and has spent many billions of dollars on cancer research, the age-adjusted total cancer mortality rate has been steadily climbing. Dr. Irwin Bross, director of biostatistics of the Roswell Park Memorial Institute for Cancer Research, stated that while "conflicting animal tests have often delayed and hampered advances in the war on cancer, they have never produced a single substantial advance either in the prevention or treatment of human cancer."[16] A 1987 report of the U.S. Government Accounting Office found that the National Cancer Institute statistics "artificially inflate the amount of 'true' progress" against cancer.[17] Important genetic, molecular, and immunological differences distinguish humans from other animals, and as cancer researcher Dr. Jerome Leavitt has explained, human cancer "may have critical mechanical differences which may in turn require different, uniquely human approaches to cancer eradication."[18]

Other medical discoveries attributed to animal use have often been made despite animal use and not because of it. Polio experiments involving monkeys, for instance, falsely indicated that the virus infected only the nervous system, and this mistake—directly related to reliance on animal "models"—delayed the discovery of the polio vaccine. Indeed, it was research with human cell cultures that led researchers to understand that the polio virus infected nonneural tissue and that the virus could be cultivated on nonneural tissue.[19] Similarly, the use of a human's own veins to replace clogged arteries was delayed because animal experiments with dogs indicated that veins could not be used.[20]

These examples could be multiplied endlessly. Although we assume that vivisection is crucial for human health, most of us base this belief on what those in the scientific establishment tell us. But the evidence supports considerable skepticism about the supposed benefits of vivisection.[21]

Fourth, even if we accept that some use of animals is both required for human health and morally justifiable, it is clear that many uses of animals cannot be described as necessary; indeed, many animal experiments can only be described as bizarre and macabre. Obtaining information about animal use in experiments is often difficult, and researchers take extraordinary measures to keep their experiments, most of which are financed by our tax dollars, from public scrutiny. Nevertheless, the available literature is replete with extraordinary instances of trivial uses of animals and the waste of federal and other public funds that could be used far more effectively. Consider the following:

- Researchers at the University of California at Berkeley spent a decade in an attempt to change female dogs into male dogs and male dogs into female dogs through the use of hormones. One of the conclusions of this research is that female dogs injected with male hormones may develop a sort of penis, but that these hormonally treated females will be unable to use these "penises" to achieve copulation with nontreated females.[22]

- Researchers studying aggression at the State University of New York at Oswego used male rats to observe the effects of castration on killing behaviors. The rats, some of whom were castrated, some injected with male hormone, and others not castrated, were placed in cages with one-day-old baby rats, and their rates of killing and cannibalizing the baby rats were recorded.[23] At Rutgers University, researchers performed aggression studies with animals whose sense of smell had been removed through surgical destruction of olfactory bulbs (located in the brain).[24] At Tufts University, researchers studied aggression in monkeys, rats, and mice, and concluded that alcohol-free animals were more aggressive toward animals who had been forced to consume alcohol.[25] These sorts of studies are still being conducted at many research facilities around the country.

- Researchers at the University of California at Davis investigated the impact of stress on the development of lambs. Three times a week for five weeks after birth, baby lambs were taken from their mothers, suspended in a hammock, and shocked. The lambs were then subjected to more stress at the age of five months to determine whether their reaction was dependent on the infliction of the earlier stress.[26]

- Experimenters at the State University of New York at Albany placed rats in two different sized tubes and gave them severe electric shocks for six hours. Rats shocked in the larger tubes, who could struggle, developed fewer ulcers than rats shocked in the smaller tubes. In a subsequent experiment, these researchers found that rats who were allowed to gnaw while being shocked had fewer ulcers than those not allowed to gnaw.[27]

- Researchers at the University of Wisconsin stitched closed the eyes of fourteen kittens before they ever opened their eyes for the first time. Their brain cells were examined between ages seven and fifteen months to ascertain whether there were nerve cell changes as a result of their blindness.[28]

- At the University of California at San Francisco, experimenters amputated the fingers of eight owl monkeys and then examined the brains of the animals to ascertain whether their perception had been altered to take account of the amputation.[29]

- A popular area of biomedical research involves using animals as "models" for drug addiction. Anyone who is at all familiar with drug addiction in humans understands that such conduct is the result of complex societal factors. Humans are the only animals who use harmful substances, such as alcohol, tobacco, and illicit drugs. In short, animal use in addiction experiments may tell us how animals react when we addict them to a substance they would never encounter, much less use, in their world, but it does not tell us much about the phenomenon of human drug use or addiction. Moreover, even if one supports animal research as a general matter, it is surely questionable whether animals should be made to suffer because humans choose to smoke, drink to excess, or use drugs. In any event, addiction studies are commonly performed on animals, and an enormous amount of federal and state funding is spent on these experiments annually. Rhesus monkeys, squirrel monkeys, baboons, chimpanzees, dogs, cats, rodents, and other animals are forcibly addicted to amphetamines, barbiturates, alcohol, heroin, morphine, cocaine, and other drugs so that their behavior can be tested and monitored. In addiction studies involving monkeys, the animals are often restrained in metal chairs for an average of more than five hours a day with their tails shaved and connected to electrodes. The monkeys are subjected to shocks or to food deprivation in order to coerce them to self-administer drugs or alcohol until they are addicted, and they are then subjected to tests that measure their response to varying levels of shock, given different levels of drug ingestion. Some of the addiction studies last for more than ten years, with the same monkeys made to participate for the entire period. Another common type of addiction study involves addicting pregnant rats to various substances and then measuring the effect of that addiction on the baby rats, who are put through punishment-avoidance tests that measure their ability to escape from water and electric shock and to withstand hypothermia. Some of the baby rats are forced to undergo as many as thirty trials a day.

Despite the use of millions of animals in experiments in which they were subjected to physical and mental suffering, many researchers performing such experiments acknowledge the considerable difficulty of extrapolating data from animal "addicts" to human drug users. For example, one researcher has written that neonatal toxicity tests of cocaine on pregnant rats "tell little about whether cocaine is capable of inducing long-term effects [in humans], which is the principal concern about this drug when taken by women during pregnancy."[30] Another researcher has acknowledged that animal models of drug addiction are ill founded: "Some 60 years of offering alcohol to animals has produced no fundamental insights into the causes of this self-destructive behavior or even a convincing analogue of pathological drinking."[31]

• The "maternal deprivation" experiments of Harry Harlow of the University of Wisconsin are infamous. In these experiments Harlow separated infant monkeys from their mothers and reared them in total isolation or with "surrogate" mothers made of wire and cloth.

Some of these "surrogate" mothers were designed to hurt the infant monkeys whenever the infants sought affection from them. Harlow concluded that the terror and subsequent psychopathology of these infants proved that nurturing maternal contact was important for humans.[32] Similar maternal deprivation studies continue today.

- In the "learned helplessness" experiments conducted by Martin Seligman and his colleagues at the University of Pennsylvania, Seligman shocked and burned dogs with such intensity and duration that the dogs just gave up trying to escape the pain. Many other researchers have performed similar experiments on animals to show that humans will also learn to be "helpless" if they are made to suffer mental or emotional distress over an extended period.[33] A number of research facilities continue to perform such experiments.

- Animals are also used for military research. For example, between 1983 and 1991, the U.S. Army spent $2.1 million for "wound" research.[34] Researchers shot hundreds of cats in the head with steel pellets in order to study the wounds. After the General Accounting Office criticized this research, the Pentagon canceled the project, only to restart it using rats instead of cats, even though the army had stated earlier that rats were an "inappropriate animal model" for these purposes. At the army's Fort Sam Houston, researchers studied the burns produced by immersing rats in boiling water for ten seconds and then infecting the burned portions of their bodies. To study the effects of temperature changes on nerve gas potency, researchers at Brooks Air Force Base exposed rats to subfreezing temperatures for eight hours and then subjected them to nerve gas and forced them to perform behavioral tasks in order to escape electric shocks. Monkeys at the Brooks facility were strapped into flight simulators and forced to maneuver them for ten hours while being subjected to radiation and electric shocks. NASA studied the effects of immobility in space by placing monkeys in full-body casts for fourteen days and then killing them to ascertain the condition of their jawbones. Many of these military experiments have been criticized by other federal agencies as redundant and wholly irrelevant to humans.[35]

- Many animals are used for agricultural research. Indeed, much of the new "high tech" science, such as cloning and transgenic engineering, is intended to facilitate meat production, an activity, as we saw in Chapter 1, that represents a wholly unnecessary use of animals.

In any event, the list of what are undeniably trivial uses of animals goes on and on.[36] The point is not that we have never learned anything of use from animal experiments; the point is only that assertions by vivisectors and their public relations organs that all animal use is concerned with finding cures for human diseases or improving human health are not only wrong but deeply, fundamentally wrong. And a doctorate in science is not required to make such a judgment—common sense suffices.

Fifth, those who defend vivisection claim that when animals are used, researchers strive to inflict no more pain than is absolutely necessary. According to the Foundation for Biomedical Research, minimizing pain and distress in laboratory animals "is an important objective of every responsible researcher." The Foundation claims to recognize the humane treatment principle and maintains that "[i]nflicting unnecessary pain is ethically unacceptable" and that "anesthetics, analgesics, or tranquilizers are routinely administered for procedures likely to be painful or highly uncomfortable." The Foundation, which relies on USDA claims that approximately 6 percent of animals used in experiments suffer pain or distress that is not relieved by anesthesia or analgesia, states that "most research projects involve no painful or potentially painful procedures."[37]

In assessing these claims we should bear in mind that because the Animal Welfare Act does not cover rats and mice—approximately 90 percent of the animals used in American laboratories—the USDA figures about animals used in painful experiments concern only 10 percent of the animals that are actually used. Therefore, assertions like those of the Foundation for Biomedical Research, which purport to describe the use of animals as a general matter and not of merely the small proportion covered by the Animal Welfare Act, are intellectually dishonest.

Moreover, the 6 percent figure represents reports that come exclusively from researchers themselves: that is, we ask researchers who are using animals in research to tell us how many animals they subject to unrelieved pain and distress. Not surprisingly, researchers rarely report that they are inflicting unrelieved pain on animals, and studies of researcher assessments of pain in the laboratory have demonstrated that vivisectors simply—and perhaps selectively—ignore animal pain and suffering. In one study, the USDA determined that Ohio State University had violated the Animal Welfare Act because approximately forty cats had been injured when identification tags became embedded in their necks. The Ohio State annual report to the USDA of animal use for the relevant period indicated that no animals (including the forty cats) were subjected to any unrelieved pain or distress. Apparently, Ohio State vivisectors did not consider that a chain embedded in the flesh caused any suffering or distress. A government inspection of laboratories at Harvard University revealed cages too small for the animals to make normal postural adjustments, rusted cages with exposed sharp wires, moldy food, monkeys entangled in chains, and unacceptable waste accumulation. The Harvard report to the USDA on animal use during the relevant period indicated that no animals (including those confined in substandard housing) were subjected to any pain or distress. In another study, researchers did not consider that placing corrosive substances into the eyes or onto the shaved skin of rabbits caused any pain or distress.[38]

Some vivisectors do not believe that pain and suffering can be measured at all, and many do not consider even intensely invasive procedures to be painful or distressing for animals. Dr. Mary Phillips, a sociologist, studied actual animal use in laboratories and found that researchers did not consider it painful or distressing to inject mice with cobra venom, use rats in acute toxicity tests, or induce cancer in mice and rats without administering pain-relieving drugs. They also did not consider it necessary to administer postoperative analgesia to animals who had undergone major surgery. The vivisectors Phillips studied reported to the government that none of these animals suffered any pain or distress. Phillips reported that "[o]ver and over, researchers assured me that in their laboratories, animals were never hurt" and that "'[p]ain' meant the acute pain of surgery on conscious animals, and almost nothing else."[39]

Moreover, the pain and distress caused to lab animals reach well beyond the confines of a particular experiment or surgery. Animals are caged and isolated, exposed to illnesses beyond those intentionally inflicted in the experiment, and subjected to a battery of invasive monitoring procedures that involve pain, distress, and sometimes death.[40] For example, blood and other bodily fluids are regularly and routinely collected from animals involved in experiments so that the effects of procedures or tests can be recorded. Blood is normally removed through venipuncture, or puncturing the animal's vein, and is sometimes removed through cardiac puncture, or puncturing the heart. The tip of a rodent's tail may be cut off when small amounts of blood are needed, and blood samples are often taken from hamsters by inserting needles into the vessels behind their eyeballs. Urine is collected from animals, often by inserting catheters into their urethras or puncturing their bladders. Experimenters obtain vaginal fluid from female animals by inserting glass pipettes or swabs into their vaginas, or by pushing saline solution into their vaginas until vaginal fluid is forced out. Semen is collected from male animals by electro-ejaculation, which entails placing an electrode in an animal's rectum and running electrical shocks through it. Pumps are used to remove milk from female animals who have been given drugs to stimulate lactation. Rats, mice, guinea pigs, and other small animals are often identified by cutting off the toes of the animals. Animals are constantly stuck with needles and frequently get injections in their footpads, which is particularly painful. Animals are killed by breaking their necks, gassing or freezing them, cutting their arteries, or injecting barbiturates into their veins or hearts. They are normally restrained during many of these procedures. Nevertheless, these procedures are considered "routine" and are virtually never reported as causing any pain or distress, reinforcing Dr. Phillips' conclusion that vivisectors conceive of animal pain as something experienced only during surgery. They disregard any pain that is incidental to these routine procedures, and Phillips reported that the vivisectors she interviewed were unable to answer her questions about the psychological or emotional suffering of animals.

Finally, in recent years, a number of clandestine trips beyond the laboratory door have revealed that researchers—even at prestigious institutions—are less conscientious and concerned about animal pain than they would like us to believe. In 1984, for example, videotapes made by researchers were stolen by animal advocates from a laboratory at the University of Pennsylvania.[41] The tapes showed researchers inflicting head injuries on conscious, unanesthetized baboons while researchers mocked the animals, who were obviously in great pain. This case, and others in which animal advocates have obtained similar evidence, indicate that researchers have little regard for the care of animals used in laboratories.

In sum, vivisectors and their public relations corporations, such as the Foundation for Biomedical Research, claim that animal use in experiments is necessary for human health and that animals used in these experiments do not for the most part suffer pain or distress. These claims are false, and you do not have to be an advocate of animal rights to reach this conclusion. Even if you believe that some animal use in experiments is important for human health and morally justifiable, it is impossible to deny that a considerable amount of animal use is unquestionably trivial and that many of the procedures performed on animals in laboratories cause pain and distress that vivisectors simply ignore.

These trivial uses, and the casual infliction of pain on animals as part of routine laboratory procedures, are compelling evidence that despite vivisectors' ostensible endorsement of the humane treatment principle, there are few if any real limits on vivisection. Animals used in experiments are regarded as nothing more than commodities.

The Use of Animals for Testing

In addition to their use to create "models" of disease or to test surgical procedures, millions of animals are used to test drugs and consumer products such as household cleaners, cosmetics, agricultural chemicals, bleach, detergents, and various industrial lubricants to determine whether they are likely to be toxic or otherwise harmful to humans. A variety of tests are used; we will consider briefly several of the primary ones.[42]

Eye irritancy is measured by the Draize test (named after its inventor, John Draize), in which researchers apply chemicals to the eyes of animals in order to observe ocular tissue damage. Albino rabbits are usually used for these tests because their eyes are large, clear, and easily observable, and because the tearing of their eyes, appreciably less than that of other animals' eyes, does not wash away or dilute the substance to be tested. The rabbits are usually restrained in stocks that immobilize their heads and bodies so that they cannot struggle or rub their eyes. Rabbits have been known to break their backs struggling to free themselves from these stocks. The test usually continues for seven days, "during which the cornea, iris, and conjunctivae are examined for signs of opacity, ulceration, haemorrhage, redness, swelling and discharge."[43] After the test is completed, the animals are either killed or recycled into another experiment.

Skin irritancy is measured by applying the substance to the shaved backs of guinea pigs or rabbits, who are then wrapped in an impervious material in order to retard the evaporation of the chemicals and to keep the substance in contact with the raw skin. The wrap is usually removed after twenty-four hours, and the skin is observed over a period of three days for swelling, scarring, and other injuries. Researchers often conduct another round of testing on previously unexposed areas of the same animals. Some dermal irritancy tests continue for three weeks, and the animals have the substance applied for up to six hours a day.

Acute toxicity testing of drugs and chemicals usually entails "lethal dose (LD)" or "lethal concentration (LC)" tests. The most common LD test, called the LD50 test, seeks to ascertain what quantity of a substance (measured in milligrams per kilogram of body weight) will kill 50 percent of the population over a period of fourteen days, and these acute tests generally continue for up to three months. The substance is force-fed to the animals (rabbits, rats, mice, dogs, or monkeys); it is poured down the animals' throats with dosing needles or syringes or is pumped into their stomachs through tubes. Symptoms experienced by animals include convulsions, paralysis, tremors, and bleeding from the eyes, nose, and mouth. If the concern is that human exposure to the tested substance will come from inhalation rather than ingestion, the LC50 test is used. The animals are placed in chambers and are forced to inhale heavy concentrations of substances such as hair spray, disinfectants, and industrial chemicals.

Chronic toxicity tests, which are called bioassays and are usually concerned with the cancer-causing potential of substances, can last for a period of years, and usually involve rats, mice, or dogs. The animals are divided into at least two groups: those that receive a quantity of the chemical (through forced ingestion or inhalation) that will produce tumors in the animal but will not kill them as in the LD tests, and those that receive half of the higher dose. In addition to developing tumors, these animals often experience lesions, respiratory problems, weight loss, change in blood clotting, and dysfunction of the nervous system, liver, kidney, or other organs. Animals are also used to test for teratogens, or substances that may cause birth defects or other damage to the reproductive system, as well as for neurotoxins, or substances that may have toxic effects on the nervous system.

For the most part, anesthetics and analgesics are withheld from animals used for all of these tests because researchers believe that pain relief may mask certain effects of the substance being tested. Moreover, studies of reports submitted to the government by research facilities confirm that many researchers do not regard these tests as causing pain or distress to the animals used, and so anesthesia and analgesia are not provided.

The controversy over the necessity of animal toxicity and irritancy tests for human health is considerable. Just as many are increasingly skeptical about the use of animals in experiments generally, many scientists and health care professionals are critical of these animal tests. In the first place, there is absolutely no agreement on how to extrapolate the results of animal tests to humans. Although the uncertainty of extrapolation affects all biomedical research involving animals, it is particularly problematic in the context of animal testing, which usually involves predicting how humans will react to exposure over a lifetime to small quantities of a substance on the basis of how animals respond to short-term exposure to large quantities of the substance. In testing the sweetener cyclamate, animals were given the human equivalent of 552 bottles of soft drinks per day; in two experiments involving trichloroethylene, which, among other things, is used to decaffeinate coffee, rats were given the equivalent of 50 million cups of coffee per day.[44] Such high dosing may damage the cells and tissues of the animals so badly that it inhibits the development of cancer that would have occurred, or it may damage the metabolism of the animal and cause a cancer that would not have occurred at lower dosing levels. The problem of extrapolation is compounded by the fact that there is no species of animal that has identical biological reactions to those of humans. For example, rats cannot vomit and, unlike humans, cannot thereby eliminate toxins. With respect to the Draize tests, humans and rabbits differ in eyelid and cornea structure and in tearing ability, and these differences cast serious doubt on any effort to extrapolate results from animals to humans. In comparing rabbit and human data on eye inflammation after exposure to fourteen household products, researchers found that the data differed by a factor of 18 to 250.[45]

Second, animal testing is inherently unreliable. Results from animal toxicity tests can vary dramatically depending on the method that is used. For example, it is not uncommon for an inhalation study of a chemical to result in the development of cancer when oral administration of the same substance does not. Moreover, variations in acute and chronic toxicity tests are also quite dramatic. These variations occur from laboratory to laboratory, within the same species of animal, and between species of animal. The LD50 values of the same chemical may show a tenfold variance within the *same* species. Different species and strains of animals respond in very different ways to the substances tested. A study comparing the carcinogenicity of 214 chemicals in rats and mice found a correlation of only 70 percent.[46] As early as 1983, it was recognized that only seven of the then-known human oral carcinogens caused cancer in nonhuman animals.[47] In addition, variables such as an animal's sex, age, weight, and the stress of the laboratory setting can have a profound impact on the results of these tests.

Putting aside the matter of the effectiveness of these tests, it is beyond doubt that the overwhelming majority of animal toxicity tests have nothing to do with human health. We are barraged by "new and improved" versions of this oven cleaner or that shampoo, and these products are tested on animals not because these products are necessary for human health but because they are necessary for corporate profits. If we maintain that we are opposed to unnecessary animal suffering, we must ask whether it is really necessary to have yet another "new and improved" product. Indeed, as Gillette stated in response to public criticism of its animal testing, the matter is not ultimately one of any moral obligation to animals; it is a matter of corporate "obligation to its stockholders to continue" to market new products.[48]

Finally, in the past twenty years, there has been an explosion of alternatives to animal tests. These include the use of human cell cultures, cell membranes, human skin substitutes, protein compounds that resemble the composition of the eye, computer programs that use molecular structure and other parameters to predict whether a chemical will produce a toxic effect, computer programs that produce models of biological systems, improvements in epidemiological studies, and other advances. These alternatives are much cheaper and faster than the use of animals. A rodent bioassay can cost over $2 million and can take years. A test using a cell culture costs about $1,000 and can be done in a day. A Draize eye-irritancy test can cost thousands of dollars. The use of a protein compound that resembles the eye and will turn cloudy if the substance would irritate the eye costs about $100.

So why are we still using animals for testing? Although there has been some reduction in the use of animals for cosmetics testing, animal testing continues largely unabated precisely *because* of the cost and the time involved in using animals. Only a small number of the approximately seventy-five thousand chemicals currently in use have been tested and there are approximately one thousand new ones coming out every year. The net effect of the cost and the time, combined with the inherent unreliability and variability of the tests that are performed and the resulting difficulty of extrapolating data from animals to humans, is to allow industry to continue marketing products whose safety has not been tested, or products that have been tested but where the animal data are inconsistent or otherwise inconclusive. In addition, because animal tests are still the norm, companies often point to the results of these tests to prove that products are safe when they are sued for injuries sustained by humans, although courts are gradually coming to recognize that animal testing may not provide a shield against liability because the results are irrelevant to humans.

In short, the pharmaceutical and chemical industries, aided by confused and confusing government testing requirements, make guinea pigs of both us and the guinea pigs, while at the same time they sanctimoniously portray themselves as searching for cures for diseases or otherwise improving the quality of human life.

Animal Use in Teaching and Education

In the United States, grammar schools, high schools, colleges, universities, medical schools, and veterinary schools use at least 5.7 million animals annually to teach students about anatomy, surgical techniques, and the effects of drugs. Is such use necessary? Consider that "in most European countries," according to *Scientific American*, "[t]here is no high school dissection."[49] And Britain has not allowed the use of animals to teach surgery skills to medical or veterinary students for over a hundred years. Yet no one claims that British doctors or veterinarians are not properly trained. Indeed, teaching universities in the United States routinely compete for graduates of British programs to participate in American internship and residency programs. A good number of doctors and veterinarians trained in Britain are on the faculties of American schools.

Over the past decade, I and my colleague at Rutgers Law School, Anna Charlton, have been involved in literally hundreds of cases in which students have objected on legal grounds to the use of animals in the classroom.[50] These cases have involved students at all educational levels. We were successful in getting nonanimal alternatives for the students, in large part because the schools were unable to demonstrate that the use of animals was necessary for pedagogical purposes. But although students who objected were offered alternatives, the schools continued to use the animals and allowed non-objecting students to perform all sorts of procedures on animals that the schools could not defend as pedagogically necessary, thus proving the point that these schools regard animals as commodities devoid of morally significant interests.

Although we tend to think of vivisection as involving issues analogous to those that confront us in the burning house scenario, we see that this is simplistic at best. At the very least, there are serious questions about the need for animal use in experiments, testing, and education. And it is clear that even in this context, there is a significant disparity between our claim that we regard animals as having morally significant interests and our treatment of them as commodities whose interests we ignore.

3

The Cause of Our Moral Schizophrenia: Animals as Property

WE MAY THINK it is acceptable or even obligatory to prefer the human over the animal in situations of true conflict or emergency, but we also claim to endorse the humane treatment principle: we recognize that it is morally impermissible to inflict unnecessary pain and suffering on animals. The problem, as we saw, is that the overwhelming portion of the suffering we inflict on animals cannot be described as necessary in any meaningful sense. Indeed, there is a profound disparity between what we say we believe about animals and how we actually treat them. In this chapter, we will explore the reason for this disparity.

Animals: Things That We Own

Animals are our *property;* they are things that we own.[1] In virtually all modern political and economic systems, animals are explicitly regarded as economic commodities that possess no value apart from that which is accorded to them by their owners—whether individuals, corporations, or governments. The status of animals as property is not new; it has been with us for thousands of years. Indeed, historical evidence indicates that the domestication and ownership of animals are closely related to the development of the very ideas of property and money. The word *cattle*, for example, comes from the same word root as the word *capital,* and the two are synonymous in many European languages. The Spanish word for property is *ganaderia;* the word for cattle is *ganado.* The Latin word for money is *pecunia,* which is derived from *pecus,* which means "cattle."[2]

The status of animals as property is particularly important in Western culture for two reasons. First, property rights are accorded a special status and are considered to be among the most important rights we have. The American Revolution was primarily a reaction against British attempts to regulate and restrict property ownership by the colonists, and the Fifth Amendment to the Bill of Rights of the U.S. Constitution prohibits the deprivation of property (or life or liberty) "without due process of law" and provides that no private property shall "be taken for public use, without just compensation."[3] Second, the Western concept of private property, or the system whereby resources are regarded as separate objects that are assigned and belong to particular individuals who are allowed to use the property to the exclusion of everyone else, is explicitly linked to the status of animals as resources that were given to us by God.[4]

The importance of property rights and the role of animals as property are illustrated clearly in the work of John Locke (1632–1704), the primary architect of our theory of property rights.[5] Like most other people of his time, Locke subscribed to the Judeo-Christian belief about the creation of the universe and the establishment by God of human supremacy. In Genesis, the first book of the Bible, we are told that God said: "Let Us make man in Our image, according to Our likeness; let them have dominion over the fish of the sea, over the birds of the air, and over the cattle, over all the earth and over every creeping thing that creeps on the earth."[6] This passage suggests that God created the earth and its resources for the common use of all humans. If, however, we all owned everything in common, how could any of us use any of these resources without infringing on the rights of others to use the same resources? If we all own the trees of the forest in common, then you might very well object when I try to chop down a tree for my own personal use. Locke sought a solution to this problem that allowed me to chop down the tree and at the same time preserve the idea that the tree was initially our common property, and he called this solution the natural right of private property based on labor.

Locke argued that God had created humans in God's image, and that although we all belonged to God rather than to other human beings, humans owned their own bodies and their own labor. Humans could acquire property by "joining" their labor with an object in nature that was otherwise held by humankind in common. If I join my labor to a piece of wood by cutting it from a tree and carving it into a piece of furniture, then I have, through my labor, made that piece of wood my property. I now have a property right in this piece of wood in that I have a claim to the exclusive use and control of the wood and you are under an obligation to respect my claim.

In protecting our interest in property with a right, Locke was saying that our exclusive use and control of things is protected from being taken away simply to benefit someone other than the owner. An owner has a legitimate claim to the possession and use of his property that excludes others from possessing or using it. We usually think of the law as the source of property rights, but Locke regarded the right to property as a "natural" right, that is, as a right stemming ultimately from God that exists independent of any government or legal system established to protect it. The right to property exists "in nature" and depends solely on the investment of human labor into a thing. If the right to property depended on human laws, then legislatures and courts could change these laws and base this right on any arbitrary standard that suited them. This, in Locke's view, would violate God's divine law.[7]

As far as Locke was concerned, because God gave humans dominion over animals, they are no different from any other resource or object that we may own.[8] Although animals have been provided in common to humans, it is necessary "to appropriate them some way or other before they can be of any use, or at all beneficial to any particular Man."[9] And humans can acquire property rights in animals just as they can acquire property rights in any other resource. When, for example, a person hunts and kills a hare, or otherwise joins human labor with an animal, the person has "thereby removed [the animal] from the state of Nature, wherein she was common, and hath begun a Property."[10] "Thus this Law of reason makes the Deer, that Indian's who hath killed it; 'tis allowed to be his goods who hath bestowed his labour upon it, though before, it was the common right of every one."[11]

Locke maintained that animals constitute "the inferior ranks of Creatures"[12] and that we owe them no moral obligation; they are merely resources, like water and trees, that God created for our use. Locke thought we should not "spoil or waste" animals—that is, use them for no purpose—just as he thought we should not "spoil or waste" any of the resources God gave us. Like Kant, whom we met in Chapter 1,

Locke believed that animals could feel pain and could suffer but that our treatment of them was relevant only to the extent that it affected our treatment of other humans. He observed, for example, that "the exclusion of butchers from juries of life and death" reflected a consensus that the practice of butchering animals might make a person less inclined to be compassionate toward people. Of course Locke did not advise that we stop eating animals in order that butchers could serve on juries. Rather, he was concerned about the "mischief," primarily of children, of the "spoiling of any thing to no purpose, but more especially the pleasure they take to put any thing in pain that is capable of it." Locke admonished parents to teach their children kindness to animals because "the custom of tormenting and killing beasts will, by degrees, harden their minds even towards men; and they who delight in the suffering and destruction of inferior creatures, will not be apt to be very compassionate or benign to those of their own kind."[13] Locke's moral compunction about "tormenting and killing beasts" for no purpose was, like Kant's, based not on the harm that *would* come to the animals but on the detriment that *could* come to humans. The child who tortures the cat and the butcher who slaughters the hog, particularly given the conditions of the seventeenth-century slaughterhouse, are both, of course, inflicting excruciating pain on animals. But the child inflicts pain for no purpose and therefore merely spoils or wastes the animal, while the butcher has some purpose based on God's supposed grant to us of animals as our property.

Locke argued, moreover, that there is a close connection between property rights in general and property rights in animals. He maintained that *all* property rights derive from God's grant to humans of dominion over animals and the resulting "Right a Man has to use any of the Inferior Creatures, for the Subsistence and Comfort of his Life" and "for the benefit and sole Advantage of the Proprietor, so that he may even destroy the thing, that he has Property in by his use of it, where need requires."[14] That is, Locke's notion that a property right gives an owner exclusive use of and control over an object—the cornerstone of the modern theory of private property—originated in the exclusive control and use of animals that God supposedly gave to humans.

Locke's theory of property, and of animals as property, had an extraordinary influence on British common law, the system of judge-made law inherited by the United States. William Blackstone, one of the greatest commentators on the common law, stated that "[t]here is noth ing which so generally strikes the imagination, and engages the affections of mankind, as the right of property; or that sole and despotic dominion which one man claims and exercises over the external things of the world, in total exclusion of the right of any other individual in the universe."[15] In discussing the philosophical foundation of the right of property, Blackstone rejected "whatever airy metaphysical notions may have been started by fanciful writers upon this subject," and, relying on Genesis, concluded that "by holy writ, the all-bountiful Creator gave to man 'dominion over all the earth; and over the fish of the sea, and over the fowl of the air, and over every living thing that moveth upon the earth.'"[16] Blackstone relied on Locke's theory and formulated a broad notion of property that would not tolerate the "least violation of it."[17]

Under our present-day law, "animals are owned in the same way as inanimate objects such as cars and furniture."[18] They "are by law treated as any other form of movable property and may be the subject of absolute, *i.e.*, complete ownership . . . [and] the owner has at his command all the protection that the law provides in respect of absolute ownership."[19] The owner is entitled to exclusive physical possession of the animal, the use of the animal for economic and other gain, and the right to make contracts with respect to the animal or to use the animal as collateral for a loan. The owner is under a duty to other humans to ensure that her animal property does not harm others, but she can sell the animal, bequeath the animal, give the animal away, or have the animal taken from her as part of the execution of a legal judgment against her. She can also destroy or kill the animal. Wild animals are generally regarded as owned by the state and held in trust for the benefit of the people, but they can be made the property of particular humans through hunting or taming and confining them.

The Failure of the Humane Treatment Principle and Animal Welfare Laws

The humane treatment principle and the animal welfare laws that supposedly incorporate it as a legal standard purport to recognize Bentham's view that because animals are like us (in that they are sentient), we have a moral and legal obligation that we owe directly to animals not to inflict unnecessary suffering on them. The status of animals as property, however, precludes any meaningful recognition of their interests.

The humane treatment principle establishes a balancing standard; we are supposed to balance our interests against those of animals in order to determine whether particular animal use or treatment is necessary. But because animals are property, and because we have great respect for property rights, we have decided—before we even start our balancing process—that it is morally acceptable to use animals for food, hunting, entertainment, clothing, experiments, product testing, and so forth. That is, we generally do not question whether particular institutions of animal use are necessary; rather, we inquire only whether particular practices that are part of those various institutions are necessary. We question not whether it is necessary to eat animals but whether the de-horning or branding or castrating of cattle is a necessary component of the process of bringing animals to our table—and we look to the commonly accepted practices of the food industry to answer the question. We question not whether it is necessary to use animals for sport, recreation, or entertainment but whether particular practices are necessary in order to use animals for those purposes; and again we look to the commonly accepted practices of those involved in such activities for the answer. In such situations, what we really balance are not the interests of animals against those of humans in some abstract way, but the *interest of the property owner* in using or treating the animal in a particular way against the *interest of the property*, which, in this case, is the animal. It is absurd, however, to talk about balancing the interests of property against those of property owners, since property "cannot have rights or duties or be bound by or recognize rules."[20] Because animals are property, we treat every issue involving the use or treatment of them as analogous to the situation of the burning house, in which we must choose between human and animal interests. The result is that we choose the human interest over the animal even in situations in which the human interest is trivial and the animal interest is fundamental, a matter, literally, of life or death. What we are *really* choosing between, however, is the interest of a property owner and the interest of a piece of property. The outcome of this "conflict of interests" is predetermined.

Although animal welfare laws, and particularly anticruelty laws, supposedly prohibit the infliction on animals of unnecessary suffering, these laws simply do not provide any meaningful level of protection. There are at least five reasons for this failure, all of which are related to the property status of animals. First, many of these laws explicitly exempt most forms of institutionalized exploitation, which account for the largest number of animals that we use. Second, even if these statutes do not explicitly exempt certain forms of animal use, courts have effectively read into them an exemption for most of our animal uses. Third, many anticruelty laws, which are criminal laws, require that a defendant act with a particular mental state, and it is difficult to prove that a defendant who inflicted suffering on an animal when engaged in a customary or accepted property use acted with the required culpable mental state. Fourth, the law presumes that owners will act in their best economic interests and will not inflict more suffering than is necessary on an animal because to do so would diminish the monetary value of the animal. Fifth, there are serious problems concerning the penalties and enforcement of anticruelty and other animal welfare laws. We are generally reluctant to impose the stigma of criminal liability on property owners for what they do with their own property, and we generally prohibit those with no ownership interest from questioning a particular use or treatment of animals.

We will briefly examine each of these reasons why the property status of animal enables us to treat them as beings that lack morally significant interests.

Cruelty Ruled Out from the Beginning: Specific Exemptions[21]

Many anticruelty laws contain explicit exemptions for activities that account for the largest numbers of animals killed in our society.

For example, California provides that its anticruelty law is not applicable to activities permitted under the game laws, laws for the destruction of certain birds, the killing of venomous reptile or other dangerous animals, the killing of animals for food, or the use of animals in experiments conducted under the authority of the faculty of a regularly incorporated medical college or university.[22] The Delaware statute exempts "accepted" veterinary practices and scientific experiments, as well as the killing of animals for food, "provided that such killing is not cruel."[23] Kentucky prohibits the killing of any animal[24]—a prohibition that on its face is the most stringent in the United States—but exempts hunting, fishing, trapping, processing animals for food "or for other commercial purposes," killing for "humane purposes," killing animals for any authorized purpose, and dog training.[25] Maryland law specifically provides that "[c]ustomary and normal veterinary and agricultural husbandry practices including but not limited to dehorning, castration, docking tails, and limit feeding, are not covered" by its anticruelty law.

The statute continues that although it is the intention of the law to protect from intentional cruelty all animals, whether "they, be privately owned, strays, domesticated, feral, farm, corporately or institutionally owned, under private, local, State, or federally funded scientific or medical activities . . . no person shall be liable for criminal prosecution for normal human activities to which the infliction of pain to an animal is purely incidental and unavoidable."[26] Nebraska exempts veterinary practices, experiments conducted by research facilities that conform to certain requirements, hunting, fishing, trapping, animal races, rodeos, pulling contests, and "[c]ommonly accepted practices of animal husbandry."[27] Oregon exempts "[a]nimals subject to good animal husbandry practices," which are defined in another section as including "the dehorning of cattle, the docking of horses, sheep or swine, and the castration or neutering of livestock, according to accepted practices of veterinary medicine or animal husbandry."[28] Pennsylvania exempts any "normal agricultural operation" from its statute and defines these activities as "practices and procedures that farmers adopt, use or engage in year after year in the production and preparation for market of poultry, livestock and their products in the production and harvesting of agricultural, agronomic, horticultural, silvicultural and aquicultural crops and commodities."[29] The most frequent exemptions from anticruelty statutes involve scientific experiments, agricultural practices, and hunting. Some statutes apply only to warm-blooded vertebrate animals.[30]

Whether or not the use of animals in experiments is exempted from the scope of state anticruelty laws, the primary law that regulates this activity, at least in the United States, is the federal Animal Welfare Act.[31] This law, which was originally passed in 1966 and was intended to stop the theft of dogs and cats—human property—for use in experiments, purports to place considerable restrictions on the use of animals in experiments. For example, as we saw in Chapter 2, the Act and its implementing regulations supposedly prohibit the use of animals if nonanimal alternatives are feasible. In addition, it requires that the experimenter minimize pain and consider alternatives to any procedure that may cause pain or distress in an animal. Although it appears that the Act establishes some sort of balance of human and animal interests, there is really no balance at all because it effectively exempts from scrutiny the actual use of animals in experiments. The Act and its implementing regulations provide certain standards for the transportation of animals and require that animals used in experiments receive adequate food, water, and shelter, but the regulation stops there. Once the laboratory door is closed, there are no meaningful legal limits on what an experimenter can do with animals. The Act does not even apply to most of the animals—rats and mice—used in experiments. Moreover, the Act explicitly forbids any interference in the "design, outlines, or guidelines of actual research" or interruption of "the conduct of actual research" or the prescribing of methods of research.[32] The law imposes no limits on the content of animal experiments or on the amount of pain or suffering that may be imposed on animals in the conduct of these experiments. As a result, the researcher or research facility decides what uses of animals are appropriate, presumably in conjunction with any public or private funding source that may be involved, and these uses are effectively insulated from meaningful regulation.

Necessary Suffering: Whatever Makes Animals "More Serviceable for the Use of Man"[33]

Even if an anticruelty statute does not explicitly exempt particular animal uses, courts have effectively exempted our common uses of animals from scrutiny by interpreting these statutes as not prohibiting the infliction of even extreme suffering, so long as it is incidental to an accepted use of animals. For example, in *Cinadr v. State*, the court, which emphasized that despite anticruelty laws "the right of property in domestic animals is not open to question," reversed the defendant's conviction for "needlessly" killing a hog, because "the exercise of judgment by the owner to slaughter [the owner's own] animals [is not] the proper subject" of the anticruelty law.[34] Moreover, the legal definition of cruel treatment differs significantly from what most of us would regard as cruel treatment in our ordinary, non-legal thinking. In *Murphy v. Manning*, the court noted that "[u]ndoubtedly every treatment of an animal which inflicts pain, even the great pain of mutilation, and which is cruel in the ordinary sense of the word, is not necessarily" prohibited by an anticruelty law.[35] And in *Lewis v. Fermor*, the court remarked that cruelty "does not mean merely inflicting pain. . . . Much pain is often inflicted where the operation is necessary, as for instance in the case of cautery, which is practised on animals. . . . That is torture, and in one sense it may be called cruel; but in my opinion, in this statute the word 'cruelly' must refer to something done for no legitimate purpose."[36]

Although anticruelty statutes supposedly prohibit the infliction of unnecessary pain and suffering, courts generally hold that any treatment that facilitates our use of animals for an accepted purpose is considered necessary under the laws. We do not balance interests in order to determine the legality of the allegedly cruel act or the legality of the animal use of which the cruelty is a part. Rather, we look to whether the activity the defendant seeks to engage in is an accepted institutionalized use of animals. If it is, we then look to whether the allegedly cruel act is considered a normal part of that use by those involved in the institution, or is intended to enable that use. Such a framework will accept the standard of "necessity" defined by animal property owners, and explains why the anticruelty laws have not been able to touch certain activities, such as animal agriculture or hunting.

In cases dealing with the treatment of animals used for food, for instance, courts have held that pain and suffering inflicted on animals is necessary "[w]henever the purpose for which the act is done is to make the animal more serviceable for the use of man."[37] When we inquire whether our treatment of animals used for food runs afoul of anticruelty laws, we do not ask whether the treatment is "cruel" as we would ordinarily use that term. Instead, we ask whether the treatment facilitates the use of the animal for the intended purpose and increases its marketability. If it does so, then the treatment is, by definition, not "cruel" under the anticruelty laws. As one court observed, "[i]t must have come to the attention of many that the treatment of 'animals' to be used for food while in transit to a stockyard or to a market is sometimes not short of cruel and, in some instances, torturable. Hogs have the nose perforated and a ring placed in it; ears of calves are similarly treated; chickens are crowded into freight cars; codfish is taken out of the waters and thrown into barrels of ice and sold on the market as 'live cod'; eels have been known to squirm in the frying pan; and snails, lobsters, and crabs are thrown into boiling water."[38]

In *Bowyer v. Morgan*,[39] the court held that branding lambs on the nose with a hot iron did not violate the anticruelty law because, although it was "cruel" in that it caused pain to the animal, it was "reasonably necessary" for identification purposes, and because the practice had become customary in Wales. Once we accept the legitimacy of eating animals, then whatever is necessary to facilitate that form of exploitation—even if it causes excruciating pain, as the veterinary experts on both sides in *Bowyer* agreed—falls outside the scope of the anticruelty statute altogether. A close examination of *Bowyer*, together with the summary of the opposing expert testimony given at trial, shows that the trial court considered the branding necessary in large part because it was customary, even though less painful alternatives existed.

In *Lewis v. Fermor*, Fermor, a veterinarian, was prosecuted under an anticruelty law that made it a crime to "cruelly abuse, ill-treat, or torture any animal." Fermor had spayed some sows, an operation that "consists in cutting out the uterus and ovaries, and removing them through an incision made in the flank of the sow for the purpose."[40] He had provided no pain relief, so the court acknowledged that he "did inflict pain, and it may be that he inflicted torture."[41] Nevertheless, the court held that Fermor did not violate the anticruelty law because he had inflicted pain and suffering in order to benefit the owners of the animals by increasing the weight and development of the sows. The court made very clear that whether severe pain or even torture was permitted by the anticruelty law depended on whether it was inflicted for a "legitimate purpose," such as to increase the weight of the animal and thereby provide a benefit to the owners of the animal. In response to evidence that spaying had no effect on the weight or development of the animals, the court noted that the practice was common among pig farmers in the region and that there was "wide-spread belief in its utility,"[42] and that as long as Fermor believed that the operation would provide an economic benefit for the owners of the sows, the procedure, although severely painful, did not violate the anticruelty law.

Similarly, an Irish court in *Callaghan v. Society for the Prevention of Cruelty to Animals* held that dehorning of cattle did not violate the anticruelty statute because the practice was common among cattle owners in Ireland. The court held that cruelty applied only to "unnecessary abuse" and stated that if the purpose of animal treatment was "'to make the animal more serviceable for the use of man,'" then the law did not apply.[43] In this case, the dehorning was supposedly done to ensure that cattle, who were being raised and transported in crowded conditions, would not injure each other, and the court found that the procedure was "necessary for the proper exercise of the system of straw yard feeding, which is a reasonable and profitable mode of cattle farming, and also an act which renders the animal more quiet and tractable, and less liable to injury from its fellows, both in the yard and in transit, and of more value to its owner."[44] According to the court, "[t]he pain caused to the animals in this case cannot be said to be an unnecessary abuse of the animal, that is reared up, tended, and fed, with the object of having it as soon as possible made ready for slaughter, if the operation by which the pain is caused enables the owners to attain this object either more expeditiously or more cheaply." Dehorning is something that farmers do "in the course of their trade, having found that they make the animals more profitable by having this operation performed on them."[45] The court emphasized that even acts that cause extreme pain are perfectly lawful if the action makes the animal more useful for human purposes.

There have been some cases that have ostensibly held that the profit and convenience of the owner do not in and of themselves justify the infliction of suffering on animals. But close examination of these cases reveals that they really hold that the imposition of suffering may be justified for economic reasons as long as the practice in question is commonly accepted by those involved in animal agriculture and not the idiosyncratic practice of a particular farmer or intended to deceive the public. For example, in *Ford v. Wiley*, an English court held that the dehorning of older cattle with saws violated the anticruelty law because it caused unnecessary suffering. The court had no difficulty with any procedure "without which an animal cannot attain its full development or be fitted for its ordinary use,"[46] and held that "[m]utilation of horses and bulls is necessary, and, if properly performed, undoubtedly lawful; because without it, in this country at least, the animals could not be kept at all."[47] In another example, the court noted that although a horse may be "designed for draught and riding purposes, [the horse] is not in its natural untutored state so fitted. To prevent it from being unruly and unsafe, it requires to be broken, sometimes with a degree of severity, occasioning pain, which without such necessity would be utterly unjustifiable."[48] The court noted that there were alternatives to sawing off the horns of older cattle, including the removal with a knife of the core of the horn before the animal was six months old, which, although still painful, would not run afoul of the anticruelty law. But the primary criterion upon which the court relied was that the practice of dehorning older cattle had been discontinued for twenty years in England, Wales, and most parts of Scotland, and was therefore no longer an accepted agricultural practice. The court noted that the owners of cattle had, with very few exceptions, including the defendants in the case, concluded as a matter of animal husbandry that dehorning of older cattle was not necessary to make the animal "fitted for its ordinary use" and that the defendants were involved in an attempt to deceive potential buyers about the quality of the cattle.[49]

Subsequent English cases have made clear that if a practice concerning animals used for food is an accepted part of animal husbandry, then the resulting suffering is necessary and the practice does not violate the anticruelty law even if there are alternatives that would cause less suffering.

For example, in a 1985 English case, *Roberts v. Ruggiero*, Roberts, a representative of an animal advocacy organization, argued that the intensive raising of veal calves violated the anticruelty law.[50] Roberts argued that *Ford v. Wiley* required that the court consider alternative ways of raising veal calves. The court in *Ruggiero* rejected this argument, stating that the intensive raising of veal calves was, unlike the dehorning in *Ford v. Wiley*, an accepted practice of animal husbandry. Although the intensive rearing of veal calves was modified in Britain by specific legislation, the court refused to find that the practice violated the anticruelty laws, even though there was no doubt that there were alternatives that would cause less suffering to the animals. In short, *Ford v. Wiley* and its progeny stand for the proposition that economic gain by animal owners justifies the imposition of suffering as long as the conduct in question is customary within the industry. Indeed, were this not the case, intensive farming, which is based exclusively on profit and convenience for animal owners, and which is prevalent throughout the United States, Great Britain, and Western Europe and is rapidly spreading throughout other parts of the world, would never have been possible.

Similarly, in the 1892 American case *State v. Crichton*, the court, following *Ford v. Wiley*, held that dehorning cattle with saws could not be justified merely by increased profit or convenience of a particular owner, but it could be justified if it facilitated the ordinary use for which the animal was designed.[51] The court stated that if the procedure could be shown to "render the flesh nutricious [*sic*] and wholesome," or if it could be proved that animals with horns cause more injury to each other than is caused by dehorning, then the procedure would be justified as facilitating the service of the animal for human purposes. The court focused on the fact that dehorning of cattle with saws was not a historically accepted practice in animal husbandry. Echoing *Ford*, it noted that the "mutilation of horses, bulls, and other male species is necessary and undoubtedly lawful, for without it, they could not be fully developed and fitted for their ordinary use to man."[52] In the years since 1892, however, dehorning of cattle, from calves to older animals, without anesthesia, has become an accepted practice of American animal husbandry; accordingly, the resulting suffering of the animals is considered necessary and is exempted from the scope of anticruelty laws, whether through explicit legislative exemptions or judicial interpretation.

Dozens of other cases support the thesis that in any inquiry into whether a particular method of husbandry or slaughter is humane, we generally look to what is customarily done; if the practice comports with custom, it is not considered cruelty. In *Commonwealth v. Anspach*, the defendant, a manager of a Sears, Roebuck & Co. store, was charged with violating the anticruelty statute by placing a small chicken in a bottle for the purpose of advertising a special chicken feed that was given to the confined chick.[53] The bottle was nineteen inches high and had wire netting on which the chick stood. The court held that so confining the chick did not constitute a violation of the anticruelty statute because the custom in the industry was, according to the court, even more inhumane. One expert witness, upon whom the court relied, stated that young chicks were routinely placed in drawers that were only eight or nine inches high and had much less space than the chick had in the bottle, that wire floors were common in brooder houses, and that commercial practice was tending toward restrictive chicken cages in any event. Moreover, the court noted that other farm animals are kept under very confined circumstances. Again, the question whether the conduct was cruel, as cruelty is ordinarily understood, did not enter the picture.

Cases involving the exploitation of animals in contexts other than food production support the thesis that our institutionalized uses of animals—however much pain and suffering they may cause—are generally outside the scope of anticruelty laws. In one of the few cases in which a vivisector was prosecuted under a state anticruelty law, *Taub v. State*, Taub's conviction for failing to provide adequate veterinary care to monkeys he was using in experiments was overturned by the Maryland appellate court because, according to the court, the state anticruelty statute was not meant to apply to animals used in scientific experiments. Although the statute did not contain an explicit exemption for animals used in experiments, the court held that "there are certain normal human activities to which the infliction of pain to an animal is purely incidental and unavoidable," and that scientific research using animals is one such activity.[54]

Animal Cruelty: A State of Mind[55]

State anticruelty laws, as opposed to regulatory statutes such as the federal Animal Welfare Act, are generally criminal laws; with most criminal laws the state must prove that a defendant engaged in an unlawful act in a culpable state of mind. In the case of anticruelty laws, the state must prove beyond a reasonable doubt not only that a defendant imposed pain and suffering on an animal but that he did so maliciously, willfully, intentionally, knowingly, recklessly, or negligently.[56] The problem is that if a defendant is inflicting pain or suffering on an animal as part of an accepted institutional use of animals, it is very difficult to prove—and prove beyond a reasonable doubt—that the defendant acted with the requisite mental state to justify the charge of criminal liability.

For example, in *Regalado v. United States*, Regalado was convicted of violating the anticruelty statute of the District of Columbia for beating a puppy. Regalado appealed, arguing that the evidence was insufficient to convict him because the state had not proved that he had intended to harm the puppy; he claimed that he had merely disciplined the puppy. The appellate court noted that the statute did not designate any particular mental state necessary for conviction, and that the trial judge had instructed the jury that it was required to find that Regalado "willfully" mistreated the puppy. The court held that this meant that the jury had to find that Regalado intended to engage in the beatings with malice or a "cruel disposition." The court recognized that anticruelty statutes were "not intended to place unreasonable restrictions on the infliction of such pain as may be necessary for the training or discipline of an animal."[57] Therefore the act of beating an animal does not in itself prove liability; the beating must be accompanied by a "malicious" mental state. In short, unless the state can prove that the defendant is a sadistic psychopath, there can be no conviction under the anticruelty law. Although the court affirmed Regalado's conviction, it recognized that "proof of malice will usually be circumstantial and the line between discipline and cruelty will often be difficult to draw."[58]

In *State of North Carolina v. Fowler*, Fowler was convicted of willfully beating and torturing his dog Ike. After Fowler beat Ike and tied him up, Fowler's wife filled a hole in the backyard with water. Fowler then submerged Ike's head under water. He continued this action for various periods of time over fifteen to twenty minutes. Then the Fowlers untied Ike, hit and kicked him, and tied him to a pole near the water hole. On appeal, Fowler argued that he and his wife were professional dog trainers, and that Ike had been digging holes in the backyard. After trying less harsh methods to no avail, Fowler consulted with Koehler, a famous dog trainer, and Koehler recommended alternative strategies, including the water submersion method that Fowler ultimately used successfully to stop Ike from digging the holes. The trial court refused to allow evidence about the Koehler method, including the fact that the Humane Society approved the Koehler method.

The appellate court reversed Fowler's conviction, holding that the violation must be "willful," which "means more than intentional. It means without just cause, excuse, or justification." If Fowler had undertaken these acts merely to torture Ike, he would have violated the law. If, however, Fowler punished the dog in "an honest and good faith effort to train it," then he would not be guilty. The court noted that a "beating inflicted for corrective or disciplinary purposes without an evil motive is not a crime, even if painful and even if excessive."[59] Since the trial court had excluded evidence Fowler had sought to introduce concerning the Koehler method of dog training, and since this evidence might have influenced the jury in Fowler's favor, the appellate court granted a new trial. As in *Regalado*, the fact of the beating and water submersion were not sufficient to prove that Fowler violated the law because the state had to prove that he undertook these acts for reasons other than discipline, punishment, or training, and that he engaged in these actions merely to torture Ike. We can be quite certain, however, that it made no difference to Ike whether his pain was caused in an effort to train him or to torture him. The court ordered a new trial, which allowed Fowler to introduce his evidence that dog trainers considered submerging a dog's head in water an acceptable part of training.

The other two states of mind that are often required for violation of anticruelty statutes are recklessness and criminal negligence, which, although seemingly easier to prove than subjective intent or willful conduct, actually make it easier for defendants to avoid liability. For example, a person acts recklessly when she knowingly or consciously disregards a substantial risk that her conduct would result in a violation of the law and where the risk represents a "gross deviation" from the conduct that a law-abiding citizen would observe in the same situation. The problem is that law-abiding farmers, hunters, dog trainers, experimenters, trappers, and other animal exploiters are permitted to inflict extreme pain and suffering on animals, and it is difficult to show that particular conduct represents a gross deviation from what we normally permit as part of these animal uses. The primary difference between recklessness and criminal negligence is that with negligence it is not necessary that the defendant knowingly disregard a substantial risk that her conduct would violate the law; it is enough that she should have known about the risk involved. The question is whether the defendant's conduct represents a gross deviation from what a reasonable person would have done under the circumstances. Again, what we regard as the acceptable conduct of "reasonable" farmers, hunters, experimenters, dog trainers, and other animal exploiters is consistent with an enormous amount of animal suffering. Since we permit the infliction on animals of severe pain for a variety of purposes, including punishment, it is difficult to see how the state can prove criminal negligence in violating an anticruelty law.

A Presumption: Property Owners Take Care of Their Property

The law presumes that property owners will act in their best economic interests and will not intentionally inflict pain and suffering on animals unless they at least believe that it will serve some purpose. This presumption helps to explain why anticruelty statutes contain exemptions for customary or accepted practices, and why courts have read into these statutes exemptions for such practices. It also accounts for why courts are reluctant to find that defendants in anticruelty cases acted with the requisite culpable state of mind.

The presumption that an owner of animal property will act rationally and not impose unnecessary suffering on his or her animals has its origins in early decisions interpreting anticruelty laws. In *Callaghan*, for example, the court held that a sensible property owner would not dehorn cattle and inflict "useless torments or gratuitous cruelties" if the owner did not think it a good use of the animal property. The court said that "self-interest" would prevent the owner from inflicting more harm than necessary, because doing otherwise would diminish the value of the cow: "Great pain and suffering would necessarily reduce the condition of the animal; and, unless they very soon recovered, the farmer would lose in the sale."[60] Although the English court in *Ford v. Wiley* held that the dehorning of older cattle was a violation of the anticruelty law, its judgment was based on the fact that the practice had been discontinued for twenty years in England, Wales, and most of Scotland by "gentlemen quite as alive to their own interests as those who have adopted this cruel practice" and that this was "abundant proof" that dehorning was not necessary "for all the legitimate purposes of [the] owner."[61] If dehorning were still widely practiced, *Ford v. Wiley* would unquestionably have come out the other way.

The presumption that animal owners treat their animal property prudently is also articulated in American cases. In *Commonwealth v. Barr*, the defendant was convicted of cruelty to animals because he fed his chickens an "experimental" grainless diet that caused his chickens to become ill and die. The conviction was reversed on the grounds that if Barr had fed the chickens this diet in the sincere belief that it was appropriate, he could not be said to have exhibited a reckless disregard for the animals. The court noted that the "[d]ead chickens, however, were the defendant's loss, and as he was their owner, the natural inference would arise that he would not deliberately or with gross carelessness bring about a result that was disastrous to himself."[62] In another case, *Commonwealth v. Vonderheid,* the defendant was convicted of cruelty to animals that he used in a traveling circus and roadside zoo because, according to humane officers, the animals were kept in a crowded condition, had insufficient food and bedding, and the building in which they were housed leaked water. The conviction was reversed, the court holding that Vonderheid "is endeavoring to make his livelihood from the use of these animals. He has expended large sums of money to secure them, and he is most certainly not about to impair his investment by improper food and shelter." The court made an explicit comparison with slave owners, who "may have cruelly treated some slaves," but "the slave that produced was well fed and housed by reason of their [*sic*] livelihood to the planter."[63]

We assume that animal owners will act in their own economic self-interest and not impose any more pain and suffering than is necessary to achieve the efficient use of the animal as an economic resource. To impose more pain and suffering would be to damage and diminish the value of that animal property without any corresponding economic gain, which would be irrational. In a system of private property, we generally assume that property owners are the best judges of the value of their property and allow them to use that property as they see fit. We assume that animal owners will not as a general matter "waste" their animal property, just as we assume that most people will not light cigars with flaming $100 bills.

Animal Laws with No Teeth: Penalties and Enforcement Difficulties[64]

Until recently, states, with few exceptions, treated violations of anticruelty laws as summary offenses or misdemeanors, which provide penalties that do not usually exceed a fine of $1,000 or a prison term of one year. For the most part, these laws were hardly ever enforced; imprisonment was rarely imposed and the usual penalty was a fine far less than the maximum authorized. The reason for this lack of enforcement was threefold. First, anticruelty laws, as we have seen, do not apply to most of our uses of animals. Second, we are reluctant to impose the stigma of criminal liability on people for what they do with their property. Third, if animals are not owned by particular individuals who value them, then, because they are property, we consider them worthless and, again, are reluctant to impose the stigma of criminal liability on those who destroy worthless property. For example, in a 1997 case, three young men broke into an animal shelter in Iowa and bludgeoned sixteen cats to death with baseball bats, seriously injuring seven others. The youths were convicted of a misdemeanor because the value of the cats did not exceed $500—the amount of property damage required for conviction of a felony. The youths maintained—and the court accepted—that cats in an animal shelter have no market value because no one wants them. Although the case received national publicity and many people expressed outrage that the cats were regarded as having no value, the outcome is completely consistent with—indeed compelled by—the characterization of animals as property.[65] So long as animals are viewed as property, if they have no market value, then they have no value at all.

In the 1990s, a number of states amended their anticruelty laws and upgraded at least certain violations to felonies with steeper fines and longer prison terms. It remains to be seen whether this change will make any real difference, since making cruelty to animals a felony does not change the fact that most animal uses will still not be covered thanks to explicit or judicially created exemptions—and because violation of these laws requires the proof of a mental state that is elusive at best. Upgrading the status of violations has nothing to do with expanding the coverage of the anticruelty statutes. Moreover, prosecutors were reluctant to pursue these crimes when they were misdemeanors, when the resulting stigma of conviction was much less serious than it will be in the case of felonies. Upgrading the penalties for these offenses may actually serve to deter prosecutors from pursuing violations of these statutes.

It is also important to understand that many regulatory laws, such as the federal Animal Welfare Act, apply to research facilities but not to individual researchers. Although the federal government can impose certain sanctions on institutions that receive federal funds for animal experiments or use animals covered by the Act, the researchers themselves are not subject to punishment under it. The Act, therefore, is not similar to a federal criminal law.

Another way in which the property status of animals affects the enforcement of animal welfare and anticruelty laws has to do with a legal doctrine known as *standing*. Standing establishes limits on who can seek redress in courts and the nature of the claims for which they can seek relief. For example, I have standing to sue you if you breach a contract that we have made; I have no standing to sue you for breaching a contract that you have made with Simon and in which I have no interest. I have no standing to seek a divorce on your behalf because I happen to think that you and your spouse are poorly matched. Only you or your spouse can seek the dissolution of your marriage. As a general matter, my status as a taxpayer does not give me standing to challenge how the government spends tax revenues. The doctrine of standing is very complicated and exceeds the scope of this book. It will suffice for present purposes to make several observations about the status of animals as property and the effect of that status on the criteria for standing in seeking enforcement of anticruelty and animal welfare laws.

First, because animals are property, they are the *object* of legal claims and not the *subject*, and they of course have no standing at all to make legal claims on their own behalf; nor does the legal system allow for the appointment of guardians to protect the rights of animals. Guardians are appointed to represent and protect the legal rights of children, the insane, and so forth, all of whom have legal rights that a guardian can assert. We may treat children or the insane poorly, but there are limits on our treatment of them because they possess a basic right, recognized by the law, that protects them from being treated exclusively as our resources. Animals are property and have no legal rights for a guardian to protect.[66]

Second, the ability of humans to get standing to enforce anticruelty and animal welfare laws, which supposedly provide some protection to animals short of rights, is very severely limited. Anticruelty laws are state criminal laws, and with few exceptions, violations of these statutes can be pursued only by the police and public prosecutors.[67] If the police refuse to take action, or if the prosecutor refuses to pursue the matter, there are few remedies available, as courts are generally unwilling to interfere with the almost unfettered discretion of police and prosecutors to administer the criminal justice system. Similarly, courts have denied standing to humans who have sought to enforce or challenge noncriminal regulatory statutes, such as the federal Animal Welfare Act, particularly when the animals in question are the property of an entity such as a research facility and the human cannot rest her claim on some legal right that she has concerning the animal.[68]

The Scope of Protection under Animal Welfare Laws

Does the humane treatment principle—as it is applied through animal welfare laws—really protect animal interests in any significant way? The short answer is no. For the most part, the law limits our use of animals only insofar as we must use animals for a "purpose." We must use them incidental to our accepted forms of institutionalized exploitation—for food, hunting, recreation, entertainment, clothing, or experiments—the primary ways in which we use animals as commodities to generate economic profit. The only time that our infliction of suffering on animals raises any sort of legal question is when we inflict that suffering outside the accepted institutions of animal use—when we inflict suffering in ways that do not generate property-related benefits and where the *only* explanation for the behavior can be characterized as torture "for the gratification of a malignant or vindictive temper."[69]

For example, in *State v. Tweedie*, the defendant was found to have violated the anticruelty law by killing a cat in a microwave oven.[70] In *In re William G.*, a cruelty conviction was upheld when a minor kicked a dog and set her on fire because she would not mate with his dog.[71] In *Motes v. State*, the defendant was found guilty of violating the anticruelty statute when he set fire to a dog merely because the dog was barking.[72] In *Tuck v. United States*, a pet shop owner was convicted of cruelty when he placed animals in an unventilated display window and refused to remove a rabbit whose body temperature registered as high as the thermometer was calibrated—110 degrees Fahrenheit.[73] In *People v. Voelker*, the court held that cutting off the heads of three live, conscious iguanas "without justification" could constitute a violation of the anticruelty law.[74] In *LaRue v. State*, a cruelty conviction was upheld because the defendant collected a large number of stray dogs and failed to provide them with veterinary care; the dogs suffered from mange, blindness, dehydration, pneumonia, and distemper, and had to be killed.[75] But these are unusual cases and constitute a minuscule fraction of the instances in which we inflict suffering on animals.

The very same act can be either protected or prohibited depending only on whether the act is part of accepted institutions of animal exploitation. If someone kills a cat in a microwave, sets a dog on fire, allows the body temperature of a rabbit to rise to the point of heat stroke, severs the heads of conscious animals, or allows animals to suffer un-treated serious illnesses, the conduct may violate the anticruelty laws. But if a researcher engages in the exact same conduct as part of an experiment at a university (and a number of researchers have killed animals or inflicted pain on them in the very same and much similar ways) the conduct is protected by the law because the researcher is supposedly using the animal to generate a benefit. Indeed, the use or treatment of animals in experiments runs afoul of the federal Animal Welfare Act or state anticruelty laws (if they are even applicable to experimenters), only if the experimenter inflicts pain and suffering that will frustrate rather than facilitate the experiment. The purpose of laboratory use of animals is to produce valid scientific data. The Animal Welfare Act requires that researchers provide animals with a minimal level of care, such as minimal food, water, and cage space, to ensure that animals will be useful as producers of reliable scientific data, and requires that researchers not impose more pain or suffering than is required, but only because animal distress could adversely affect the validity of data and thereby result in a waste of animal resources. We do not base our judgment of whether vivisection is humane or inhumane on some abstract notion of what constitutes cruel treatment. Inhumane treatment of animals in experiments is understood exclusively as treatment that results in the waste of animal resources in experiments that do not produce reliable scientific data. Therefore, if the researcher who microwaves the cat fails to provide adequate food and water to the animal before the animal is killed in the microwave oven, or after the animal is severely injured but is still alive for further study, the researcher may violate the law because the stress she causes the animal through dehydration and starvation may render the experimental data invalid and the animal may thereby be wasted.

A video that we show to the students in our course on animals and the law depicts a government-funded experiment in which researchers applied a blowtorch to an unanesthetized pig. The stated purpose of the experiment was to ascertain the effects of severe burns on a pig's subsequent eating habits. The pig was kept alive for several weeks and was given no pain relief. If teenagers performed this act merely to satisfy sadistic impulses, they would have wasted the animal and run afoul of anticruelty laws. But researchers performing the very same act are exempt from the anticruelty laws because they are considered to be using the animal productively. The interest of the pig is exactly the same in both cases, but protection for that interest depends solely on whether the use is considered to be productive or a waste of animal "resources." Protection of the animal's interest is completely irrelevant under the law; the law is concerned only to protect human property interests.

Similarly, a farmer can brand, dehorn, castrate, and otherwise mutilate animals intended for food, and can raise these animals in situations of severe confinement. We allow farmers, food vendors, and slaughterhouses to decapitate and cut the throats of conscious animals—as occurred in *Voelker*—without even suggesting that such conduct violates anticruelty laws. All of these actions cause extreme suffering and distress to animals, but they are considered part of normal animal husbandry and are therefore protected under the law. If, however, a farmer imposes suffering on livestock for no reason—the farmer does not use livestock as property and merely wastes them—then the anticruelty laws may apply. In *State v. Schott*, Schott was convicted of cruelty to animals when police found dozens of cows and pigs dead or dying from malnutrition and dehydration on Schott's farm.[76] Schott's defense was that bad weather prevented him from caring for his livestock. The jury found Schott guilty of cruelty and neglect, and the appellate court affirmed. Schott surely inflicted a great deal of suffering on his animals by neglecting them, but had Schott followed normal practices of animal husbandry, he would also have inflicted an enormous amount of suffering on them. The only difference is that had Schott followed normal farming procedures, his infliction of suffering would have occurred within the context of institutionalized exploitation that we regard as acceptable and as productive.

In sum, anticruelty and other animal welfare laws provide precious little protection to animals. As long as the animal use can be characterized as part of an accepted practice of animal exploitation, then we generally permit the use—however trivial—because these practices are based on the economic status of animals as property. We may object to your giving your dog an excessive beating for your own sadistic pleasure, but we do not object if your purpose is to punish the dog for digging a hole in your back garden or to train your dog to attack intruders. We may object to your setting your dog on fire merely because you enjoy watching her burn, but we do not object if you perform the very same action as an experimenter at your local university.

If the humane treatment principle merely prohibits our use of animals outside of accepted institutions of exploitation and with no resulting economic benefit, then the principle was historically unnecessary. The point of the position articulated by Bentham was to establish that animals had morally and legally significant interests, and that we had obligations that we owed directly to animals. The humane treatment principle was a moral and legal repudiation of the views of Descartes and Locke, both of whom regarded animals as things without any protectable interests. But to the extent that Bentham's principle was expressed in laws that assumed from the outset that animals were the property of humans, it was doomed to go no further in protecting their interests than did the positions of Descartes or Locke. Although Descartes did not believe that animals were sentient or conscious of pain, we can assume that he would not have used animals gratuitously, just as he would not have gratuitously destroyed any other property he owned. Locke regarded animals as merely another resource that God gave to humans, but he argued that it was morally wrong for humans to "spoil or waste" them and that we should be limited in our use or treatment of animals by our obligations to God and other humans, a limitation no different from that imposed on our use of any other resource, such as land or water or wood, provided by God. In short, by defining animals as property, we deny the very foundation of the humane treatment principle—that animals are not the moral equivalent of inanimate objects.

Valuing Animal Property as Other Than Property?

The failure of animal welfare laws should not come as any surprise. If the animal is property, how *can* that animal be anything other than a commodity? How can an animal's interests be assessed or valued at any level higher than is necessary to ensure efficient exploitation of the animal property for its designated purpose? How can anticruelty or animal welfare laws apply to anything but animal use that is wholly gratuitous and that represents a completely unproductive use of animal property? In order to understand this point, consider the following example. In 1985, Congress amended the Animal Welfare Act and directed the U.S. Department of Agriculture, which enforces the Act, to require standards for the exercise of dogs used in experiments and for the psychological well-being of primates.[77] In keeping with the position, discussed above, that the actual content of experiments is not regulated by the Act, these amendments did not in any way interfere with the content of permitted experiments, but had only to do with improving husbandry standards. The USDA originally proposed uniform and specific standards, requiring, for example, that dogs receive thirty minutes of exercise per day and that primate housing meet the social needs of the animals. The research community objected strongly to these specific standards. Researchers did not dispute that dogs had interests in exercise or that primates were complicated beings with interests in psychological well-being. Rather, they claimed that they could obtain valid scientific data from their use of these animals without the more rigorous standards proposed by the USDA, and that these more rigorous standards would make research more expensive.

Under pressure from the research community, the USDA capitulated and adopted less rigorous standards that accord discretion to the attending veterinarian to determine the appropriate standards of canine exercise and primate psychological well-being in light of the needs and resources of a given research facility. In short, the animals' interests were compromised because it was not cost-effective to respect those interests. If researchers are getting valid data from a dog whose maintenance costs $1 a day, why should they spend $2 a day? If your car runs as well with oil costing $1 a quart as it does with oil that costs $2 a quart, why would you spend the extra dollar? If you were a rational property owner, you would not waste your money on the more expensive oil. Why make animal experiments more expensive if animal researchers are satisfied with the quantity and quality of data they already obtain from their animals under a less rigorous standard that imposes a much lower compliance cost?

Indeed, in ultimately adopting the less rigorous standards, the USDA balanced the compliance costs for regulated facilities against what it regarded as the "anthropomorphic" value represented by the public perception that animals used in experiments were being treated better—a value that could not be quantified in the way that increased costs for regulated facilities could be. In other words, the position that prevailed, which follows from the view that animals are property, was that the only interests of animals that mattered or that could matter were those that researchers had to respect to avoid wasting the animal or using the animal in a way that would produce scientifically invalid data. If, in an experiment involving a dog, we determined that the dog needed ten minutes of exercise per day in order not to develop a level of stress that would interfere with the experiment, then ten minutes is all that should be required. A requirement of thirty minutes of exercise per day would represent an "unnecessary, unreasonable, or unjustified financial burden."

It is unreasonable to expect that animal welfare laws will mandate a level of care for animals that exceeds the minimal level needed to ensure that animals are used in the most cost-effective way for the intended purpose: as a "food" animal, a "laboratory" animal, a "circus" animal, a "zoo" animal, a "rodeo" animal, a "fur" animal, and so forth. Despite a plethora of animal welfare laws, animal exploitation today is worse—in terms of both the numbers of animals exploited and the ways in which they are exploited—than ever before. If we regard animals as our property, we will disregard their interests whenever it is in our interest to do so. This is particularly true in countries such as the United States, which regards property ownership as a natural right—a right that has its origin in religious doctrine and that is considered an absolutely essential cornerstone of social organization.

But animals are also treated as little more than commodities in countries where private property concepts are not quite as strong. For example, although the modern concept of private property originated in Britain, the concept of private property under British law is not as strong as it is under American law, in part because British law is more secular than American law is, and because Britain has had a more progressive political system that allows for greater regulation of property rights. Nevertheless, although Britain has more restrictions on the use of animals than does the United States, the differences in the treatment of animals are more formal than substantive. For example, in discussing British laws requiring the "humane" slaughter of animals, one British commentator has noted that although these laws suggest that "the suffering of farm animals in the last moments of their lives should be minimal," the laws do little to alleviate animal pain and suffering. The use of electric stunning equipment requires a certain amount of skill and accuracy that mass slaughter makes difficult: "the need to get animals through as quickly as possible results in inaccurate, or (in the case of electric tongs) insufficiently lengthy, use of equipment and the failure to ensure that each animal is stunned in isolation from others." Moreover, "animals may regain consciousness before, during or after having their throats cut." Slaughterhouse staff "are often inexperienced and may care little for animal welfare." In short, "animal welfare often takes second place to cost-cutting."[78] This echoes the observations about the American Humane Slaughter Act, which does not even apply to chickens and other birds, who account for approximately 8 billion of the 8.3 billion animals we slaughter annually, and for the most part requires only those practices that are "more efficient in labor utilization," result "in lower costs," and will "not impose any significant financial burden on the government which enforces [the regulations] on the livestock industry, the meat-packing industry, or consumers."[79] Whether in America, Britain, or anywhere else where animals are economic commodities, the observation holds that "much of the animal welfare agenda has been obstructed and it is difficult to think of legislation improving the welfare of animals that has seriously damaged the interests of the animal users."[80]

We may regulate the use of any property, and thereby limit property rights, in order to protect human interests that we think are even more important. We may and often do prohibit the destruction or alteration of historical buildings because we believe that such structures are important for future generations of human beings. We do not, however, generally regard it as appropriate to impose restrictions on the use of property for the benefit of the property itself. Although in theory the law may seek to impose restrictions on the treatment of animals that go beyond the minimum level of care required for the intended purpose, the law has rarely done so, and there are powerful economic incentives against doing so.[81] Countries that adopt more restrictive agricultural practices, for example, will no longer be competitive with those that do not, and local farmers who adopt such practices put themselves at a competitive disadvantage with others who do not. Although animals suffered a great deal on the "family farm," they did generally, at least, have more space in which to move. The family farm has given way to intensive agriculture because it produces animal products more cheaply and on a much larger scale. As technology continues to develop, the infliction of animal suffering will only increase, and the creation of regional and global markets will militate against any effort to treat animals as anything more than economic commodities.

The Market Value of Your Dog or Cat

At this point, you may be looking at your dog sleeping soundly in front of the fireplace, or your cat lounging decadently on the couch, and thinking that although food animals, animals used for experiments, or other forms of animal property may be valued only as economic commodities, we treat some animals—our "pets"—as more than that. In many cultures, humans have by tradition maintained certain animals as companions, animals with whom one has a relationship that is entirely different from one's relationship with inanimate property.

Although many of us live with companion animals whom we love and regard as members of our families, most of us have little idea about where these animals come from. The "pet" industry is really no different from the "food" animal industry or the "laboratory" animal industry. The majority of dogs sold in pet shops—about 500,000 per year—come from what are called "puppy mills," or breeding factories in which animals are kept in filthy and cramped conditions. Puppy mill kennels are usually small wood or wire cages or crates. Female dogs are bred continuously until they can no longer produce enough puppies and are then killed. The puppies are taken from their mothers at ages ranging from four to eight weeks and are shipped in crates by truck, trailer, or airplane to pet shops and pet distributors. About half of the dogs bred at puppy mills die as the result of unsanitary conditions at mills or during transport. Although the USDA is supposed to regulate breeding kennels as part of its enforcement of the federal Animal Welfare Act, such inspection is virtually nonexistent, and there is very little regulation of these kennels at the state level. Cat and bird breeding occurs under similar conditions but on a smaller scale. Exotic animals such as birds, lizards, monkeys, tigers, and bears, are smuggled into the United States and end up in pet shops or are sold through private dealers. Exotic birds account for most of this trade and up to 80 percent of the smuggled birds die in transit.

The fact that some of us value our companion animals highly does not mean that they are no longer property. Indeed, it is precisely *because* pets are our property that we can choose to value them as more than economic commodities. Property owners can, of course, choose to treat any of their property well or poorly. I may wash and wax my car regularly, or I may ignore the finish and let the paint fade and the body corrode away. Similarly, many of us who live with dogs and cats choose not to treat our animals solely as economic commodities and instead accord them a level of care that exceeds their market value. But as we saw in cases such as *Fowler*, we may also choose to treat these animals as nothing more than property. Many owners keep their dogs in cramped quarters and provide only a minimal amount of food or exercise and little if any companionship. Dogs used for guarding purposes often spend a great deal of their lives on short chains and receive human contact only when a dish of food or water is placed before them. These dogs are of ten beaten in order to make them more vicious. Cats are used by restaurants or farmers to eradicate mice. These cats are often not fed at all by humans in order to keep them hungry and make them effective hunters. Many dogs and cats receive little if any veterinary care, and the owners of these animals may at any time "humanely" kill the dog or cat or have a willing veterinarian do so. For the most part, anticruelty laws are unable to regulate such conduct; indeed, the courts have explicitly held that dog owners have the right to kill their dogs in order to avoid punishment under the anticruelty laws for not providing the required minimal care to their animals. In *Miller v. State*, the court held that the owner of a dog has the privilege "of killing in some swift and comparatively painless manner" a dog that the owner considers to be worthless and that if the owner has the privilege to kill the dog, "he may also consent that another person may do the execution."[82] The court reasoned that if the owner could not kill his own animal, he might incur unwanted financial burdens because he would be required under the anticruelty laws to expend funds for the care of the animal. In any event, the status of animals as property means that the choice of how to treat the animal is by and large left to the owner, and the law will generally protect that choice because we assume that the property owner will act in his or her best interest and is the best judge of the value of the property.

In addition, when companion animals are injured as a result of the negligent conduct of others, the law generally limits recovery to the fair market value of the animal. For example, in *Richardson v. Fairbanks North Star Borough*, the Richardsons discovered that their dog, a mix named Wizzard, was missing. They called the local shelter and were told that Wizzard had been found and that they could reclaim him before 5:00 P.M., when the shelter closed. The Richardsons arrived at the shelter at 4:50 P.M. and were told that the shelter had closed for the day. They were able to see Wizzard chained in the rear of the facility. When they returned the next day, they found that he had been killed by the shelter, which acknowledged that it had kept inadequate records and had improperly killed the dog before the required three-day waiting period had passed.

The Richardsons sued the shelter for killing their dog. They argued that they had an emotional bond with Wizzard; he was a member of their family. The court rejected this claim, holding that "[s]ince dogs have legal status as items of personal property, courts generally limit the damage award in which a dog has been wrongfully killed to the animal's market value at the time of death."[83] The court awarded $300 to the Richardsons and ordered the Richardsons to pay $3,763 to the shelter, an amount representing its attorney's fees and other costs, because the Richardsons had no legal basis for their claim of emotional and mental distress. Wizzard was just a piece of property the Richardsons owned. Some cases have allowed for punitive damages that go beyond market-value damages in cases involving animals, but as a general matter only when defendants acted intentionally or maliciously in damaging or destroying the animal property of others, or acted with gross or extreme negligence.[84] An award of punitive damages may be considered by a court in the face of wanton or morally outrageous conduct that damages any type of property, whether an animal or an inanimate object, and therefore represent no change in the property status of animals or any recognition that humans can have relationships with dogs and cats in a way that they cannot with cars or stereos.

In recent years, some courts have expressed a willingness in some instances to allow recovery that goes beyond market value and includes compensation for an owner's emotional distress at the loss of an animal. But such cases do nothing to change the status of animals as property; indeed, they reinforce that status because such recovery depends solely on whether the owner values that animal more highly and are similar to instances in which courts have allowed greater recovery when the damaged property in question is a family heirloom to which the owner has a sentimental attachment that cannot be fully compensated through market value recovery alone.[85]

The status of animals as property renders meaningless our claim that we reject the status of animals as things. We treat animals as the moral equivalent of inanimate objects with no morally significant interests or rights. We bring billions of animals into existence annually simply for the purpose of killing them. Animals have market prices. Dogs and cats are sold in pet stores like compact discs; financial markets trade in futures for pork bellies and cattle. Any interest that an animal has is nothing more than an economic commodity that may be bought and sold when it is in the economic interest of the property owner. That is what it means to be property.

Consider the following comments about animals in meat-industry trade magazines, all of which indicate that we, like Descartes, still regard animals as nothing more than automatons, or moving machines:

The modern layer is, after all, only a very efficient converting machine, changing the raw material—feedstuffs—into the finished product—the egg—less, of course, maintenance requirements.[86]

Forget the pig is an animal. Treat him just like a machine in a factory. Schedule treatments like you would lubrication. Breeding season is like the first step in an assembly line. And marketing like the delivery of finished goods.[87]

Broilers blooming to market size 40 percent quicker, miniature hens cranking out eggs in double time, a computer "cookbook" of recipes for custom-designed creatures—this could well be the face of animal production in the 21st century.[88]

In light of the status of animals as property, there can be no real balance between human and animal interests—and there is none. We regard all animal interests as having a "price tag" in that these interests may be "sold" by the property owner. This means that there is virtually no limit on what humans can do with animals.

In the next chapter, we will consider what we must do if we truly mean to take animal interests seriously.

4

The Cure for Our Moral Schizophrenia: The Principle of Equal Consideration

Our Two Choices

WE HAVE TWO CHOICES—and only two—when it comes to the moral status of animals.

We can continue to permit the infliction of suffering on animals for virtually any purpose that provides a benefit to us, including wholly unnecessary purposes. If we exercise this option, then we should at least admit that our claim that animals have morally significant interests is a sham and that we in fact recognize only their value as things, as means to our ends.

Or we can maintain that animals have morally significant interests in not being subjected to unnecessary suffering. This option requires that we rethink the moral status of animals and provide some meaningful content to the humane treatment principle that we claim to accept. It is important to understand that this second option does not require that we treat animals in the same way that we treat humans, or that we regard animals and humans as the "same," or that we give up the idea that in situations of true emergency or conflict—where necessity requires—we may prefer human over animal interests. All that is required is that we accept that animals have a morally significant interest in not suffering and that we must justify the necessity of inflicting any suffering on animals.

In this chapter, we will explore what we need to do if we want to give content to our moral and legal prohibition against the infliction of unnecessary suffering on animals. If we are to take animal interests seriously, then we can do so in only one way: by applying *the principle of equal consideration* to animal interests in not suffering. There is nothing exotic or particularly complicated about the principle of equal consideration. Indeed, this principle is part of every moral theory and, like the humane treatment principle, is something that most of us already accept. To put the matter simply, we ought to treat like cases alike. Although there may be many differences between humans and animals, there is at least one very important similarity that we all already recognize: our shared capacity to suffer. If our supposed prohibition on the infliction of unnecessary suffering on animals is to have any meaning at all, then we must interpret the concept of necessity in a way similar to the way that we interpret it when it comes to inflicting unnecessary suffering on other human beings.

We will begin with some observations about the principle of equal consideration as a general matter, and we will then examine the application of this principle to humans and nonhumans.

The Principle of Equal Consideration: Some General Comments

The principle of equal consideration tells us that if Simon has an interest and Jane has the same or a reasonably similar interest, we should treat Simon and Jane alike unless there is a good reason not to do so. Assume that Jane has an interest in attending a university and that Simon has this interest as well. If we are going to give Simon a place at the university, then, according to the principle of equal consideration, we should provide a place for Jane as well unless there is a good reason not to. A good reason might be that Simon is a much better student than Jane and that there is only one place open at the university. A bad reason would be that Simon is a man and Jane a woman, facts of gender that generally bear no relationship to qualification for university study. The principle of equal consideration reflects the view that sound moral judgments must be universal and cannot be based on self-interest or the interests of a "special" or elite group. If we make a moral judgment that Simon ought to receive a benefit, then we ought to make the same judgment about Jane—or anyone else—in circumstances that are relevantly similar.[1]

There are three general points to keep in mind about the principle of equal consideration:

First, it is a *formal* principle, which means simply that it tells us only that we ought to treat like cases alike. The principle tells us about the *form* of moral reasoning, not about its *content*. It does not tell us what particular benefits we ought to bestow on anyone, or even that we ought to bestow any benefits at all (other than equal consideration). For example, if Simon and Jane are my children and they both misbehave in the same way, then I should respond to their behavior similarly. If I decide to punish Simon by not giving him his allowance for a week, then I should also dock Jane's allowance for a week. If I do otherwise without a good reason, then Simon would be correct to criticize me for treating him differently from Jane. Similarly, if I deprived Jane of two weeks' allowance and Simon of only one week's allowance, then Jane would have a good claim that my unequal treatment of her was unfair. She and Simon may also object to my punishing them at all, but if I punish them differently, they have an additional objection—I have not treated them equally.

Second, the principle of equal consideration does not necessarily direct us to treat everyone as "equals" or as "the same" for all purposes. For example, Simon may have moderate musical talent; Jane may have no musical talent at all. Jane may be a brilliant mathematician; Simon may be hopeless at mathematics. Simon and Jane are equals only to the extent that they are alike for some particular purpose; they are entitled to be treated alike with respect to that particular similarity unless there is a good reason not to so treat them. Jane's superior ability at mathematics may be valuable to a computer firm, and that firm may be willing to pay her a large sum of money to write computer languages. If Simon decides to become a professional musician, his moderate talent may result in his receiving less compensation.

Third, the principle of equal consideration is a necessary component of any moral theory; any theory that rejects the principle is unacceptable as a moral theory. Assume, for example, that Simon believes that capital punishment is morally justifiable and that the state should execute any person—of whatever color or sex—found guilty of premeditated murder. Jane disagrees; she believes that capital punishment is morally unjustifiable in any case. Both of these moral positions accord with the principle of equal consideration in that they treat like cases alike. Simon supports capital punishment and makes no exception based on race, gender, or any other criterion. Jane is opposed to the death penalty in all cases. Jane may have other reasons to believe that Simon is morally wrong in supporting capital punishment; Simon may base his support for capital punishment on its supposed deterrent effect and Jane (and most criminologists) may reject any causal connection between the death penalty and deterrence. But she cannot say that his position violates the principle of equal consideration.

If Simon took the position that capital punishment was morally justifiable when blacks murdered whites or when women murdered men but never when whites murdered blacks or men murdered women, then his position would fail to be a moral one, arguments about moral justifications for capital punishment aside. If capital punishment is to have any moral justification at all, it must be applied equally.

The reason why we object to racism and sexism is precisely that these viewpoints require that we treat like cases in different ways simply on the basis of race or gender. The racist says, "I do not care whether a black human and a white human have the same interest. I attach more weight to the white human's interest because whites are morally superior, or more important as a general matter." The sexist says, "I do not care whether a man and a woman have the same interest. I attach more weight to the male's interest because men are superior, or more important as a moral matter." Racism and sexism make equality impossible because they use irrelevant criteria systematically to devalue or disregard the interests of people of color or women.

Whether interests are similar or dissimilar, or whether particular reasons for differential treatment are morally sound or unsound, will remain open to dispute. But everyone who cares about morality agrees that whatever position is taken must be justifiable in light of the principle of equal consideration. Opponents and advocates of affirmative action may disagree about whether race or sex constitutes a morally relevant reason for favoring people of color or women, but they both accept the principle that we ought to treat like cases alike unless there is a morally relevant reason not to. Supporters of affirmative action argue that because of historical discrimination against people of color and women, and the resulting imbalance in the present distribution of political and socioeconomic power, preferences based on race and sex are required in order to achieve a "level playing field" where sex and race per se are in fact regarded as irrelevant. Opponents believe that historical discrimination against people of color or women does not justify differential treatment based on race or gender because it places white males who did not participate in this historical discrimination at a disadvantage.[2] But no one—except extremists—argues against racial preferences on the ground that people of color, as a group, are inferior, or that white people, as a group, are superior. No one argues for or against gender preferences based on the inherent inferiority of women or the inherent superiority of men. People of good faith accept the principle of equal consideration, which requires that we reject racist and sexist notions as factors in any acceptable moral theory.

The Principle of Equal Consideration and the Humane Treatment Principle

The humane treatment principle is a moral theory that requires us to balance the interests of animals and humans. Like every moral theory, it must include the principle of equal consideration. We have seen that when human interests are similar, they should be treated in the same way. We should protect the respective interests of humans to the same degree unless there is some other difference that justifies treating similar interests in dissimilar ways.

The analysis is exactly the same in the context of the humane treatment principle. We are supposed to weigh human interests in using animals against animal interests in avoiding suffering. If the human interest weighs more, then the animal suffering is justifiable. If the animal interest weighs more, then it is not. And if the interests are similar—if the scales are equally balanced—then we should treat those interests in the same way unless there is some other difference between the human and the animal that justifies differential treatment. The balancing required by the humane treatment principle logically implies acceptance of the principle of equal consideration applied to human and animal interests.

Moreover, the humane treatment principle as it developed historically explicitly included the principle of equal consideration. Bentham rejected the views of those who, like Descartes, Locke, and Kant, regarded animals as things that possessed no morally significant interests and to whom we could have no direct moral or legal obligations. Bentham recognized that the only way to ensure that animal interests were treated as morally significant was to apply the principle of equal consideration to animals, and Bentham therefore "incorporated the essential basis of moral equality into his system of ethics by means of the formula:

'Each to count for one and none for more than one.'"[3] He explicitly applied this formula to animals when he maintained that the supposed inability of animals to think rationally or to use language did not justify their exclusion from the protection afforded by the principle of equal consideration: "the question is not, Can they *reason?* nor, Can they *talk?* but, Can they *suffer?*" Although Bentham believed that animals and humans were very different from each other, he also believed they both suffered and that an animal's suffering should not be discounted or ignored simply because the animal was an animal. Otherwise animals would be "degraded into the class of *things*," and Bentham very explicitly rejected the view that animals were things.

In sum, the humane treatment principle that most of us accept already logically and historically embodies the principle of equal consideration. It assumes that animals and humans may not be the "same" or "equals" in all respects (just as humans are not), but that they are similar in at least one respect: unlike stones, plants, and everything else in the world, animals and humans are sentient and, therefore, they have similar interests in not suffering. We claim to require a balancing of animal interests and human interests, but in fact no true balancing occurs. No animal interest is ever considered as similar to, let alone as exceeding, any human interest in our balancing act. Even when animals have significant interests in not suffering and humans have only an interest in amusement, animals lose because their status as property is *always* a good reason not to respect their interests in not suffering. *The interests of property will almost never be judged as similar to the interests of property owners.* The principle of equal consideration has then essentially *no* meaning in the context of any balance of human and animal interests required by the humane treatment principle.

The Principle of Equal Consideration: Humans as Property

The application of the principle of equal consideration similarly failed in the context of American slavery, which allowed some humans to treat others as property.[4] The institution of human slavery was structurally identical to the institution of animal ownership. Because a human slave was regarded as property, the slave owner was able to disregard all of the slave's interests if it was economically beneficial to do so, and the law generally deferred to the slave owner's judgment as to the value of his slave property. As chattel property, slaves could be sold, willed, in-sured, mortgaged, and seized in payment of the owner's debts.[5] Slave owners could inflict severe punishments on slaves for virtually any rea-son. Those who intentionally or negligently injured another's slave were liable to the owner in an action for damage to property. As a gen-eral rule, slaves could not enter into contracts, own property, sue or be sued, or live as free persons with basic rights and duties.[6] The law sup-posedly required that slaves be treated "humanely." Slaves "are not ra-tional beings. No, but they are the creatures of God, sentient beings, capable of suffering and enjoyment, and entitled to enjoy according to the measure of their capacities. Does not the voice of nature inform every one, that he is guilty of wrong when he inflicts on them pain with-out necessity or object?"[7] The law purported to regulate the use of slave property and in principle recognized that slaves had some interests their owners were obligated to protect, and it thereby established some limit on the use and treatment of slave property. The law, however, failed to accord any moral status to slaves or to set any effective limits on the use and treatment of slave property—and for precisely the same reason that the humane treatment principle fails to establish any meaningful limit on our use of animal property. The property status of the slave always trumped any interest that the slave supposedly had under the law. The principle of equal consideration could not apply because the interests of slaves and the interests of slave owners were virtually never judged to be similar.

Legislation enacted in 1798 in North Carolina, for example, pro-vided that the punishment for maliciously killing a slave should be the same as that for the murder of a free person. This law, however, "did not apply to an outlawed slave, nor to a slave 'in the act of resistance to his lawful owner,' nor to a slave 'dying under moderate correction.'"[8] Tennessee had a similar law. A law that prohibits the murder of slaves but permits three general—and easily satisfied—exceptions, combined with a general prohibition against the testimony of slaves against free persons, is certainly not an effective deterrent to the murder of slaves. Moreover, despite the fact that the North Carolina law superficially supported the idea that slave owners could not kill their own slaves with impunity, courts were unwilling to hold owners liable for serious harm inflicted on their slaves. In one case, *State v. Mann*, the court held that a master is not liable for a battery of his slave because the law cannot protect a slave from her own master. Mann had leased for one year a slave named Lydia, who ran away one day while he was beating her. When Mann ordered Lydia to stop running and she refused, Mann shot at and wounded her. Mann was convicted at trial, but the appellate court reversed the conviction because even a "cruel and unreasonable battery" on one's own slave was not indictable. The court held that it could not "allow the right of the master to be brought into discussion in the Courts of Justice. The slave, to remain a slave, must be made sensible, that there is no appeal from his master."[9]

There are many reasons why the law was reluctant to impose criminal liability on slave owners for brutal acts committed on their slaves. As mentioned above, the law was concerned that slaves not think that they could appeal the exercise of dominion by the master. Another reason, which, as we saw in Chapter 3, was explicitly articulated in anticruelty cases involving animals, was the presumption that the master had a self-interest in his property that would militate against the infliction of unnecessary punishment. "'Where the battery was committed by the master himself, there would be no redress whatever, for the reason given in Exodus 21:21, "for he is his money." The powerful protection of the master's private interest would of itself go far to remedy this evil.'"[10] Indeed, a Virginia law stated that a slave owner who killed a slave in the course of disciplining the slave could not be said to have acted with malice, and could therefore not be convicted of murder, because of this presumption that an owner would never intentionally destroy his property.[11] As Professor Alan Watson, the leading expert on slavery and slave law, has noted: "At most places at most times a reasonably economic owner would be conscious of the chattel value of slaves and thus would ensure some care in their treatment." This is related to the notion, expressed by the Roman jurist Justinian, that "'it is to the advantage of the state that no one use his property badly.'"[12]

Although free persons could be punished under criminal law for battering another's slave (as well as be liable for damages in a civil action for damaging another's property), it was clear that the concern in such cases was for the property interest of the owner. In State v. Hale, the court held that slaves were protected from wanton abuse by strangers because "[i]t is a more effectual guarantee of [the master's] right of property when the slave is protected from wanton abuse . . . for it cannot be disputed that a slave is rendered less capable of performing his master's service when he finds himself exposed by the law to the capricious violence of every turbulent man in the community."[13] Although most southern states by the middle of the nineteenth century had laws intended to protect the "welfare" of slaves that provided for substantial punishment for the cruel treatment of them, "few Southerners suffered the penalties of these laws, since juries were reluctant to convict, and slaves, who were often the only witnesses to such crimes, were barred from testifying against white men."[14]

We may disagree about what level of human exploitation is appropriate and what particular rights humans have, but none of us defends human chattel slavery, or the buying and selling of humans as commodities. Although many of the men who drafted the U.S. Constitution were slave owners, the Constitution was later amended to prohibit the institution of slavery. And it does not matter whether enslaving some humans will result in great benefits for the rest of us. Even conservative economic theorists, such as Richard Posner, reject human slavery: "we do not permit degrading invasions of individual autonomy merely on a judgment that, on balance, the invasion would make a net addition to the social wealth. And whatever the philosophical grounding of this sentiment, it is too deeply entrenched in our society at present for wealth maximization to be given a free rein."[15] Indeed, although we disagree internationally and intranationally about the scope of human rights and about what constitutes discrimination, our agreement regarding the unacceptability of human slavery is virtually unanimous. The laws of almost every nation in the world prohibit chattel slavery, and the international community condemns slavery as a violation of basic human rights. This is not to say that slavery does not still exist in some places in the world, just as murder still occurs despite every nation's moral and legal proscriptions against homicide.[16] Practices such as child labor and forced prostitution persist. The important point is that as a bedrock moral principle reflected in national and international law, we accept without question that slavery and murder are wrong. We condemn slavery when it is exposed. We recognize that if human interests in not suffering are to have any moral significance, then humans must have at least one basic right: the right not to be enslaved.

Moreover, we do not allow "humane" slavery while prohibiting "inhumane" slavery. Although more brutal forms of slavery are worse than less brutal forms, we prohibit human slavery in general because humans have an interest in not suffering *at all* as a consequence of use as the property of others. A rational person who found herself a slave would obviously prefer a less harsh form of slavery to a more harsh one. Given a choice between a master who would beat her five times a week and one who would beat her ten times a week, she would choose the former. But that does not mean that it is in her interest to be a slave under the more "humane" master in the same way that it is in her interest not to be a slave at all.

Treating Other Humans Exclusively as Means to Our Ends

Not only do we reject the formal institution of chattel slavery, we also reject the notion that it is appropriate to treat any human *exclusively* as a means to an end. We think that it is morally impermissible, for example, to use homeless human beings as forced organ donors in order to benefit middle-class or wealthy humans.[17] We no longer believe that it is appropriate to use humans—irrespective of their race, gender, intelligence, beauty, talent, and so forth—as unconsenting experimental subjects. We may, however, treat humans as means to the ends of other humans in some respects. When we call a plumber to fix our faucet, we are treating that person as a means to our end of getting the faucet fixed. The plumber is also using us as a means to her end of making a living. We may also attach an economic value to people in certain circumstances. Jane's value as a plumber is determined in part by how other people estimate and reward her services. If she is valued more highly as a means to the ends of those who need her skills, she will be paid more money.

We can, however, go only so far in treating or valuing other humans as means to an end. There is a "red light" that curtails that valuing process and that limits our use and treatment of humans. We can value our plumber as a means to the end of repairing our faucet, and it is all right to compensate a good plumber more highly than we do a lesser plumber. But if we no longer value the plumber as a plumber and moreover do not like her or value her in any other way, we cannot treat her solely as an economic commodity; we cannot enslave her in a forced labor camp; we cannot eat her, use her in experiments, or turn her into a pair of shoes. A factory owner may treat his or her workers in an instrumental way; that is, the factory owner, concerned primarily about the "bottom line" of profit, may regard the workers as economic commodities. We may allow the factory owner to disregard a worker's interest in a mid-morning coffee break, or even to disregard a worker's

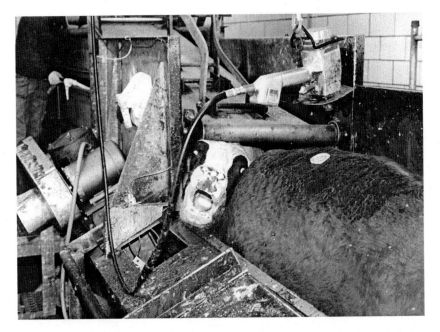

Modern mechanized slaughter unquestionably causes terror to animals, such as this cow, who is riding up in a restrainer to be stunned before she is shackled, hoisted, and slaughtered. This process complies with the requirements of the Humane Slaughter Act. Credit: Photo courtesy of Gail A. Eisnitz/Humane Farming Association (HFA).

The pig sticker cuts the animal's throat.
Credit: Photo courtesy of Humane Farming Association (HFA).

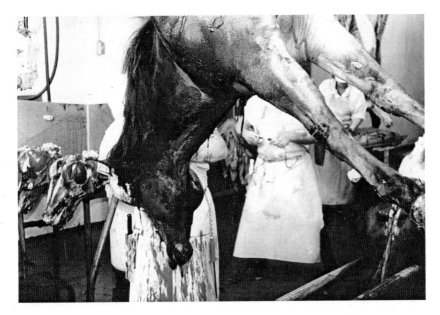

Many people do not realize that horses end up in the slaughterhouse.
Credit: Photo courtesy of Gail A. Eisnitz/Humane Farming Association (HFA).

Vast mechanized factory farms produce "farm-fresh" broilers.
Credit: Photo courtesy of Animal Emancipation, Inc.

"The modern layer is, after all, only a very efficient converting machine, changing the raw material—feedstuffs—into the finished product—the egg—less, of course, maintenance requirements." *Farmer and Stockbreeder*, January 30, 1962. Credit: Photo courtesy of Humane Farming Association (HFA).

In order to produce "white veal," calves are tethered in small stalls to stop muscle development and are fed a diet that induces anemia and prevents them from ruminating. Credit: Photo courtesy of Humane Farming Association (HFA).

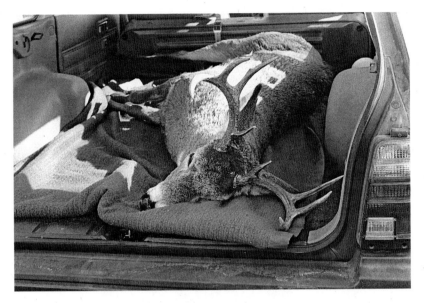

The morning's trophy kill.
Credit: Photo courtesy of Joy Bush. Copyright 1987 Joy Bush.

Although an increasing number of countries have banned leghold traps, millions of animals continue to be caught in such devices. Credit: Photo courtesy of The Fur-Bearers Association.

Steer wrestling: one of the cruelties of that favorite American entertainment, the rodeo. Credit: Photo courtesy of Animal Emancipation, Inc.

Circus life reduces magnificent animals to depressed and neurotic creatures. Credit: Photo courtesy of Animal Emancipation, Inc.

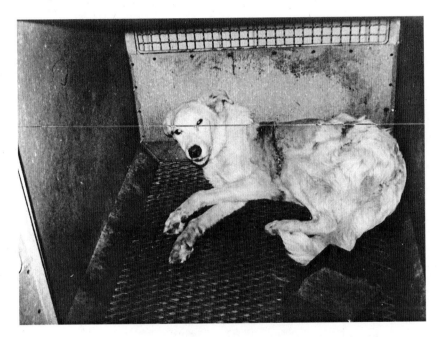

Dogs: some are members of our families, some are research tools.
Credit: Photo courtesy of Friends of Animals.

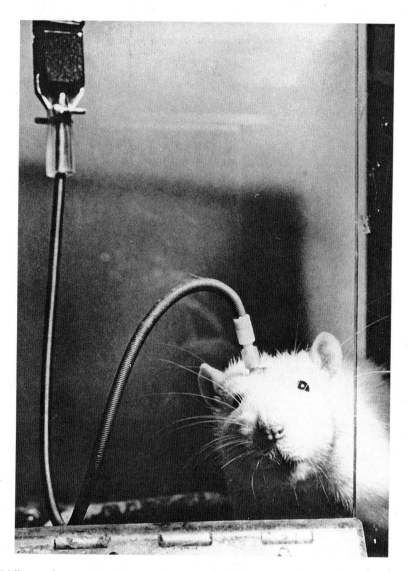

Millions of rats are used in experiments annually but are not even considered "animals" under the federal Animal Welfare Act. Credit: Photo courtesy of The American Anti-Vivisection Society.

interest in health care, in the name of profit. But this does not mean that the factory owner may disregard all of the worker's interests. Pharmaceutical companies cannot test new drugs on employees who have not consented. Food processing plants cannot make hot dogs or luncheon meats out of workers.

Consider the following example. Assume that Simon the researcher has designed an experiment that will in all likelihood yield data crucial in finding a cure for cancer. The experiment, however, will work only if he uses a human being as a test subject. There is no feasible alternative. No animal subject will do; no computer model will work. The human used in the experiment will suffer excruciating pain and eventually die. No volunteers offer to participate. An unwilling human—a severely retarded homeless adult with no family or friends—is chosen. Is it morally acceptable to use one severely retarded human being in a painful experiment that may produce a cure for cancer?

Before you answer, consider the fact that every year millions of humans around the world die from cancer. Think about their pain and suffering. Think about the pain and suffering of their loved ones. Surely the benefits of a cure for cancer would be inestimable. Would such benefits not outweigh the detriment to a single human, especially a severely retarded homeless human?

Consider also that if Simon is after data applicable to human illnesses, he would do much better to use humans rather than animals in his biomedical experiment. After all, data derived from animals must be extrapolated to humans if that data is to be at all useful. And extrapolation is always inexact.

For most of us, the answer to this question is no. It does not matter how large a benefit we will receive from exploiting the person. It does not matter whether the human is retarded or brilliant, rich or poor, able to speak or to perform on a test better than a chimpanzee. We simply do not consider it appropriate to use sentient humans in this way.[18] It does not matter whether there is a feasible alternative to using humans: to use a human being in this way would be to treat him or her as a thing—exclusively as a means to an end. The law forbids such a trade-off, and most of us would agree with this absolute prohibition. Indeed, I have posed this hypothetical question in lectures in medical schools throughout the world, and I have asked those who would allow severely retarded homeless humans to be used in finding a cure for cancer to raise their hands. *No one* has ever raised a hand.

We simply do not allow humans to be used in biomedical experiments without informed consent, and we uniformly condemn such conduct whenever it is brought to light. The Nazis' use of humans in experiments prompted the international community to embrace the Nuremberg Code, which forbids research on unconsenting subjects. In 1964, the World Medical Association adopted the Helsinki Declaration, which similarly prohibits the use of humans as unconsenting or ill-informed research subjects. And in May 1997, President Clinton apologized to survivors of federally funded syphilis experiments conducted by the government on poor men of color in Tuskegee, Alabama, from 1932 to 1972. These human subjects were allowed to develop advanced syphilis symptoms even though penicillin existed and could have been used to treat the men, who were not even told that they had syphilis.[19] Similarly, the government condemned radiation experiments that were conducted between 1944 and 1974 on military personnel, hospital patients, children, pregnant women, and prisoners who were not properly informed about the nature of the experiments.[20]

The reason that we must protect the interest of humans in not being treated as the resources of other humans—despite the beneficial consequences of such treatment and irrespective of the particular characteristics of those whom we may seek to use as resources—is simple. If we do not protect this interest across the board, then some humans will be treated as things whenever it is determined to be in the interests of other humans. If the human interest in not suffering has any moral significance, then we cannot treat humans merely as resources. If some humans are treated as the resources of others, then the principle of equal consideration can never apply to their interests in not suffering. Humans who are for whatever reason regarded only as resources will never have interests similar to those of humans who are not regarded as resources.

The Principle of Equal Consideration: Basic Rights and Equal Inherent Value

If the principle of equal consideration is to have any application to humans, then we must, at the very least, recognize that all sentient humans have an interest in not suffering *at all* as the result of their use as the resources of others. We can express this idea in two different but related ways. We can say that all humans have a *basic right* not to be treated exclusively as means to the ends of others. Alternatively, we can say that all humans have *equal inherent value* that prevents our valuing them only as our resources. But however we say it, we are asserting that the principle of equal consideration *requires* that we not treat human beings as property or exclusively as resources; humans *must* receive some minimal baseline protection if they are to have *any* morally significant interest in not suffering.

We will now briefly examine the basic right not to be treated as a thing and the concept of equal inherent value. We will see that neither of these concepts involves anything that requires our acceptance of any metaphysical doctrines. All that is required is *logic:* if human interests in not suffering are to have moral significance, then humans *cannot* be resources. If one human is a resource of another, then that other human gets to value the interests of the resource in not suffering, and this valuation may be based solely on what will benefit the valu*er* and with absolutely no regard for what will benefit the valu*ed*. The interest of the human who is the resource, and the end or interest of the human for whom this other serves exclusively as a means, can *never* be similar for the purposes of applying the principle of equal consideration.

The Basic Right Not to Be Treated as a Thing

As we saw in the Introduction, a right is a way of protecting an interest.[21] To say that my interest is protected by a right is to say that it is protected against being abrogated merely because such abrogation produces beneficial consequences for someone else. Although there is certainly a great deal of disagreement about precisely what rights human beings have, it is clear that we now regard every human being as holding the right not to be treated exclusively as a means to the end of another. This is a basic right, and it is different from all other rights; it is a pre-legal right in that it is a necessary prerequisite to the enjoyment of any other right. If we do not recognize that a human has the right not be treated exclusively as a means to the ends of another, then any other right that we may grant her, such as the right of free speech, or of liberty, or to vote or own property, is completely meaningless. In this sense, the basic right not to be treated as a resource is different from what are normally referred to as "natural" rights, although the two concepts are sometimes used interchangeably, which contributes to the confusion. For the most part, natural rights are those rights that are considered to exist apart from their recognition by a particular legal system, and they are often but not always grounded in religious doctrines. For example, we have seen that Locke (and Western law) regarded the right to own property as a natural right grounded in God's grant to humans of dominion over the earth and animals. Although there can be no doubt that the right to own property is considered very important, we can imagine a society in which humans do not have property rights, or in which property rights are regarded as much less important. A socialist society may regard certain other rights, such as the right to free education or health care, as more important than property rights per se. But in *any* society, be it capitalist or communist or whatever, humans must possess a basic right not to be a resource as a minimal prerequisite to being a moral and legal *person* within that society. Anyone who does not possess that basic right is not a person but a thing, precisely because the principle of equal consideration cannot apply to the interests of a human whose only value is as a resource for others.[22]

This concept of a basic right has been expressed by philosophers throughout the centuries. Kant, for example, maintained that there is one "innate" or pre-legal or pre-political right—the right of "innate *equality*," or the "independence from being bound by others to more than one can in turn bind them; hence a human being's quality of being *his own master*."[23] This "innate" or basic right "grounds our right to *have* [other] rights."[24] A modern version of the theory of basic or "innate" rights is found in *Basic Rights* by political theorist Henry Shue.[25] Shue maintains that a basic right is not a right that is "more valuable or intrinsically more satisfying to enjoy than some other rights."[26] Rather, a right is basic if "any attempt to enjoy any other right by sacrificing the basic right would be quite literally self-defeating, cutting the ground from beneath itself." Shue states that "non-basic rights may be sacrificed, if necessary, in order to secure the basic right. But the protection of a basic right may not be sacrificed in order to secure the enjoyment of a non-basic right." The reason for this is that a basic right "cannot be sacrificed successfully. If the right sacrificed is indeed basic, then no right for which it might be sacrificed can actually be enjoyed in the absence of the basic right. The sacrifice would have proven self-defeating."[27]

Shue emphasizes that basic rights are a prerequisite to the enjoyment and exercise of nonbasic rights, and that the possession of nonbasic rights in the absence of basic rights is nothing more than the possession of rights "in some merely legalistic or otherwise abstract sense compatible with being unable to make any use of the substance of the right."

Although Shue identifies several basic rights, the most important of these is the "basic right to physical security—a right that is basic not to be subjected to murder, torture, mayhem, rape, or assault."[28] While acknowledging that it is not unusual in a given society for some members of at least one ethnic group to receive less physical protection than others, Shue argues that "few, if any, people would be prepared to defend in principle the contention that anyone lacks a basic right to physical security."[29] If a person does not enjoy the basic right to security, and may be murdered at will by any other person, then it is senseless to consider what other "rights" she might have. In other words, if I have no right to physical security and you have the right to kill me at any time, then my possession of the right to drive or to vote becomes meaningless.

If we are going to recognize and protect the interest of humans in not being treated as things, then we *must* use a right to do so; if we allow the interest of humans in not being treated as things to be traded away because the consequences of doing so will benefit others, then, by definition, we will no longer respect the interest of those humans in being treated as ends in themselves, and those humans will be at risk of being treated merely as commodities. The basic right not to be treated as a thing is the minimal condition for membership in the moral community. This is the one right that we all agree is inalienable; you can get greater protection, but if you are going to be a member of the moral community—if you are not going to be a thing that has no protected interests—then you cannot get less protection than this right affords. If you are a thing, then you have no rights at all, and your value can be determined exclusively and completely by someone else—and that person is your owner. Once you are a slave, then you are no longer a member of the moral community, because you no longer have any interests that can be protected in any meaningful way. Your owner may choose to treat you well—and we will protect that choice. Your owner may choose to treat you poorly—and we will protect that choice as well. Indeed, we will protect your owner's decision to inflict pain and suffering on you as long as your owner derives a benefit thereby.

It is important to understand that the basic right not to be regarded as a thing is very limited and in no way provides protection against being used to some degree as a means to the ends of others, against every form of discrimination or unfair treatment. But the basic right provides essential protections. It means that we may not buy or sell humans, or use humans in biomedical experiments without their consent, or make shoes out of them, or hunt them for sport. To possess the basic right not to be treated as a thing means that the holder is included in the moral community; it does not specify what other rights that human may have.[30]

Equal Inherent Value

Another way of expressing the idea that we protect the interest of humans in not being treated as the resources of other humans is to say that we recognize that all humans—regardless of their personal characteristics—have value beyond their value as the resources of others. The concept of inherent, or intrinsic, value is, like the basic right not to be treated as a thing, a necessary starting point if we are going to treat human interests as morally significant. If things have any value at all, that value is extrinsic or conditional—that is, they have value only insofar as we regard them as valuable. Things have a price that reflects the value we place on them, and money is the ultimate standard of the value of things. If humans have no inherent or intrinsic value, then they will be regarded merely as things, their value will be determined solely in monetary terms, and they will become outcasts from the moral community.[31] Any "humane" treatment of such unvalued humans will be a matter of *our* charity, not of *their* right.

Although the notion of inherent value is often associated with religious doctrines, there is nothing necessarily mystical or metaphysical about it. It is a very commonsensical and logical notion integral to the structure of morality. Inherent value is merely another name for the minimal criterion necessary to be regarded as a member of the moral community. If you do not have inherent value, all of your interests—including your fundamental interest in not experiencing pain and your interest in continued life—can be "sold away," depending exclusively on someone else's valuation. In order for the concept of inherent value to protect humans from being treated as things, we must regard all humans as having *equal* inherent value. This does not mean that all humans must be valued equally for all purposes. We may decide to allocate a greater share of wealth to a brain surgeon than we do to a bricklayer because we value the skills of the one more highly than we do the skills of the other. But for purposes of deciding whether we should use either the brain surgeon or the bricklayer as a forced organ donor, or should intern either in a concentration camp, both have exactly the same value: we are not permitted to value either exclusively as a means to the ends of others. The concept of equal inherent value reflects the fact that all human beings value themselves even if no one else values them. And it is not necessary that one be able to think explicitly about one's interests in such terms in order to have interests. A baby, a severely retarded human, and an insane person all have an interest in not suffering, even if others do not value their interests at all.[32]

As in the case of the basic right not to be treated as a thing, it is important to understand exactly the scope of protection that is provided by the recognition of inherent value. We may still value other humans instrumentally. We may still choose to pay a brain surgeon more than we pay a janitor. The recognition of inherent value does, however, protect the individual from being sold into slavery or used in biomedical experiments. Inherent value must be "equal" in that it merely stops us from valuing certain humans exclusively as commodities. Any human who has "lesser" inherent value than others will be treated no better than a human who is regarded as having no inherent value at all: the interests of such humans will necessarily be deprived of moral significance. The principle of equal consideration will not apply to them, we will have no moral obligations that we owe directly to them, and they will risk being treated solely as economic commodities.

In sum, the basic right not to be treated as a thing and equal inherent value define the bare minimum needed for membership in the moral community. We might compare the moral community to a large theater. Once you are admitted into the theater, you are guaranteed a space somewhere to watch the performance, but not necessarily the best seat or a particularly good seat, or even any seat at all. Maybe we will make you stand. But to be in the theater is to have some space in which to watch the performance; otherwise admission is meaningless. As a logical matter, admission to the theater for the purpose of seeing the performance means that you will have some access—however imperfect relative to that of those sitting in the front row.

And that is what inherent value and the basic right not to be treated as a thing are all about. In order to be a member of the moral community, a human has to have some value that is protected against being assessed by others exclusively in terms of what will benefit them. We do not permit humans to own others as slaves, or arrogate to themselves the privilege of valuing all of the interests of other humans. We do not permit humans to be used in biomedical experiments without informed consent. We do not exhibit human beings in zoos and circuses, although we once did.[33] If we do not accord every sentient human the basic right not to be treated as a thing, or equal inherent value, then those humans whom we do not value will risk being excluded completely from the moral community. The principle of equal consideration *requires* that we reject the use of humans as resources if human interests in not suffering are to be morally significant. We cannot have a "hybrid" system that requires us to balance the interests of slave owners against slaves, and expect the interests of slaves to be morally significant.

Applying the Principle of Equal Consideration to Animals

The humane treatment principle was intended to overturn the view that animals are merely things and to recognize that animals have a morally significant interest in not suffering. The property status of animals, however, precludes the recognition of any animal interests beyond those required to ensure that humans benefit from the exploitation of animals. Animals are treated in precisely the same way that slaves were. We do not want property owners to "waste" animal property any more than we wanted slave owners to "waste" human property—to inflict suffering on animals or slaves for no purpose whatsoever. But as long as there is a purpose, however trivial it may be, the suffering of the animal is considered justified, just as it was in the case of the slave.

Although there are laws that supposedly protect animals, just as there were laws that supposedly protected slaves, these laws require that we balance the interests of right holders, and, in particular, holders of property rights, against the interests of their property. This sort of "hybrid" system did not work for slaves and it does not work for animals. In the case of animals, the law has presumed that the owners of animals will act to protect their economic interest in the animal property, and that this self-interest will provide a sufficient level of protection for the animal. Such a presumption did not provide much protection for slaves, and, as we saw in Chapter 3, it does not provide much protection for animals. Although animal welfare laws were originally intended, at least in part, to recognize that humans had at least some obligations directly to animals, this purpose was quickly forgotten, with the result that the law now defines the primary object of anticruelty laws as "to prevent outrage to the sensibilities of the community."[34] The very same thing happened with laws that supposedly protected slaves: their primary object became the protection of community sensibilities. In a Virginia case, *Commonwealth v. Turner*, the court determined that it had no jurisdiction to try the defendant slave owner, who beat his slave with "rods, whips and sticks," and held that even if the beating was administered "wilfully and maliciously, violently, cruelly, immoderately, and excessively," the court was not empowered to act as long as the slave did not die.[35] The court distinguished private beatings from public chastisement, which might subject the master to liability "not because it was a slave who was beaten, nor because the act was unprovoked or cruel; but, because ipso facto it disturbed the harmony of society; was offensive to public decency, and directly tended to a breach of the peace. The same would be the law, if a horse had been so beaten."[36]

If we agree with the underlying premise of the humane treatment principle and disagree that animals are merely things to which we can have no direct moral or legal obligation, we must go back to the drawing board. We must be committed to the idea that when animals and humans have a similar interest, we must treat them in a similar way unless there is a morally sound reason not to do so. And despite any interspecies or intraspecies differences, all sentient beings have interests, in particular an interest in not suffering. Animals, like humans, have an experiential welfare in the sense that things can go better or worse for them depending on whether their interest in not suffering is respected, and on whether other interests they have as sentient beings are facilitated or frustrated.[37]

We do not, and in some cases cannot, protect humans from all suffering. Humans suffer from diseases; they suffer from natural disasters; they suffer from accidents; and to a greater or lesser degree, in every nation in the world, they suffer from a lack of resources, such as food, clothing, medical care, and shelter. Indeed, there is not even agreement about which human interests in not suffering ought to be protected. Yet, whatever other rights humans may have, and although we may not treat humans in the same way, it is generally agreed that all humans— babies, the elderly, the retarded, the poor, the brilliant, the person of color, the white—have at least one right: a right not to be valued exclusively as a means to the ends of others.

In the case of animals, the principle of equal consideration tells us that if we are going to take animal interests seriously and give content to the prohibition against unnecessary suffering that we all claim to accept, then we must extend the same protection to animal interests in not suffering unless we have a good reason for not doing so. Just as we cannot protect humans from all suffering, we cannot protect animals from all suffering. Animals in the wild may be injured, or become diseased, or may be attacked by other animals. But the principle of equal consideration requires that unless we have a morally sound reason not to do so, we must protect animals from suffering at all from use as human property. We must accord to animals, as we do to humans, the basic right not to be treated as a resource.

There is no "third" choice: either animal interests are morally significant and are subject to analysis under the principle of equal consideration, or animals are merely things that have no moral status. We could, of course, treat animals better than we do, but, as we saw in Chapter 3, there are powerful economic forces that militate against better treatment in light of the status of animals as property. But simply according "better" treatment to animals has nothing necessarily to do with making their interests morally significant. It may have been "better" to beat slaves three rather than five times a week, but this "better" treatment did not remove slaves from the category of things. The similar interests of slave owners and slaves were not accorded similar treatment because the former had a right not to suffer at all from being used as a resource that the latter did not possess.

Animals as "Persons"?

If we extend the principle of equal consideration to animals, does that mean that they will become "persons"? Yes, it does. But we should be careful about what we mean by that term. We tend to use "persons" and "humans" synonymously, but such usage is incorrect. The best current example of this misuse can be found in the debate on abortion, where much of the controversy focuses on whether the fetus (at whatever stage, including at conception) is "human." This is the wrong question. Whatever your religious or moral beliefs about abortion, there can be no doubt that the fetus is human in that if there is no abortion or miscarriage, a human fetus will not gestate into a giraffe or a squirrel. The moral question is whether the human fetus is a "person"—is the principle of equal consideration applicable to the fetus—at any stage in the gestation process?

In any event, we should not think that our considering animals as persons means that animals are the same as humans or that they have all of the same rights humans have. To say that a being is a person is merely to say that the being has morally significant interests, that the principle of equal consideration applies to that being, that the being is not a thing. In a sense, we already accept that animals are persons; the humane treatment principle represented a historical shift that established that we could have direct obligations to animals. Their status as property, however, prevented their personhood from being realized.

The same was true of human slavery. Slaves were regarded as chattel property. Laws that provided for the "humane" treatment of slaves did not make slaves persons because, as we saw above, the principle of equal consideration could not apply to them. For a while, we tried to have a three-tiered system: things, or inanimate property; persons, who were free; and, depending on your choice of locution, "quasi-persons" or "things plus"—the slaves. But, as we saw, that system could not work. We eventually recognized that if slaves were going to have morally significant interests, they could not be slaves anymore. We recognized that the moral universe is limited to only two kinds of beings: persons and things. "Quasi-persons" or "things plus" will necessarily risk being treated as things because the principle of equal consideration cannot apply to them.

Similarly, we cannot regard animals as "quasi-persons" or as "things plus." They are either persons, beings to whom the principle of equal consideration applies and to whom we have direct moral obligations, or things, beings to whom the principle of equal consideration does not apply and to whom we have no direct moral obligations. As we will explore further in Chapter 7, our considering animals as persons does not mean that we cannot prefer humans to animals in situations of true emergency or conflict; it means only that we must stop creating those conflicts by treating animals as our property. If we are going to apply the principle of equal consideration to animals and treat animal interests in not suffering as morally significant, then we must extend to animals the basic right not to be treated as our resources. This does not require that we treat animals in the same way that we treat humans. No one argues that we should extend to animals the right to vote or to drive a car or to own property or to attend a university, or many other rights that we reserve to competent human beings. Nor does this mean that animals have any sort of guarantee of never suffering or that we must protect animals from harm from other animals in the wild or that we can protect animals from accidental injury by humans. But just as we believe that humans should not suffer from use as the slaves or property of other humans, animals should not be made to suffer from our use of them as resources.

Yet the extension of this one right to animals will profoundly affect our use and treatment of animals. We will no longer be able to justify our institutional exploitation of animals for food, biomedical experiments, entertainment, or clothing. All of these uses *assume* that animals are resources and have no moral status.

In the next chapter, we will consider whether there are any morally sound reasons—reasons that do not themselves violate the principle of equal consideration—that justify our treatment of animals as property and our consequent denial to animals of the basic right not to be treated exclusively as a resource. That is, we will ask whether there is any sound reason to account for why we accord this basic right to all humans irrespective of their age, intelligence, or any other characteristic, yet deny this right to all nonhumans, despite the fact that they, like humans, are sentient.

5

Robots, Religion, and Rationality

WE SAW IN CHAPTERS 1 and 2 that although the humane treatment principle purports to reject the infliction of unnecessary suffering on animals, the overwhelming amount of suffering that we do inflict cannot be described as necessary and occurs merely to facilitate the pleasure, amusement, and convenience that we derive from using animals. In Chapter 3, we saw that the humane treatment principle fails to accord moral significance to animal interests because animals are viewed as property. Even though we claim that animals have moral value and morally significant interests and that we have direct obligations to them, their status as property means that we nevertheless consider them things.

In Chapter 4, we saw that the principle of equal consideration requires that we treat likes alike. The humane treatment principle recognizes that humans and animals, however different, are alike in that they are sentient and have an interest in not suffering. The principle of equal consideration says that if we are going to take this interest seriously, we must extend to animals the basic right not to be treated as things unless there is some reason that justifies this differential treatment. We must provide a reason that is neither arbitrary nor a violation of the principle of equal consideration why we accord this basic right to all humans yet deny it to all nonhumans, despite the fact that they, like us, are sentient.

In this chapter, we will consider four different reasons that have been advanced for denying to animals the basic right not to be treated as things. The first reason, sometimes connected with religious belief, is that animals have no interests at all, and that it therefore makes no logical sense to accord them a basic right to protect their interest in not suffering. The second reason is that animals are our "spiritual inferiors," and that although they may have an interest in not suffering, God has given us license to ignore that interest. The third reason, often but not always related to the second, is that there is some natural characteristic, such as the ability to think rationally, to use abstract concepts, or to be self-aware, that animals lack, and that justifies our denial to them of the basic right not to be treated as things. The fourth reason is that although animals have inherent value, they have less inherent value than do humans and therefore do not merit our according them the basic right not to be treated as things.

Animals Are Really Robots

In Chapter 1, we met French philosopher René Descartes. Descartes maintained that animals are nothing more than automatons, or robots, created by God. According to Descartes, animals do not possess souls, which are required for consciousness, and therefore lack minds altogether and cannot experience pain, pleasure, or any other sensation or emotion. Descartes reasoned that animals lack consciousness because they do not use verbal or sign language. If Descartes is correct, then we can no more speak sensibly about animals having interests than we can about clocks having interests. If animals are not sentient and cannot experience anything, then by definition they have no interests and it would be absurd to believe that we have any moral or legal obligations to them.[1]

The humane treatment principle explicitly rejects the Cartesian idea that animals are not sentient. Indeed, the foundation of the principle is precisely that *because* animals can suffer, we have a moral obligation that we owe directly to animals not to impose unnecessary suffering on them. But just as there is a still a Flat Earth Society and a resurgence of belief in alchemy, there are still those who, almost four hundred years later, serve as standard-bearers for seventeenth-century Cartesian mechanism and who deny that animals can, as a matter of fact, have interests.

A stunning example of this denial is found in the work of philosopher R. G. Frey. Frey claims that although animals may have interests in the same sense that an automobile engine has an "interest" in being oiled, animals do not have desires and cannot have "wants which can be satisfied or left unsatisfied."[2] So, according to Frey, when I beat my dog, my dog *cannot* have a desire not to be beaten. Animals cannot have desires, because desires presuppose beliefs about the truth or falsity of sentences. For example, if I want to acquire a particular Van Gogh painting, it is necessary, according to Frey, that I believe that the sentence, "I presently own this particular Van Gogh painting," is false. And to have a belief about the truth or falsity of a sentence requires that I have a grasp of the relationship between language and the actual state of affairs in the world—in this case, the state of my collection of paintings. And since animals lack language, Frey reasons, they cannot have such a grasp and therefore have no desires and cannot have any interests.

Frey's argument is, of course, nothing more than a regurgitation of the Cartesian position minus God—that because animals supposedly lack the ability to use words or sign language, they are nothing more than machines that lack consciousness and the ability to experience pain. In fact, however, there is simply no reason to assume that in order to have a desire to avoid pain, a being must have a belief about the truth of sentences, and there is every reason to believe that a being can have desires and preferences in the absence of beliefs about sentences. If I am sleeping deeply and you apply a flame to my skin, I will awaken in a fit of pain. I will undoubtedly desire that you stop burning me; I most definitely have an interest in your not burning me—indeed, my consciousness would probably consist of nothing more than my desire to have the pain stop. But I doubt very much whether I would be consciously experiencing or having a belief that the sentence "I am not in pain" is false or that the sentence "I am in pain" is true. Moreover, many human beings—the very young, the very old, the senile, the severely retarded, those with various neurological diseases, and so on—are unable to have beliefs, *any* beliefs, about the truth value of sentences, yet we still regard these beings as members of the moral community, replete with interests.

The fact that Descartes and the seventeenth-century mechanists believed that animals were nothing more than machines may have been excusable given the state of scientific knowledge in the 1600s and the risk that the Catholic Church might excommunicate or execute anyone who blasphemed that animals are similar to humans in morally significant ways. That there are still those today who believe that an animal who is unable to form beliefs about the truth or falsity of sentences is therefore unable to have desires or interests (other than in the sense that an engine needs oil) is rather astounding.

Philosopher Peter Carruthers is another who claims that animals may lack consciousness. He argues that all animal behavior may be non-conscious and that pain "may help to control behaviour without being felt by the conscious subject." Although Carruthers acknowledges that on balance it may be "too highly speculative" to argue that animals are not conscious, it is quite paradoxical, to say the least, that he suggests that pain controls behavior but that animals are not conscious of pain.[3] Although we might formulate many arguments to refute Carruthers' position, common sense is all that is necessary. If Carruthers is correct, then an animal who is rendered unconscious with an anesthetic is still not conscious when the anesthetic wears off. Carruthers would be forced to say that the unconscious animal regains unconsciousness. Such a position is charitably characterized as most implausible.

Frey and Carruthers attempt to characterize animals as beings that lack minds or consciousness of pain, just as Descartes did in the seventeenth century. But we got over that hurdle several hundred years ago when, as a result of simple empirical observation, we recognized that sentient animals, like sentient humans, are conscious of pain and therefore have an interest in avoiding it. If we do not believe that animals are conscious of pain, then why have a humane treatment principle? Why not have a humane treatment principle for rocks and plants, as well?

Animals as Spiritual Inferiors

The second reason for denying animals the basic right not to be treated as things is that although animals are sentient and have an interest in not suffering, God has given us permission to ignore those interests.[4] Although we post-Enlightenment types like to think of Western culture as secular and as upholding the separation of church and state, Western culture has its roots in the Judeo-Christian tradition, and that tradition has had a profound influence on our thinking about animals and on their legal status as property. As we saw in Chapter 3, although the concept of property is ancient and has taken different forms, and although animals have long been regarded as property, the primary architect of our current concept of private property, and of animals as private property, was John Locke. Moreover, we saw that Locke maintained that the origin of property rights as a general matter was the absolute right that God had supposedly given to humans to use and kill animals. Locke's theory of private property and his view that animals are property, both of which have had an enormous effect on British and American law, were based directly on the Book of Genesis, in which God created humans in his image and gave "dominion" to us over the earth and all of the animals with whom we share the planet. Locke argued that because humans were made in God's image, there cannot be any "Subordination among us, that may Authorize us to destroy one another, as if we were made for one anothers uses, as the inferior ranks of Creatures are for ours."[5] Locke opposed treating humans as property and therefore opposed slavery. He interpreted God's grant of dominion as a license for human domination over the "Inferior Creatures" intended for the "benefit and sole Advantage" of humans, who may use and "may even destroy" them.[6] For Locke, God's grant of dominion over animals meant that we had divine permission to exercise *domination* over them.

According to Locke and others in the same theological tradition, the Bible established that animals could have *no* moral significance; we could have no direct moral or legal obligations to them. As we saw earlier, to the extent that Locke regarded inflicting gratuitous suffering on animals to be morally problematic, his only concern was that such conduct would tend to make us treat each other less kindly. Locke's theory is inconsistent with Bentham's humane treatment principle—and with any standard that accords moral significance to animals. One cannot simultaneously maintain that animals are inferiors created by God as human resources and that animals have moral significance. If we believe that animals and humans can never have similar interests.because animals are our spiritual inferiors, created by God exclusively as means to human ends, then the principle of equal consideration can *never* be applicable to animal interests. Indeed, this is exactly the problem we encountered in the context of the animal welfare laws. We claim to accord animals some moral status through the humane treatment principle, but because we regard animals as property, the balance of interests required by the humane treatment principle is never realized through animal welfare laws.

Locke's view that God's grant of dominion sanctioned our domination of animals as things is at the very core of our supposedly secular view of animals as property and remains the prevailing view of animals in Western culture. Although Locke articulated the view of animals as a sort of divine commodity in the context of his theory of private property as based on the labor theory of value, he inherited a religious tradition that had long equated dominion with domination. According to the tradition of Christian theology, animals, unlike humans, do not have immortal souls and we may therefore exclude them from the moral community, regardless of their sentience and moral status as beings with interests. The New Testament generally expresses no concern for animal interests. Indeed, in one story, Jesus exorcizes demons from a man and then casts the demons into a herd of swine, causing the animals to run into the sea and drown themselves.[7] Christian theologians such as Saint Augustine (354–430) and Saint Thomas Aquinas (c. 1225–74), both of whom acknowledged that animals could experience pain and suffering, were quick to combine God's grant of dominion over animals in the Old Testament with Jesus' apparent indifference to animals, and to conclude that animals existed only for the benefit of humans and had no moral significance whatsoever. Augustine denied that animals have souls and stated that "it is by a just arrangement of the Creator that their life and death is subordinated to our needs."[8] Aquinas likewise denied that animals possess immortal souls and argued, therefore, that "it is not wrong for man to make use of them, either by killing or in any other way whatever." Like Locke and Kant, Aquinas maintained that any prohibition on cruelty to animals is intended "to remove man's thoughts from being cruel to other men, lest through being cruel to animals one become cruel to human beings."[9] Although some Christian thinkers, among them Saint Basil and Saint Francis of Assisi, voiced moral concern about animals, the various denominations of organized Christianity have largely rejected the notion that animals have any moral significance whatsoever. In the mid-nineteenth century, the pope prohibited the establishment in Rome of a society to prevent cruelty to animals, stating that we cannot have any moral duties to animals because they do not possess souls.

We may make the following observations about the view that God created animals as spiritual inferiors for the use of humans and that animals have no moral significance per se.

First, a view such as Locke's requires that we accept as facts the existence of God; that God literally created humans as a finished product (rather than creating matter that evolved into human and other life forms); that God endowed only humans with souls; that the possession of a soul is a necessary prerequisite for possessing any moral significance; and that God created animals exclusively as means to our ends. If we do not accept a very literal creation story, then Locke's justification for the status of animals as property has no basis. Indeed, it is ironic that the animal rights position is often characterized as a "religious" position. Although there are some Eastern religions that promote the sanctity of all life, and although there are at least some believers in every religion that adopt the view that animal interests are morally significant, it is the concept of animals as property, rather than the sanctity of animal life, that is explicitly and inextricably rooted in religious doctrine.

Second, even if we accept the biblical creation story, the meaning of "dominion" in Genesis has generated serious disputes. Locke and most of the rest of us have simply assumed that dominion means domination.[10] At least some theologians, however, maintain that "dominion" as used in Genesis means *stewardship*, a concept that is inconsistent with treating animals merely as things and may, indeed, be quite consistent with recognizing that they have moral value and morally significant interests.[11] Although Genesis unambiguously established a spiritual hierarchy—God over humans, and humans, made in God's image, over everything else—it is not at all clear that the dominion God granted was intended to give us a license to use animals in any way that we wished, or even to kill animals for food. In the two verses of Genesis that immediately follow God's grant of dominion over animals to humans, it appears that, at least at the outset of creation, God did not intend humans to eat animals or animals to eat other animals. In Eden, *everyone* was a vegetarian: "And God said [to Adam and Eve] 'See, I have given you every herb that yields seed which is on the face of all the earth, and every tree whose fruit yields seed; to you shall it be for food. Also, to every beast of the earth, to every bird of the air, and to everything that creeps on the earth, in which there is life, I have given every green herb for food'; and it was so."[12]

This emphasis on the use of plants for food recurs when Adam and Eve are ejected from Eden after Eve, acting in conspiracy with a snake, persuades Adam to disobey God's command that they not eat from the tree of the knowledge of good and evil. When God reprimands Adam for his disobedience, God curses the ground and says to Adam that from that point forward, he will have to toil to obtain his food. But again, the food of which God speaks does not include animals: "Cursed is the ground for your sake; In toil you shall eat of it [a]ll the days of your life. Both thorns and thistles it shall bring forth for you, [a]nd you shall eat the herb of the field. In the sweat of your face you shall eat bread [t]ill you return to the ground."[13] The first mention of humans killing animals comes only later in Genesis.[14] So even if God created humans as spiritual superiors to animals, such a hierarchy does not necessarily mean that God did not intend animals to have at least that amount of inherent value required for their possession of a basic right not to be treated as our resources.[15] Moreover, some passages in the Old Testament express concern about our treatment of animals. In Deuteronomy, humans are enjoined from muzzling the ox while the animal treads out the grain.[16] Proverbs tells us that "[a] righteous man regards the life of his animal."[17] Isaiah condemned animal sacrifice and had a vision of the coming of the Messiah when the "wolf also shall dwell with the lamb, [t]he leopard shall lie down with the young goat," "a little child shall lead them" and "[t]hey shall not hurt nor destroy in all My holy mountain."[18]

Third, any reliance on the Old Testament to justify the treatment of animals as things requires that we explain our rejection of other forms of discrimination clearly present in the Bible. Numerous passages in the Old Testament assume that human slavery is a legitimate institution,[19] and Noah's curse of Canaan (the son of Noah's son Ham) to be a "servant of servants,"[20] as well as Abraham's ownership of slaves, were explicitly cited by defenders of slavery in the antebellum American South.[21] Slave owners and their supporters claimed that "[i]t is the order of nature and of God, that the being of superior faculties and knowledge, and therefore of superior power, should control and dispose of those who are inferior. It is as much in the order of nature, that men should enslave each other, as that other animals should prey upon each other."[22] Similarly, patriarchal society has used the Bible to justify discrimination against women. To punish Eve for leading Adam astray, God declares that man shall "rule over" woman.[23] Throughout the Bible, and particularly the Old Testament, women are regarded as the property of their husbands, and prostitutes, divorced women, and non-virgins are generally regarded as unfit for marriage (and therefore as outcasts from society). Even in the New Testament, Jesus' choice of twelve men to be his apostles has been used to justify exclusion of women from the priesthood or from holding significant positions in many Christian denominations.

We accept that human slavery is no longer a moral option, and most of us reject the sexism that is rampant in the Bible and particularly the Old Testament. To the extent that we continue to believe that our treatment of animals as things is warranted and required by religious authority, the burden is on us to explain why we reject the Bible on the matter of human slavery but accept it in the case of the treatment of animals as commodities. As a general matter, reliance on the Bible as a sufficient justification for a given moral position is almost always arbitrary. Proponents of the death penalty, for example, often point to scriptural authority, quoting the passage in Exodus stating that a murder should be punished "life for life."[24] Although the Old Testament states in numerous places that the death penalty is the appropriate penalty for murder, it is also prescribed for striking or even reviling parents, kidnaping and selling another into slavery, trespass on sacred ground, incest, homosexuality, witchcraft, and prostitution. But not even proponents of the death penalty today accept that we ought to execute people for all of these offenses. Once again, the burden is on those who cite the Bible to explain why it should be authoritative in some instances but not in others.

Similarly, any reliance on the parable of Jesus and the swine to justify denying moral status to animals requires that we explain why we otherwise ignore the much more plentiful and far less ambiguous references to Jesus' concern for the poor, his counsel that the rich should give away their possessions, and his general condemnation of violence and promotion of peace. Indeed, it is a supreme irony that Christianity has been used to justify the death penalty, war, and the capitalist economic system with its resulting inequitable distribution of resources.

Animals as Natural Inferiors

The third major reason for our differential treatment of human and animal interests concerns supposed natural characteristics that are possessed by humans (though not necessarily by all humans), but not by any animals. According to this view, there is some *qualitative* distinction between humans and animals (all species considered as a single group)—a difference of *kind* and not merely of *degree*—that purportedly justifies our treating animals as nothing but means to our ends.[25] Those who have supported this view have for the most part, unlike Descartes, recognized that animals are sentient and therefore have interests on some level in not being made to suffer. They have, however, maintained that because animals lack some special characteristic, we can ignore those interests and treat animals *as if* they were inanimate objects.

These special characteristics have almost always concerned some difference between human and animal minds; we have some mental characteristic that animals lack, or are capable of certain actions of which animals are incapable as a result of our supposedly superior cognitive capabilities. The list of posited differences between humans and animals includes:

- animals lack the ability to reason; they do not think about what they do;
- animals lack general concepts or general ideas;
- animals may be conscious of sensations such as pain but are not self-conscious;
- animals lack beliefs;
- animals lack language and cannot communicate;
- animals lack emotion;
- animals cannot transform their environment and create objects in the way that humans can;
- animals are not moral "agents"; they are not capable of making or responding to moral claims and they do not have a sense of justice;
- animals lack the ability to make agreements or contracts and since morality is a matter of a social contract, animals cannot be members of the moral community.

Some of those who have espoused the view that animals lack certain mental characteristics possessed by humans and are thereby naturally inferior to humans also subscribe to the Judeo-Christian view that animals are our spiritual inferiors because we are made "in God's image," and they have linked natural inferiority with spiritual inferiority. Aquinas, for instance, maintained that animals do not have immortal souls because they are not rational. Locke, who believed that animals were "inferior Creatures" created by God for our use, recognized that animals have a complex psychology and that they possess basic reasoning ability, but argued that they do not have language and are incapable of "abstraction, whereby ideas, taken from particular beings, become general representatives of all of the same kind." In that sense "the species of brutes are discriminated from man, and it is that proper difference wherein they are wholly separated and which at last widens to so vast a distance."[26]

For others, these supposedly special human characteristics are not connected to the religious doctrines that dominate Western thought about animals. The Greek philosopher Aristotle maintained that animals are sentient, but he denied that they possess rationality or beliefs and he concluded that "animals exist for the sake of man."[27] Aristotle also believed that some humans lack rationality and are the "natural slaves" of those who are rational, and that men are superior to women.

Although Aristotle's views about animals had a profound influence on Aquinas, who linked rationality with the possession of an immortal soul, Aristotle's denial of reason to animals was related to his views about biology rather than religion. Kant maintained that animals are merely means to human ends and that we can have no duties directly to them. Kant was a deeply religious man, but his views about animals were not based on religion but on his belief that animals are neither rational nor self-aware and lack moral value because they are unable to understand or apply moral rules. More recent philosophical theories about differences between humans and animals, such as John Rawls' view, discussed below, that animals have no sense of justice and cannot participate in a social contract (which supposedly determines membership in the moral community), are also not explicitly connected with religious doctrines.

But irrespective of whether there is a religious connection, the implication of these supposed mental differences is the same as it was with the view that animals are our spiritual inferiors, intended by God exclusively as means to our ends: humans and animals have no similar interests in the first place. And if animals have no similar interests, then the principle of equal consideration can have no application, and animal interests cannot have any moral significance. As in the case of those who maintain that animals are our spiritual inferiors, here too any limit on our use or treatment of animals can be based only on the negative effect that cruel treatment might have on our treatment of other humans or on our charitable impulses.

There are two reasons why these supposed differences between humans and animals are unsound reasons for denying animals the basic right not to be treated as our resources.

What about Darwin?

It is empirically difficult to deny that animals possess many of the mental characteristics that we have regarded as unique to humans. Indeed, the proposition that humans have mental characteristics wholly absent in animals confounds the theory of evolution, which, although disputed by some religious extremists, is generally accepted by most educated people throughout the world. Charles Darwin made quite clear that there are no uniquely human characteristics when he wrote that "the difference in mind between man and the higher animals, great as it is, is certainly one of degree and not of kind." Darwin had no doubt that dogs, cats, farm animals, and other animals are able to think and possess many of the same emotional responses as do humans: "the senses and intuitions, the various emotions and faculties, such as love, memory, attention, curiosity, imitation, reason, &c., of which man boasts, may be found in an incipient, or even sometimes in a well-developed condition, in the lower animals." Darwin maintained that female animals exhibited maternal affection and he noted that "associated animals have a feeling of love for each other" and that "[m]any animals . . . certainly sympathise with each other's distress or danger."[28] Any differences between humans and animals, Darwin maintained, are differences of degree, or quantitative differences, not differences in kind, or qualitative differences. In short, humans possess no characteristic unique to themselves that can justify differential treatment solely on the basis of species.

Darwin's position is supported by both common sense and science. For example, one of the primary differences between humans and animals that has historically been offered to justify excluding the animals from the moral community is that they lack self-consciousness or self-awareness. But this position is clearly indefensible. As Harvard biologist Donald Griffin has observed in his book *Animal Minds*, if animals are conscious of anything, "the animal's own body and its own actions must fall within the scope of its perceptual consciousness." Yet we deny animals self-awareness because we maintain that they "cannot think such thoughts as 'It is *I* who am running, or climbing this tree, or chasing that moth.'" Griffin correctly observes that "when an animal consciously perceives the running, climbing, or moth chasing of another animal, it must also be aware of who is doing these things. And if the animal is perceptually conscious of its own body, then it is difficult to rule out similar recognition that it, itself, is doing the running, climbing, or chasing." Griffin concludes that "[i]f we grant that animals are capable of perceptual awareness, denying them some level of self-awareness would seem to be an arbitrary and unjustified restriction."[29] Griffin's reasoning is unassailable, and indeed, as we will see in Chapter 6, this argument can be taken even further to demonstrate that any sentient being is by definition self-aware, because to be sentient means to be the sort of being who recognizes that it is *that* being, and not some other, who is experiencing the suffering that it has an interest in not experiencing. Any being who is conscious of pain must have some awareness of *self*.

Griffin's position on self-awareness is supported by the work of neurologist Antonio Damasio in his book *The Feeling of What Happens: Body and Emotion in the Making of Consciousness*. Damasio, who works with humans who have suffered stroke, seizures, and conditions that cause brain damage, maintains that such humans have what he calls "core consciousness." Core consciousness, which does not depend on memory, language, or reasoning, "provides the organism with a sense of self about one moment—now—and about one place—here."[30] Humans who experience transient global amnesia, for example, have no sense of the past or the future but do have a sense of self with respect to present events and objects. Damasio maintains that many animal species possess core consciousness. He distinguishes core consciousness from what he calls "extended consciousness," which requires reasoning and memory, but not language, and involves enriching one's sense of self with autobiographical details and what we might consider a representational sense of consciousness. Extended consciousness, "of which there are many levels and grades," involves a self with memories of the past, anticipations of the future, and awareness of the present.[31] Although Damasio argues that extended consciousness reaches its highest level in humans, who have language and sophisticated reasoning abilities, he maintains that chimpanzees, bonobos, baboons, and even dogs may have an autobiographical sense of self.[32] In any event, most of the animals we routinely exploit undoubtedly have core consciousness, which means that they are self-conscious. And if dogs have some extended or autobiographical sense of consciousness as well, it would be difficult to deny that some degree of extended consciousness is present in other mammals and in birds.

Moreover, in the past twenty years, cognitive ethologists (scientists who study the thought processes and consciousness of animals), such as Griffin, Marc Bekoff, and Carolyn Ristau, have produced a vast literature illustrating that animals, including mammals, birds, and even fish, possess considerable intelligence and are able to process information in sophisticated and complex ways.[33] Studies indicate, for example, that animals are able to communicate with other members of their own species as well as with humans. Indeed, the evidence that chimpanzees and orangutans have the ability to learn and use human language has become indisputable. A pygmy chimp and an orangutan have been taught to speak through a computer that produces a synthetic voice and displays words on a screen in response to pressing symbols on a keyboard. These animals construct sentences and have conversations with their keepers. The pygmy chimp Panbanisha has a vocabulary of three thousand words and has begun to write words on the floor with chalk after apparently learning them from their display on the computer screen. Panbanisha has begun to teach human language to her one-year-old son, who has the vocabulary of a human child of the same age. The director of the research project has stated that Panbanisha and the orangutan Chantek have the cognitive and language skills of a four-year-old human child.[34] Chimpanzees, elephants, and dolphins have been shown to demonstrate artistic ability. As Jeffrey Masson has argued persuasively, many animals have rich emotional lives; some develop lifelong bonds with their partners and suffer tremendous grief when a partner dies.[35]

The similarities between humans and animals are not limited to cognitive or emotional attributes alone. Animals exhibit what is clearly moral behavior as well. Ethologist Frans de Waal states that "honesty, guilt, and the weighing of ethical dilemmas are traceable to specific areas of the brain. It should not surprise us, therefore, to find animal parallels. The human brain is a product of evolution. Despite its larger volume and greater complexity, it is fundamentally similar to the central nervous system of other mammals."[36] There are numerous instances in which animals act in altruistic ways toward unrelated members of their own species and toward other species, including humans. In 1996, for example, a child fell eighteen feet into a moat surrounding the gorilla exhibit at a Chicago zoo. A female gorilla, Binti, protected the child from the other gorillas and then picked him up and delivered him to the zoo keepers.[37] There are many documented instances in which dogs have engaged in behavior perilous to themselves, such as entering a burning house or deep water, in order to rescue a human. Indeed, animal behavior is often more altruistic than is human behavior. In one experiment with macaque monkeys, 87 percent of the group preferred to go hungry rather than pull a chain that would deliver food but would also deliver a painful electric shock to an unrelated macaque housed in a neighboring cage. Compared to the monkeys, humans, as they demonstrated in their own experiments, seem far more willing to impose pain on other humans.[38] Nor is a sense of justice unique to humans. De Waal notes that chimps who shared their food with other chimps were more likely to receive food when in need, whereas those who were stingy with their food were treated less generously.[39]

There are, however, four difficulties with relying on the similarities (beyond sentience) between humans and animals to justify the moral significance of animals. First, even when there is overwhelming evi-

dence that some animals are recognizably close to us and exhibit behaviors that we can understand as proof that they possess virtually every
characteristic that we possess, we have a tendency simply to ignore that
evidence. For example, the similarities between the great apes and humans are unmistakable. Chimpanzee DNA is 98.5 percent the same as
ours; chimpanzees unquestionably have a cultural life and mental characteristics very close to ours. Chimpanzees can add and subtract numbers and can learn and use human language and recognize themselves
in mirrors. They have complex social relationships and exhibit behaviors that are considered cultural because they are transmitted by social
learning as opposed to instinctive behavior that is genetically transmitted. Researchers have identified thirty-nine behavior patterns that are
passed from generation to generation in some chimpanzee populations
but are absent in others.[40] These behaviors involve tool usage, grooming, and courtship. Nevertheless, we still imprison chimpanzees in zoos
and use them in painful biomedical experiments. If we do not recognize
that even chimpanzees possess whatever characteristics we think make
us special and are members of our moral community, then it is unlikely
that we are going to recognize the cognitive similarities between us and
dogs, cats, chickens, pigs, cows, or rats and include them in that moral
community as well.

Second, we are completely unclear as to how much of a characteristic an animal must have before we consider that animal to be "like us"
in a morally relevant way. For example, a "growing body of evidence
seems to show that parrots, like chimps and dolphins, can master complex intellectual concepts that most human children are not capable of
mastering until the age of 5."[41] How intelligent does a parrot have to be
before we conclude that the parrot possesses general concepts or
ideas—a characteristic that historically has been offered as a qualitative
difference between humans and animals? Does the parrot have to have
the conceptual ability of an eight-year-old? A twenty-one-year-old?
How large must the vocabulary of Panbanisha or Chantek be, how complex do their conversations have to be, before we conclude that there
may be quantitative differences between animals and most humans, but
not qualitative differences? How many times does Binti have to defy
members of her own species in order to protect and rescue a human
child before we recognize that she possesses a sense of altruism? In
short, we do not consider it sufficient that an animal possess a characteristic that we have for centuries denied them—they must possess some

undetermined quantity of that quality, and this allows us to up the stakes every time we encounter proof that animals possess such a characteristic. When we find out that parrots or chimps have the capacity to understand and manipulate single-digit numbers, we demand that they be able to manipulate beyond single digits to be "like us." In this game of special characteristics, animals can never win. The irony, of course, is that some animals may possess the special characteristic to a greater degree than do some humans. Some animals may have more intelligence, or greater ability to engage in rational thinking, than some humans, such as infants or severely retarded adults. A parrot with the conceptual ability of a five-year-old child by definition has more cognitive ability than a four-year-old child and may have more than some brain-damaged adults. Some animals display a greater range of altruistic behavior than do some humans. Indeed, there are probably more dogs that have rushed into burning houses to save humans than the other way around. But we still treat animals as our resources based on some supposed qualitative difference between them and us.

It is not enough that animals exhibit behaviors that provide compelling proof that they possess cognitive and emotional capabilities *similar* to those of "normal" or "average" humans. If these animals do not display the characteristic in *exactly* the way that we do, then we are reluctant to conclude that the animals have the special characteristic. But the failure to act in exactly the ways in which we do does not mean that they are not "like us" in that there are qualitative distinctions that separate us from them. We come to that conclusion because we assume from the outset that only identical demonstrations of a quality count as a morally relevant similarity. If anything, acceptance of evolutionary theory should lead us to adopt a starting point of similarity marked by differences between and among species, and not a qualitative distinction in which no animals possess some special mental characteristic that is regarded as uniquely human.

Third, the entire enterprise of trying to determine whether animals are "like us" in ways beyond their being creatures who, like us, can experience pain and pleasure, tends to lead to circular thinking and in any case ultimately begs the question. We arbitrarily identify some characteristic we think distinguishes us from animals, and we then declare that because animals do not have that characteristic, we are justified in treating them as resources. We have historically focused on the use of human language, for example, as a unique characteristic that separates us from animals and makes us "better." Who says? In the first place, there is, as we have seen, compelling evidence that animals other than humans can learn human language. Moreover, there is a great deal of empirical evidence that animals are able to communicate, often in very sophisticated ways, with members of their own species. The more relevant question, however, is what is *inherently* better about a species that uses human words and symbols to communicate? Birds can fly; we cannot. What makes the ability to use words and symbols better for moral purposes than the ability to fly? The answer, of course, is that *we* say so.

Fourth, the attempt to identify whether animals, or certain animals, possess characteristics that we have historically thought to be the sole province of human beings may be interesting from a scientific point of view. But it has absolutely nothing to do with the moral issue of how we should treat animals who are sentient but who lack a given characteristic. Although the work of cognitive ethologists has been very important, it is also dangerous in that it threatens to create new hierarchies in which we move some animals, such as the great apes, into a "preferred" group based on their similarity to humans, and continue to treat other animals as our property and resources.[42] The problem is that we do not require that humans have any particular characteristic—beyond sentience—before we accord them a basic right not to be treated as resources. We will discuss this matter in the next section.

At Least Some Humans Do Not Possess the Special Characteristic

Even if all animals other than humans lack a particular characteristic as an empirical matter, what *moral* conclusion concerning the treatment of them as resources could thereby be drawn? The answer is that there is absolutely no logically defensible relationship between the lack of a particular characteristic in animals and our treatment of them as resources. Philosopher and classical scholar Richard Sorabji has observed how "bad were the arguments designed to show that animals are very different from us" advanced by the Greeks in their debate over whether only humans had reason and syntactical linguistic ability (the ability to use language to form sentences and phrases). The very same debate remains unresolved to this day, and Sorabji correctly concludes that the language ability of animals, "of course, is a question of great scientific interest, but of no moral relevance whatsoever."[43] In 1974, philosopher Thomas Nagel wrote an essay entitled "What Is It Like To Be a Bat?" in which he maintained that we could never understand the consciousness of a bat, whose perception of the world is dominated by echolocation (which, by the way, is also true of dolphins).[44] From a moral point of view, the short answer to the question posed by Nagel's essay is *who cares what it is like to be a bat?* As long as the bat is sentient, then whatever other characteristics the bat has or does not have are *irrelevant* for the moral purpose of whether we should treat the bat exclusively as our resource.

Differences between humans and other animals may be relevant for other purposes, such as whether we allow animals to drive cars or vote or attend universities, but the differences have no bearing on whether animals should have the status of property or of things morally equivalent to inanimate objects. We recognize this inescapable conclusion whenever humans are involved. Whatever characteristic we identify as possessed only by humans will not be possessed by *all* humans. Some humans will have the exact same deficiency that we attribute to animals, and although we may not allow such humans to drive cars or to attend universities, most of us would shudder at the prospect of enslaving such humans, using them as unconsenting subjects in biomedical research, or otherwise using them exclusively as means to our ends.[45]

Even if animals cannot use language or reason abstractly, the same is true of humans who have suffered severe neurological disease—yet we do not use such people in biomedical experiments or as forced organ donors. Nor should we: the ability to communicate may be relevant to whether we make you the host of a talk show, or give you a job teaching in a university, but it is not relevant to whether we should kill you and remove your organs for transplant into another human, or whether we should enslave you so that you may labor for those without your particular disability.

Consider emotion. Again, the overwhelming evidence is that animals other than humans possess emotions. But so what? There are some humans, such as the severely autistic as well as those with other affective psychological disorders, who may not possess or display emotions in the same way that the rest of us do. Such characteristics may be relevant for certain purposes—we might not think it a good idea to license someone with a severe affective disorder as a teacher or psychologist. But we would not think of enslaving her or "sacrificing" her for the benefit of those without affective disorders.

Consider too the supposedly unique human characteristic of self-consciousness. If we reject Griffin's argument that any being that is perceptually aware is probably self-conscious, and require more than perceptual awareness in order to have self-consciousness, then some humans must also be considered as lacking self-consciousness. Peter Carruthers, who maintains that animals may not be conscious at all, also maintains that even if they are conscious, they are not self-conscious because they are incapable of having a "conscious experience . . . whose existence and content are available to be consciously thought about (that is, available for description in acts of thinking that are themselves made available to further acts of thinking)."[46] Once again, plenty of human beings are also unable to describe conscious experiences "in acts of thinking that are themselves made available to further acts of thinking," yet we do not enslave such humans or in general treat them exclusively as means to other humans' ends. Damasio, whose work on consciousness is based on his experience as a neurologist, argues that stroke victims may have core consciousness in that they are self-aware as beings in the present, but that they have lost the extended consciousness that allows them to contemplate themselves in the autobiographical way that Carruthers posits. But these stroke victims are certainly self-aware; they are just self-aware in a different way from the one Carruthers arbitrarily describes. In any event, self-awareness in the way that Carruthers describes it may be a useful characteristic for some purposes. It may not be advisable, for instance, to allow a severely retarded but sentient human, or a stroke victim, to have a driver's license. But that does not mean that we should use them in painful biomedical experiments. If we want the interests of Carruthers and the retarded human or the stroke victim to have moral significance, we cannot use any of them exclusively as our resource.

The argument that animals cannot transform their environment and create objects in the ways in which humans can has been made by a number of thinkers, including Karl Marx (1818–83). Marx believed that the distinguishing feature—the infamous qualitative distinction—between humans and animals was that humans were what he called "species-beings" and animals were not.[47] By this Marx meant that humans consciously transform their environment not merely in response to need, as do birds when they create nests and beavers when they create dams, but free from immediate need and for the benefit of all species. In short, bees build hives to satisfy immediate needs; humans build factories and cities and create commodities and art and thereby transform their environment for reasons that go beyond immediate need.

We can make two observations about Marx's position. First, some argue that the use of resources to satisfy immediate need, as opposed to what is effectively the overconsumption of resources to satisfy non-immediate or non-essential needs, is a virtue and not a vice. But more important, there are humans who cannot transform their environment and create objects in the way that Marx identified as the primary characteristic of a species-being. Those who have suffered strokes or other forms of brain damage are often unable to think beyond their present activities. Surely Marx would not have argued that such humans ought to be treated as the property or the resources of those who can make their labor the object of their thought.

Finally, many have argued that because animals have no sense of justice, and that only humans can respond to moral obligations or claims of right, we can have no moral obligations to animals and can exclude them from the moral community. We can think of this as a sort of "reciprocity" theory: animals cannot respond to us morally so we have no direct moral obligations to them. There are two versions of this reciprocity thesis, both of which can be traced to the ancients.[48] First, the Stoics, one of the dominant Hellenistic-Roman schools of philosophy, claimed that rational beings (i.e., humans) can extend justice only to other rational beings because only rational beings can understand the requirements of justice and participate in the community formed by rational beings. Kant accepted this view and maintained that we cannot have moral duties to beings other than rational beings. More recently philosopher John Rawls, whose book *A Theory of Justice* is considered one of the most influential treatises on ethics and moral philosophy of the later twentieth century, has argued that we are required to include in the moral community only those who "are capable of having (and are assumed to acquire) a sense of justice, a normally effective desire to apply and to act upon the principles of justice, at least to a certain minimum degree." Rawls concludes that "it does seem that we are not required to give strict justice" to animals because they lack the capacity for a sense of justice.[49] Similarly, Carl Cohen argues that we can exclude animals from the moral community because they are not "capable of exercising or responding to moral claims."[50]

A second version of this reciprocity theory is that moral rights and duties flow from a social contract; that is, morality is determined as a result of an imaginary or hypothetical contract between beings who can agree on rules that govern their behavior. Since animals are incapable of making or responding to moral claims, they are, by definition, incapable of participating in the formation of any social contract, and therefore we have no moral obligation not to harm them. Again, the origin of the idea that the moral community is limited to those who can participate in the formation of this imaginary contract may be found in Greek philosophy. The Epicureans maintained that justice extends only to those who can make contracts to avoid causing harm or suffering to others—an ability limited to humans. The English philosopher Thomas Hobbes (1588–1679) followed the Epicurean theory and maintained that there can be no injustice in the absence of a social covenant or contract, and that because animals do not have language, they cannot make covenants with humans and there can be no such thing as injustice to animals.[51] Rawls, who also defends a contractual view of justice, maintains that the social contract is based on what rational humans, who knew that they were going to be members of a society, would agree to before they knew what position they would occupy in that society. Rawls argues that since animals cannot participate in such an arrangement, "it does not seem possible to extend the contract doctrine so as to include them in a natural way."[52]

Again, however, there are many human beings who are not able to exercise or respond to moral claims, and, assuming that moral rights and duties are properly viewed as arising from a social contract—a very big assumption given the obvious fiction of any such ubiquitous contract—there are plenty of human beings who lack the capacity to participate in such contractual arrangements. The ability to respond to or make moral claims may be useful for some purposes, such as deciding whether we will allow you to make a legally binding contract or whether we will appoint a guardian to look after your interests. But these characteristics are wholly irrelevant to whether a human should be treated as a thing. For purposes of not being treated as a resource, as the property of another, as a being without morally significant interests, there is *no difference* between a human who is capable of making a contract and an insane human who does not understand what a moral or legal obligation is.[53]

Peter Carruthers, who also defends a contractual view of moral rights and duties, argues that animals lack the rational agency to participate in forming the social contract and, like Rawls, concludes that they therefore have no moral status. But Carruthers specifically and at length addresses the problem of what to do with humans who also lack the rational agency to participate in the social contract. Carruthers argues that for two reasons we can accord such humans moral status without extending moral status to animals. The first is a "slippery slope" argument: "if we try to deny moral rights to some human beings, on the grounds that they are not rational agents, we shall be launched on a slippery slope which may lead to all kinds of barbarisms against those who *are* rational agents."[54] Note that Carruthers does not think that all humans (the insane, the retarded, and so forth), deserve to have moral rights, but rather that we risk denying rights to "normal" humans if we start making such distinctions. Carruthers argues that this approach depends on the fact that there are no "sharp boundaries" between an adult who is not very intelligent and one that is severely retarded, or between a normal elderly person and an extremely senile one, but that there are such "sharp boundaries" between humans and animals.[55]

There are, however, at least two difficulties with Carruthers' slippery slope approach. First, his view that the boundary between a normal elderly person and an extremely senile one is less sharp than that between an extremely retarded human adult and a normal chimpanzee is empirically dubious. Second, his protection for retarded or senile humans depends on our not being able to make distinctions among humans without the threat of abuse. But what if we *could* distinguish between a rational human and an unequivocally nonrational one—what if we had a rule that defined a nonrational human as having an IQ less than twenty and administered that rule fairly? The answer for Carruthers must be that it would be morally acceptable to deny moral status to such humans.

The second reason Carruthers gives for according moral status to all humans, including nonrational ones, is that social instability would result were we to deny moral status to such humans, because "many people would find themselves psychologically incapable of living in compliance"[56] with such an arrangement. Again, there are two objections to Carruthers' theory. First, if the stability of the society were not threatened by excluding such beings from the moral community, then it would be perfectly acceptable to treat such humans as resources and to deny them moral status altogether. For example, no significant social instability resulted in Germany as a result of the Nazi view about the undesirability of the retarded and their exclusion from the moral community. Second, if social stability is threatened by denying moral value to animals, then Carruthers would presumably have to make his theory accommodate animals, which only reveals that Carruthers' reasoning is merely an endorsement of the moral values of the status quo. Carruthers has failed to advance a satisfactory solution to the problem faced by the contract theorist who wishes to include within the moral community those humans unable to understand or consent to the social contract, but to exclude all nonhumans because they are unable to participate in the contract.

Some people argue that membership in a species whose "normal" members have a special characteristic is enough to mandate that all members of that species should be treated as having the special characteristic, whether or not they actually have it. Carl Cohen argues that humans "who are unable, because of some disability, to perform the full moral functions natural to human beings are certainly not for that reason ejected from the moral community. The issue is one of kind."[57] This argument, however, begs the question, since the problem is how to distinguish humans from other animals by some characteristic that may be shared by some animals but that is most definitely not possessed by all humans. We do not solve that problem by pretending that all humans have the special characteristic that animals supposedly lack when some in fact do not possess it.

In sum, there is no special quality that only humans possess. Whatever the characteristic at issue, there are some nonhumans who exhibit the characteristic and some humans who do not. Of course it is possible to identify certain abilities, such as the ability to do calculus or write symphonies, that are peculiar to human beings, but those abilities are also peculiar to a very small percentage of human beings. Shall we, on the basis of their inability to do calculus or write symphonies, exclude the remainder of humankind from the moral community? Whatever defect we believe justifies our differential treatment of nonhumans, there are some human beings who suffer from these defects as well. And it is unnecessary for humans to possess any special characteristics in order not to be treated as things. That we do not require them to possess special characteristics demonstrates that we recognize that these characteristics have nothing to do with humans' susceptibility to suffering or with their right not to be treated as a resource.

The only time that we even consider suspending a human's basic rights is when we are sure that she is no longer functioning cognitively at all, as when a person is irreversibly comatose or is nonsentient, as are early-term fetuses. And even then, uncertainties about whether an irreversibly comatose human is really nonsentient or whether fetuses feel pain make many people uneasy about euthanasia and abortion apart from any religious objections they might have. But if a human is sentient, we generally regard certain use and treatment as impermissible from the outset. Our proscription of that use or treatment is not a matter of charity but a protection extended to all human beings as a matter of *right*. We do not accord children a basic right not to be treated as resources because they have the potential to be rational, or self-aware, or to make contracts. Children are members of the moral community because, apart from any potential that they have for the development of other capacities, they are already sentient beings who possess interests in not suffering. They may very well acquire other interests as they mature, but our obligation not to treat them as resources is based on the fact that they currently have interests in not suffering at all from their use as our resources.

We are left with *one* reason to explain our differential treatment of animals: that we are human and they are not, and that species difference alone justifies differential treatment. But this criterion is entirely arbitrary and no different from maintaining that although there is no special characteristic possessed only by whites, or no defect possessed by blacks that is not also possessed by whites, we may treat blacks as inferior to whites merely on the basis of race. It is no different from saying that although there is no special characteristic possessed only by men, or no defect possessed only by women, we may treat women as inferior to men based merely on sex.

As we saw in Chapter 4, racism and sexism are objectionable precisely because these forms of discrimination accord differential consideration to humans in violation of the principle of equal consideration. Both forms of discrimination have rested historically on religious justifications, or on supposedly qualitative distinctions between whites and blacks or males and females. American slavery, which was race-based, was justified on the ground that people of color were created by God as "inferiors," with inferior mental abilities, and that they had physiological differences, such as head shape, that distinguished them from whites. According to the medical and scientific views of those who supported slavery, "the negro, or Canaanitish race, consume less oxygen than the white, and that as a necessary consequence of the deficient aeration of the blood in the lungs, a hebetude of mind and body is the inevitable physiological effect; thus making it a mercy and a blessing to negroes to have persons in authority set over them, to provide for and take care of them."[58]

Similarly, patriarchal society has justified discrimination against women on the basis of supposed physical differences between men and women that made the latter the "natural inferiors" of men. Throughout the nineteenth century (and well into the twentieth), women were denied educational opportunities on "scientific" grounds. A popular theory proposed by Edward H. Clarke, M.D., was that women were incapable of supplying energy to their brains and uteruses at the same

time and that if women were allowed to pursue the same higher education as men, their uteruses would atrophy and they would become ill.[59]
Alleged biological differences were also used to justify the exclusion of
women from all forms of civil life. In *Bradwell v. Illinois*, the Supreme
Court upheld the exclusion of women from the practice of law because
"[t]he natural and proper timidity and delicacy which belongs to the female sex evidently unfits it for many of the occupations of civil life. . . .
The paramount destiny and mission of woman are to fulfil the noble and
benign offices of wife and mother. This is the law of the Creator."[60]

In both cases—race-based slavery and the treatment of women as sub-
ordinate to men—the principle of equal consideration required that we
recognize nothing morally significant per se about race that justified slavery or about sex that justified treating women as the property of their husbands and fathers. Although we have certainly not yet achieved a color-
blind or gender-blind society, most of us at least acknowledge that race
and gender ought not to be used to deny humans full participation in political and civil society. Similarly, there is nothing morally significant per
se about species membership that justifies speciesism, or the exclusion of
animals from the moral community and their treatment as our resources.
This is not to say that animals are the "same" as blacks or women; indeed,
as I have emphasized throughout, according animals the basic right not to
be treated as resources does not mean that we are obligated to give them
the same rights that we give humans. Equal consideration for blacks and
women required that we accord both groups the right to vote, a right that
would be meaningless to animals (as it is to some humans, such as the severely retarded or the insane). Equal consideration for animals requires
that we not treat animals as property and, as we will explore more in Chapter 7, this means that we should stop treating animals as our resources. To
reject speciesism is only to say that species is no more morally relevant in
determining who is a member of the moral community than is race or sex.
Admission to the moral community may not have the same meaning for
animals as it does for humans, except insofar as such membership rules out
the treatment of any member exclusively as the resource of others.

A Difference in Inherent Value?

There are those who agree that we ought to accord some inherent value
to animals but maintain that animals have a lesser degree of inherent
value and that this difference justifies our treating them as the resources

of humans.[61] But this is no different from stating that women have less inherent value than men, or that people of color have less inherent value than white people. Such a position simply assumes, rather than argues, that the principle of equal consideration cannot apply to animals (or to women or people of color). Although there are certainly differences among people and we value humans in different ways, we regard all humans as having an interest in not being valued exclusively as a resource, an interest protected by a right that cannot be violated simply because it would benefit someone else to do so. As we saw in Chapter 4, this notion of equal inherent value has both a logical and factual basis.

The logical basis is that equal inherent value is *required* for moral significance. Without the notion of equal inherent value, some humans would be excluded altogether from the moral community and their interests in not suffering ignored. Inherent value, like the concept of a basic right, places brakes on the balancing process and prohibits us from deciding whether purported benefits justify using certain disfavored humans as slaves or unconsenting biomedical subjects. Inherent value defines the minimal conditions for membership in the moral community. To say that a human has moral significance but has less inherent value than other humans is self-contradictory. The being who has less inherent value will *necessarily* be at risk of being treated as a thing. Similarly, if animals have less inherent value than humans, then their interests may be ignored when it is in our interests, and they risk being excluded entirely from the moral community and treated as things—exactly as they are treated now. Their interests, like the interests of slaves, cannot be morally significant because animal interests will almost always be regarded as dissimilar to and of lesser weight than the interests of humans, and the principle of equal consideration will be inapplicable.

The factual basis for equal inherent value is that all sentient humans value themselves even if no one else does. This does not mean that all sentient humans necessarily sit around thinking about their value; it means that sentient humans are not indifferent to what happens to them and have an interest in not suffering and in their continued existence. They care about those interests because they are the ones who experience suffering inflicted on them, regardless of whether others acknowledge it. On this level, severely retarded humans and human infants value their interests in not suffering even if no one else does. But this is also true of animals. This is the similarity between humans and animals that causes us to regard animal suffering as morally relevant in the first place.

If we accord equal inherent value to all humans, irrespective of their characteristics, and we deny that same value to animals, then our failure to apply the principle of equal consideration is arbitrary and unjustified.

In this chapter, we have seen that there are no morally sound reasons—no reasons that do not themselves violate the principle of equal consideration—that justify our not according animals the basic right not to be treated as resources. The acceptance of this basic right for animals has profound effects for the human/animal relationship in that we must be prepared to abolish the institution of animal property rather than merely regulate the system of slavery we impose on animals. But as I have argued, this outcome is really one whose seeds were sown by Jeremy Bentham and the humane treatment principle, which established that we have a direct obligation not to cause animals unnecessary suffering.

The question remains: why did we not see the implications of the idea that animals were not merely things? Why have we continued to believe that the regulation, and not the abolition, of animal exploitation will suffice to provide for the moral significance of animal interests? How could we ever have maintained that we take animal interests seriously at the same time that we eat them? Before we feel too perplexed about our moral schizophrenia about animals, we should consider that Bentham himself believed that we could provide for the moral significance of animal interests while we continued to eat them. In the next chapter, we will consider how, as a historical matter, Bentham and the humane treatment principle failed to eliminate the status of animals as things in order to give animals the status of persons, that is, of beings to whom the principle of equal consideration applies.

6

Having Our Cow and Eating Her Too: Bentham's Mistake

JEREMY BENTHAM, the principal architect of the humane treatment principle, rejected the view that we could exclude animals from the moral community because they lacked some particular characteristic, such as rationality, language ability, or self-consciousness. Bentham claimed that this view degraded animals "into the class of *things*"[1] that would be "abandoned without redress to the caprice of a tormentor."[2] He maintained that sentience was the only characteristic necessary for moral significance: "a full-grown horse or dog is beyond comparison a more rational, as well as a more conversable animal, than an infant of a day, or a week, or even a month, old. But suppose the case were otherwise, what would it avail? the question is not, Can they *reason?* nor, Can they *talk?* but, Can they *suffer?*"[3]

Bentham's theory, which established that we have a direct obligation not to cause animals unnecessary suffering, represented a most dramatic turn in our thinking about the moral status of animals. Before Bentham, there was no widely accepted view that animal interests were morally significant at all or that we had any moral obligations to them. Bentham's theory became so widely accepted and uncontroversial that it was incorporated into animal welfare laws that purported to take animal interests seriously and to prohibit the unnecessary suffering of animals.

As I argued in Chapter 3, these laws have failed to provide any meaningful protection to animals and will do so as long as we regard animals as our property.[4] The interests of property will never be deemed similar to the interests of the property owner, and the animal will always lose in any supposed balance of human and animal interests. Despite our acceptance of the humane treatment principle, we still treat animals as if they were things, Cartesian automatons without morally significant interests. In this chapter, I will explore why Bentham's theory failed to deliver on its promise and did not provide for the moral significance of animal interests.

Bentham on Slavery and the Property Status of Animals

Bentham subscribed to a moral theory known as *utilitarianism*, which holds that what is morally right or wrong in a particular situation is determined by the consequences of our actions, and that we should choose that action which brings about the best results for the largest number of those affected. There are two primary types of utilitarian theory. "Act-utilitarianism is the view that the rightness or wrongness of an action is to be judged by the consequences, good or bad, of the action itself. Rule-utilitarianism is the view that the rightness or wrongness of an action is to be judged by the goodness and badness of the consequences of a rule that everyone should perform the action in like circumstances."[5]

In order to understand the distinction between these two forms of utilitarian theory, consider the following example. Assume that Simon lends his car to Jane and then asks her to return it because, he tells her, he wants to take Sue out for a romantic evening. The problem is that Sue is married to Bill, a close friend of Jane's, and Simon's intended evening with Sue is to take place without the knowledge of Bill, who would be crushed to discover Sue's infidelity. Should Jane lie and tell Simon that she has lost the keys and cannot return the car that evening? If Jane is an act-utilitarian, she will weigh the consequences of lying in that particular case and not returning the car (Simon lives far from Sue and cannot have the rendezvous with Sue without his car) against the consequences of not lying and returning the car (Bill might find out and would be emotionally devastated). Jane may very well determine that, under the circumstances, lying to Simon about the car is the right thing to do. If Jane is a rule-utilitarian, she will weigh the consequences of a general rule about lying and ask what would happen if everyone lied under these circumstances. Jane may well conclude that even though returning the car to Simon will have negative consequences in the particular case, if all borrowers of property lied when asked to return the property, no one would lend property any longer. The difference between act-utilitarianism and rule-utilitarianism is the difference between whether the consequences of a particular act or the consequences of following a general rule determine the rightness or wrongness of actions.

Utilitarians as a general matter are not fond of rights because, as we have seen, a right places a sort of wall of protection around an interest, even if the consequences of abrogating that interest will benefit others. The utilitarian, and particularly the act-utilitarian, hold that *only* consequences matter, and that we ought to breach the wall of protection afforded by a right whenever the expected consequences demand it. The rule-utilitarian position is, however, at least a distant cousin of the rights view because rule-utilitarianism, like rights theory, requires that we follow a general rule even if the consequences of doing so in a particular case would be undesirable. In my example with Simon and the car, Jane may decide to respect Simon's "right" and return his property to him even though the consequences of doing so might be undesirable in that particular case; Jane respects the wall around Simon's property interest in his car. True, she does so only because the consequences of respecting Simon's interest will at least arguably bring about the best overall consequences (people will continue to lend their property to others), but she nevertheless does respect that wall of protection.[6]

Bentham is generally regarded as an act-utilitarian who believed that in any particular situation the morally correct action was that which maximized the greatest pleasure for the greatest number of those affected by the action.[7] Bentham rejected the concept of innate moral rights and claimed that any human interest could be ignored if the consequences of doing so outweighed the consequences of protecting the interest.[8] This would suggest that slavery might be morally permissible under certain circumstances depending on whether the detriment to the slave was outweighed by the pleasure of the slave owner. But Bentham rejected the institution of human slavery; he believed that the slave's interest in not being property outweighed the benefits of slavery for slave owners. With respect to the morality of slavery, Bentham was at the very least a rule-utilitarian (he thought the consequences of the institution of slavery undesirable), and he effectively recognized that humans had what was equivalent to a basic right not to be treated as property and that this precluded the use of humans as the slaves or resources of others.[9] He maintained that although some forms of slavery were more "humane" than others, slavery as a widespread institution had the inevitable effect of treating humans as economic commodities. Bentham recognized that if humans were to have morally significant interests and not be treated merely as things, if humans were not to be "abandoned without redress to the caprice of a tormentor," slavery had to be abolished.

Bentham explicitly compared the treatment of slaves and animals. In the same passage in which he argued that it is only the sentience of animals that matters for purposes of their moral significance, he stated: "The day has been, I grieve to say in many places it is not yet past, in which the greater part of the species, under the denomination of slaves, have been treated by the law exactly upon the same footing as, in England for example, the inferior races of animals are still." Using the language of *rights*, he expressed the hope that "[t]he day *may* come, when the rest of the animal creation may acquire those rights which never could have been withheld from them but by the hand of tyranny." Bentham believed that both slaves and animals were "degraded into the class of *things*," but he never even questioned the status of animals as the property or resources of humans.

The principle of equal consideration, the notion that each counts for one and none for more than one, was a cornerstone of Bentham's philosophy. Why, then, did Bentham not reject the treatment of animals as property as he had rejected the treatment of humans as property? Why did Bentham think that the humane treatment principle would or could impart moral significance to animals and their interests while animals remained the property of humans?

The answer is related to Bentham's view that animals, like humans, had interests in not suffering but, unlike humans, had no interest in their continued existence. In essence, Bentham argued that it was possible to have our cow and eat her too; it was morally permissible to retain our ownership and use of animals as our resources, and to kill them for our purposes, as long as we could do so in a way that respected the principle of equal consideration as applied to animal interests in not suffering

He maintained that our use of animals as property could be made consistent with the principle of equal consideration, and that we did not have to abolish the property status of animals.

According to Bentham, animals do not care whether we eat them because, although they could suffer, they were not self-aware:

> If the being eaten were all, there is very good reason why we should be suffered to eat such of them as we like to eat: we are the better for it, and they are never the worse. They have none of those long-protracted anticipations of future misery which we have. . . . If the being killed were all, there is very good reason why we should be suffered to kill such as molest us: we should be the worse for their living, and they are never the worse for being dead. But is there any reason why we should be suffered to torment them? Not any that I can see.[10]

Bentham explicitly rejected the view that because animals were not self-aware, we could treat them as things—as beings with no morally significant interests to whom we could have no direct moral obligations. But Bentham did agree that animals were not self-aware and he accepted in effect that there was a qualitative distinction between humans and animals that allowed us to treat them as things as far as their *lives* were concerned, but not to treat them as things as far as their *interests in not suffering* were concerned. If, as Bentham maintained, it were possible to apply the principle of equal consideration and accord moral significance to animal interests in not suffering while continuing to treat animals as human resources, then we would not be compelled to extend to animals the basic right not to be treated as a thing and to abolish our institutionalized exploitation of animals.

There are, however, at least two serious flaws in Bentham's approach. First, the factual assertion that animals are sentient but have no self-awareness or interest in continued existence is conceptually problematic. Second, once Bentham accepted that humans and animals were qualitatively dissimilar, allowing us to use animals as replaceable resources but not to use humans as such, he made it impossible for us to treat animal interests as morally significant. That is, we cannot apply the principle of equal consideration if humans have an interest in not suffering at all from their use as resources and animals have no such interest. The result is that although Bentham regarded his view of animals as more progressive than that of those who denied any moral significance to animal interests altogether, his theory, which was incorporated into animal welfare laws, landed us in exactly the same place as the views he purported to reject.

Peter Singer: Bentham's Modern Proponent

In order to see the problems inherent in Bentham's approach, we will consider his theory from the perspective of his modern proponent, philosopher Peter Singer. Singer, author of *Animal Liberation*,[11] bases his views directly on Bentham's theory and maintains that we need not extend to animals the basic right not to be property in order to accord moral significance to their interests.[12] Singer maintains that animals have morally significant interests in not suffering and that we deny moral significance to these interests when we treat animals as nothing more than economic commodities. What Singer proposes is that we continue to treat animals as our property but not treat them solely as economic commodities, as is the case under current animal welfare laws.

Singer argues that most humans, with the exception of the severely retarded, irreparably brain-damaged, and extremely senile,[13] are self-aware and have a "continuous mental existence."[14] "Normal" humans have "'a life' in the sense that requires an understanding of what it is to exist over a period of time."[15] They are the sorts of beings who have "the capacity to think ahead and have hopes and aspirations for the future."[16] What moral implications does this have for human beings?

Singer, like Bentham, is an act-utilitarian; that is, he believes it is the consequences of the contemplated act that matter, not the consequences of following a more generalized rule. Unlike Bentham and other classical utilitarians who maintained that pleasure is the primary value, Singer subscribes to "preference," or "interest," utilitarianism, which provides that what is intrinsically valuable is "what, on balance, furthers the interests of those affected."[17] Again, although Singer claims as a utilitarian to reject moral rights as a general matter, he, like Bentham, is at least a rule-utilitarian when it comes to using humans as resources and may be said to accept that normal humans have what is tantamount to a basic right not to be treated as things or valued in a completely instrumental manner. Although Singer claims not to recognize rights, he certainly accepts a very strong presumption that the principle of equal consideration means that we should not use normal humans as resources.[18] That is, even in the absence of a formal basic right not to be used as a resource, Singer recognizes that I have an interest in not being made a slave or killed to have my organs transplanted into others, and that my interests ought to be respected. It does not matter whether the form of slavery to which you want to subject me is "humane," or whether you anesthetize me before you remove my organs; although less pain and suffering are always better than more, I have an interest in my life, and that interest is protected by the principle of equal consideration. In all but the most extreme cases, this means that a normal, self-conscious human should not be used as a resource for others. Singer maintains that because humans are self-aware and have desires for the future, it is "particularly bad" to take the life of a normal human because we cannot make up for that loss simply by replacing one human with another. We do not judge the utilitarian worth of normal humans on a case-by-case basis; that is, we do not go around asking whether we ought to kill this particular normal human and transplant her organs into these five other humans or use this particular human as an unconsenting subject in a biomedical experiment. We presume against such use in all but the most extreme circumstances.

Singer maintains that animals—with the exception of chimpanzees, orangutans, and gorillas—are not self-aware and have neither a "continuous mental existence" nor desires for the future.[19] Animals have an interest in not suffering, but they have no interest in continuing to live or in not being regarded as the resources or property of humans. They do not care whether we raise and slaughter them for food or use them for experiments or exploit them as our resources in any other way, as long as they have a reasonably pleasant life. According to Singer, because animals do not possess any interest in their lives per se, "it is not easy to explain why the loss to the animal killed is not, from an impartial point of view, made good by the creation of a new animal who will lead an equally pleasant life."[20]

Singer strongly condemns the practices of intensive agriculture that we encountered in Chapter 1 because he believes that the amount of pain and suffering that animals experience under such conditions outweighs whatever benefits accrue to humans. He claims to reject the notion that animals have value only as economic commodities, but he does not conclude that eating animals per se is morally unacceptable; rather, he maintains that it may be morally justifiable to eat animals who "have a pleasant existence in a social group suited to their behavioral needs, and are then killed quickly and without pain." Singer states that he "can respect conscientious people who take care to eat only meat that comes from such animals."[21] Singer regards most animals as replaceable resources and regards most humans as irreplaceable resources.

Therefore, although Singer identifies a supposedly special human characteristic—self-awareness—he claims that his position is different from that of Kant and others who exclude animals from the moral community on the basis of such a characteristic. For Singer, the fact that most animals are supposedly not self-aware neither permits us to ignore animal interests whenever it suits us nor frees us from direct duties to animals. Singer maintains that because animals are not self-aware, we may use them as property and kill them because death causes them no harm, but we do have a direct duty to prevent them from suffering. And how do we protect their interest in not suffering? We apply the principle of equal consideration to that interest, which means that, barring sound justification, we should not inflict suffering on an animal if we would not inflict similar suffering on a similar human. In most cases, the only humans who will be similar to animals are those who are not self-aware, such as the severely retarded or impaired.

In assessing Singer's position, we should consider two aspects of his theory that directly parallel Bentham. First is Singer's view that animals have no interest in life (as distinct from an interest in not suffering) because they are not self-aware or self-conscious. Second is his position that we may meaningfully apply the principle of equal consideration to the interest of animals in not suffering without extending to them similar rights-type protection for their interest in not being regarded as the property of humans.

Self-Awareness and an Interest in Life

Singer's view of the relationship between sentience, self-consciousness, and an interest in life is problematic in a number of respects.

First, although he maintains that killing a sentient being does not inflict harm on that being, it would seem that the opposite is true: that death is the greatest harm for any sentient being and that merely being sentient logically implies an interest in continued existence and some awareness of that interest. To be a sentient being means to have an experiential welfare. In this sense, all sentient beings have an interest not only in the quality of their lives but also in the quantity of their lives. Animals may not have thoughts about the number of years they will live, but by virtue of having an interest in not suffering and in experiencing pleasure, they have an interest in remaining alive. They prefer or desire to remain alive. Sentience is not an end in itself—it is a means to the end of staying alive. Sentient beings use sensations of pain and suffering to escape situations that threaten their lives and sensations of pleasure to pursue situations that enhance their lives. Just as humans will often endure excruciating pain in order to remain alive, animals will often not only endure but inflict on themselves excruciating pain—as when gnawing off a paw caught in a trap—in order to live. Sentience is what evolution has produced in order to ensure the survival of certain complex organisms. To deny that a being who has evolved to develop a consciousness of pain and pleasure has an interest in remaining alive is to say that conscious beings have no interest in remaining conscious, a most peculiar position to take.

Singer acknowledges that an animal "may struggle against a threat to its life," but he does not regard this as compelling evidence that the animal has an interest in her life.[22] Common sense tells us, however, that if an animal struggles against a threat to her life, the animal does prefer or desire to remain alive. Is it necessary that the animal express that interest and preference, if only to herself, in words of English or another human language, "Oh, I am going to die. I really am upset that I am going to die. I am dying before my time"? No, of course not. Is the animal's behavior consistent with an interest in continuing to live? Yes, of course.

Second, it would seem that any being who is sentient, and therefore conscious, is also self-conscious in a morally relevant sense. All sentient beings can be said to have interests in their lives in that they are not indifferent to what happens to them. A dog may have an interest in life different from that of a normal human adult, but that does not mean that the dog is indifferent to what happens to her. Because the dog is sentient, she uses the survival mechanisms of pain and pleasure to protect her life. Following the same line of reasoning that Donald Griffin uses, in the argument that we encountered in Chapter 5, we may say that when the dog experiences pain, the dog necessarily has a mental experience that tells her that "this pain is happening to me." In order for pain to exist, some consciousness—someone—must perceive it as happening to her and must prefer not to experience it. That perceiver necessarily has some sense of self because consciousness of a painful sensation, for instance, cannot occur as some sort of ethereal experience; a painful sensation can occur only to a being who can have such an experience and who prefers not to do so. The notion that consciousness might exist without self-consciousness suggests that a being might perceive pain without perceiving that the pain was happening to that being, or that a being might perceive pain yet remain indifferent to the experience. These, however, are merely convoluted restatements of the notion that a being might perceive pain without perceiving pain, which is absurd on the face of it.

If, as Singer maintains, animals are not self-aware, then it is difficult to explain how an animal learns anything, unless we regard all animal behavior only as a matter of stimulus-response conditioning. After a dog places a paw on a hot plate and pulls away, she will avoid the plate when she sees it later. How can this be explained if the dog does not have some sense that it was her paw she had placed on the surface and that it was she who felt pain? If animals had no sense of self-awareness, we would be hard-pressed to explain much animal behavior. None of this implies, however, that a dog thinks of herself as beautiful or ungainly or wishes that she were more talented or more capable. The latter are merely particular ways in which humans may be self-conscious. To say that an animal is self-conscious does not mean that the animal necessarily has a visual image of herself. Thus, the fact that dogs may not recognize themselves in a mirror does not prove that dogs are not self-conscious or that they cannot recognize themselves. If I take my dog on a walk through a park, she will be able to identify a bush that she has visited days before. I may recognize myself by a reflection in a mirror; she recognizes herself by a scent. There may be differences in how we recognize ourselves, but this does not mean that self-recognition is something of which only humans are capable.

The claim that most animals are not self-aware because they do not have a representational or autobiographical sense of consciousness ignores the fact that self-consciousness in humans need not be representational or autobiographical. Antonio Damasio, whom we encountered in Chapter 5, distinguishes between core consciousness or an awareness of self in the present, and extended consciousness, or an awareness of self that is embellished with autobiographical details. Damasio describes humans who, through stroke or seizure, suffer damage to the brain that impairs extended consciousness and the ability to form new memories or envision the future, but who retain core consciousness and are quite aware of the self in the present. In any event, core consciousness is a form of self-consciousness. There is someone who has subjective experiences and who has desires and preferences. Damasio concedes that many species of animals have core consciousness, and that apes, monkeys, and even dogs may have some form of extended consciousness, which requires reasoning ability and memory but does not require language.

A dog may not be able to think to herself, "my human companion is coming home on Wednesday at 4:00 P.M.," but she can surely anticipate the return of her companion and anticipation requires a sense of the future. If a dog were unable to anticipate the future, she would not get happily excited when she hears her human companion on the other side of the door, inserting a key into the lock. It is because the dog anticipates a reunion with her companion that she exhibits happy excitement rather than aggression or defensiveness. The fact that humans anticipate the future by looking at calendars and clocks and that dogs anticipate the future by focusing on other aspects of their environment no doubt makes for an interesting subject of study, but it does not bear on the question whether either being should be treated exclusively as a means to the ends of others. Moreover, the ethological evidence suggests that other mammals, birds, and even fish possess memory and some reasoning ability, which would suggest that many species of animals have some form of extended consciousness and some autobiographical sense of self, in addition to core consciousness.[23]

Singer argues that because humans have a representational sort of self-awareness, they have "superior mental powers" and can have plans for the future, and that they therefore have more interests than do animals, who do not make plans for the future. Putting aside the fact that the ethological evidence clearly indicates that many animals do anticipate and plan for the future, Singer's view suggests that the lives of humans who make more future plans than other humans and who have more interests than other humans have greater moral "worth." Once again, the arbitrariness of such a moral hierarchy seems painfully obvious. Assume that Simon enjoys traveling and has very concrete travel plans to visit twenty places in the next five years. Jane has only one interest in life—taking care of her disabled child. Why should Simon's life count for more than Jane's simply because he has more future desires, or because he has more interests than Jane does?

More important, Singer assumes that because humans have a representational sense of self-awareness, they have more interests or preferences than animals and suffer greater harms than animals do. These assumptions are not necessarily sound. A very bright human being with only core consciousness may have more interests than a dull one with extended or representational consciousness. Similarly, even if animals have only core consciousness, they may have many interests that humans simply do not have. For example, I do not have the keen sense of smell and hearing that my dogs have. Their heightened senses mean that their experiences are different from mine, and their interests are different in light of those experiences. I have no desire to go sniffing trees in the neighborhood; I could learn nothing from that experience in light of my significantly weaker senses. Fish, to cite another example, have an interest in breathing under water that I not only do not share but that is dangerous to me. Moreover, because animals have interests different from those of humans, they are susceptible to harms to which humans are not. If the fire hydrant in my neighborhood is removed, this would harm my dog in a way that it would not harm me and that harm may be very significant as far as my dog is concerned. Singer assumes that human self-awareness is "superior" in some sense. But it is precisely this sort of normative characterization that begs the question from the outset. Human self-awareness may be different, but "different" does not necessarily translate into "better" in any moral sense.

Third, there is something very peculiar from a psychological point of view about regarding animals as replaceable resources. If the death of one animal is, as Singer maintains "from an impartial point of view, made good by the creation of a new animal who will lead an equally pleasant life," then why do we feel grief when one of our companion animals dies? The answer is that we do not view at least some animals (our dogs and cats) as replaceable resources, and our recognition that our companion animals have unique *personalities* is a factual observation and not anthropomorphism. I presently live with seven canine companions, all different from one another. When one of my companions dies and I adopt another, I certainly do not regard the newly adopted dog as "replacing" the dog who died any more than I would regard a human child as "replacing" a human child who had died.

But then the same observation could be made about cows, pigs, and chickens. A friend of mine lives with a number of rescued farm animals, including three chickens. An hour or two of observing and interacting with these animals made it clear to me that the three birds were quite different from one another and had distinct personalities. If we bothered to relate to chickens, cows, or pigs in the way that we do to our companion animals, we would no more see "food" animals as merely replaceable resources than we do our dogs or cats. The problem is that most of us relate to farm animals only as food, only when we sit down to consume their bodies, and in that way of relating there is not much difference between one chicken or cow or pig and another. To say, as Singer does, that animals are replaceable resources again begs the question about the moral status of animals and provides no answer at all.

Fourth, and perhaps most important, is that if self-awareness, as Singer understands it, is necessary in order for sentient beings to have an interest in life, then we must conclude—and Singer accepts—that a number of humans have no interest in life and may be treated as resources. For example, retarded humans who lack the representational sense of self that Singer requires can have no greater an interest in life than do cats or dogs and may even have less of an interest. Nevertheless, we do not believe that it is appropriate to treat such beings as resources or exclusively as means to the ends of others, although Singer suggests that it may be morally permissible to do so as long as we take seriously their interests in not suffering. In Singer's view, assuming we could accomplish the deed painlessly, it would be permissible to kill severely retarded humans in order to transplant their organs into other humans or animals (such as the great apes) who do have an interest in life. Moreover, Singer maintains that newborn infants, who will eventually become self-aware but who are disabled, should be regarded as replaceable: "[w]hen the death of a disabled infant will lead to the birth of another infant with better prospects of a happy life, the total amount of happiness will be greater if the disabled infant is killed."[24] Singer advocates that under certain circumstances, parents should have the right to kill newborns afflicted with Down's syndrome or hemophilia. Most of us do not, however, accept such views any more than we accept Aristotle's view that it was acceptable to enslave less rational humans or the Nazi view that the lives of the disabled were somehow worth less than the lives of others.

Singer never explains why a representational sense of self-consciousness has any more relevance than does a nonrepresentational sense for the purpose of treating most animals and some humans exclusively as the resources of others. The differences between normal human self-awareness (assuming that among humans this means the same thing), and animal self-awareness may be interesting from a scientific perspective, but they are of no moral relevance at all when the issue is whether to treat animals and certain impaired or disabled humans as resources for others.

The Equal Consideration of Animal Interests

Although Singer believes that animals lack self-awareness and have no interest in life, he does not think that this justifies the exclusion of animals from the moral community. That is, although, like Kant and others, he thinks that there is a difference between humans and animals involving self-awareness, Singer, unlike Kant and like Bentham, claims that the fact that animals are not self-aware does not allow us to treat their interests in not suffering as morally insignificant. Indeed, Singer explicitly criticizes Kant and others for failing to accord moral significance to animal interests in not suffering. He argues that we must apply the principle of equal consideration to those interests even though animals are not self-aware, and that we should not discount or ignore animal suffering simply because it is an animal who suffers, any more than we should discount or ignore the pain of a human because that human is a woman or person of color or a member of some other disfavored group. Although we may use and kill animals for our purposes, we should not impose suffering on an animal that we would not impose on a similar human—unless we have a good reason to do so, a reason that does not itself violate the principle of equal consideration.

Singer claims that his theory does not exclude animals from the moral community, but his notion that animals lack an interest in life and may be regarded as replaceable resources makes it difficult to apply the principle of equal consideration to animal interests in not suffering. There are in fact several problems with Singer's theory that prevent this application.

First, Singer requires that we make interspecies comparisons in order to apply the principle of equal consideration to human and animal interests in not suffering, and this requires some method—however imprecise—for measuring interspecies experiences. For example, Singer observes correctly that a slap that would cause virtually no pain to a horse may very well cause considerable pain to a human infant. "But there must be some kind of blow—I don't know exactly what it would be, but perhaps a blow with a heavy stick—that would cause the horse as much pain as we cause a baby by slapping it with our hand."[25] The difficulties with making such assessments are obvious: it is difficult enough to compare pain intensity when we are concerned only with humans who can give detailed verbal reports of the sensation they are experiencing. It becomes virtually impossible to make even imprecise assessments when animals are involved. Moreover, Singer acknowledges that because humans are self-aware and have "superior mental powers," this will, "in certain circumstances, lead them to suffer more than animals would in the same circumstances."[26] This makes interspecies comparisons of suffering even more difficult to perform

Second, because, according to Singer, most humans have an interest in their lives while most animals do not, it is difficult to understand how humans and animals can ever be regarded as similarly situated for purposes of applying the principle of equal consideration. Singer does not advocate that we should perform a case-by-case examination of humans in order to determine whether we ought to treat a particular human exclusively as a resource for others. Singer assumes that all normal (i.e., self-aware) humans have an interest in not being treated as resources and that this interest ought to be respected in all but the most extreme cases. According to Singer, many animals lack that same interest. Because animals are replaceable resources, they have an interest only in a reasonably pleasant life and a relatively painless death. We may, in Singer's view, ask on a case-by-case basis whether our use as a resource of this or that particular animal can be justified by a utilitarian consideration of consequences. In short, I have an interest in not suffering *at all* from resource use, but animals have an interest only in not suffering *too much*.[27] An animal and I can *never* be similarly situated with respect to our relative interests in not being used as resources.

Moreover, Singer maintains that we can always override the interest of the animal in not suffering, depending on the consequences for all affected. Once again, animal interests will almost always be trumped by human interests because the consequences for humans of not making animals suffer will almost always be judged more weighty than will the interests of animals.

Third, Singer recognizes on some level that we are unlikely to regard animal and human interests as similar in the first place and are therefore unlikely to find any guidance in the principle of equal consideration.[28] But that is tantamount to admitting that animal interests are not morally significant per se, because moral significance *requires* the applicability of the principle of equal consideration. Singer avoids this conclusion by claiming that even if the principle of equal consideration is inapplicable, it is still clear that much animal suffering is not morally justifiable. He states, for example, that we need not apply the principle of equal consideration in order to conclude that intensive agriculture is wrong.

It remains unclear how Singer can arrive at this conclusion other than through personal stipulation. That is, his objections to intensive agriculture are based on his empirical assessments of the consequences of particular acts in light of his theory that individual acts ought to further the interests or preferences of those affected. As with all such assessments, different people may evaluate the consequences of such acts differently. Singer thinks that the negative consequences of factory farming for animals outweigh its benefits, but when we consider all the negative consequences for humans, should factory farms be abolished, his empirical judgment is at least questionable. Consider the negative economic consequences that would befall those directly involved in the raising and killing of animals, such as farmers and butchers; those involved indirectly in the food business, such as food retailers; those involved in the dairy industry; those involved in restaurants, the pet food industry, the pharmaceutical industry, and the leather goods and wool industries; those involved in agricultural and veterinary research incidental to agriculture; those involved in publishing books about animal agriculture; and those involved in advertising the products of animal agriculture.[29] It is clear that the abolition of factory farming would have a profound impact on the international economy. This is not to say that these negative consequences would outweigh the interests of the animals involved. It is only to say that if the issue hinges on the aggregation of consequences, and if the consequences for self-aware humans weigh more than the consequences for non-self-aware animals, it is not clear whether it would be morally right under Singer's theory to abolish factory farming.

Fourth, to the extent that we regard human and animal interests as similar, that similarity is likely to be found most often between those humans who are not self-aware, such as the severely retarded, and animals, most of whom are also not self-aware, according to Singer. Again, this places particularly vulnerable humans at risk in a way that most of us regard as unacceptable because we regard all humans as having morally significant interests.

Fifth, even if Singer's theory would lead to the more "humane" treatment of animals, it would still permit us to use them in ways we do not think it appropriate to use any humans. I agree with Singer that it would be better for "food" animals if we adopted true "free-range" farming and discontinued factory farming.[30] This would reduce but by no means eliminate the pain, suffering, and distress of animals used for this purpose. Putting aside that any such change would be vociferously challenged by property owners, who would claim an invasion of their property rights, and by consumers, who would be required to pay a great deal more for meat, it is important to understand that such a change would *not* mean that animal interests are morally significant in the sense that the principle of equal consideration would apply to such interests.[31] Animals, like humans, have an interest in not suffering *at all* from use as resources, however "humane" that use may be. A more "humane" form of human slavery is less morally objectionable than a less "humane" form. But all forms of slavery are morally objectionable because all humans are accorded a right not to be treated as the property of others. To the extent that we do not protect the similar interests of animals in a similar way, we fail to accord the principle of equal consideration to animal interests, and we thereby deprive animal interests of moral significance.

The Failure of the Humane Treatment Principle: A Historical Note

We are now in a position to understand why the humane treatment principle has failed to protect animal interests. Until Bentham, Western moral and legal thought generally regarded animals merely as things without any protectable interests. Bentham maintained that since animals can suffer, and since we all regard suffering as undesirable, a civilized and just society recognizes that animals have morally significant interests in not suffering and that we have a direct moral obligation not to inflict suffering on them.

Although Bentham maintained that animals had morally significant interests, his understanding of "moral significance" differed between humans and animals. In the case of human slavery, Bentham maintained that a particular slave owner might treat a slave well and that the benefit to the slave owner might exceed the detriment to the particular slave, but that "slavery once established, was always likely to be the lot of large numbers. 'If the evil of slavery were not great its extent alone would make it considerable.'"[32] Bentham assumed that the institution of human property was morally unacceptable because although a particular owner of slaves might treat those slaves very well, slavery presented the serious risk that humans would be treated as nothing but economic commodities, and would be "abandoned without redress to the caprice of a tormentor." Bentham also believed that slave labor was ultimately less productive than the labor of free people: the latter will have more incentives to produce than the former.[33] But more important, Bentham accepted the principle of equal consideration and recognized that if each human were really to "count for one and none for more than one," then slavery presented a problem: the interests of a slave were unlikely ever to be perceived as counting as much as the interest of a slave owner. Slaves would always count for *less* than "one."

Bentham therefore assumed that our starting point was that the institution of human slavery could not be morally justified, and this had the effect of providing to all humans a rights-type protection against being treated exclusively as a means to the ends of others. Bentham most certainly believed that the principle of equal consideration applied to animals. Indeed, Bentham's humane treatment principle and his utilitarian theory required that we balance human and animal interests in order to assess the morality of our use and treatment of animals, but such a balance necessarily assumed that if human and animal interests had similar weight, they should be accorded similar treatment. Bentham, however, never questioned the institution of animal property. He maintained in effect that animals had no interest in not being used as resources by humans—they just had an interest in not suffering from that use. Bentham never recognized that although a particular owner of animal property might choose to treat her animal "resources" very well, the various institutions of animal exploitation would become the "lot of large numbers," and the overwhelming majority of animals would be treated as nothing but economic commodities. As a result, Bentham—and Singer—ask us to do something that is difficult if not impossible to do: balance the interests of humans, who are protected from use as resources, against the interests of animals, who are only resources.

We cannot simultaneously regard animals as resources and as beings with morally significant interests. In an effort to provide humane treatment for animals, we tried to prohibit the infliction of unnecessary suffering through animal welfare laws that assumed from the outset that animals were resources for human use. As we saw in Chapter 3, what became regarded as unnecessary was, as a general matter, only that suffering which was not required (in the judgment of the property owner) for whatever purpose or use was involved. But there was no real limit on animal use or treatment. Bentham's theory of equal consideration, as incorporated into animal welfare laws, did little to change the status of animals as things. Indeed, in *Callaghan v. Society for the Prevention of Cruelty to Animals*, discussed in Chapter 3, the court held that dehorning cattle did not violate the anticruelty law, which was based on Bentham's theory, because "Bentham denounces the brutal depravity that causes useless torments or gratuitous cruelties to animals subject to the use of man." The court held that ripping the horns from cattle was not "useless" or "gratuitous" because it was necessary to facilitate the use of these animals for food.[34]

The animal welfare laws that were intended to embody Bentham's theory failed to impose any meaningful limits on our use and treatment of animals because they embodied what we saw in Chapter 3 is a "hybrid" system. We are required to balance the interest of a right holder (a legal right to own and use property), against the interest of a being without any legal rights (animals are property and cannot hold rights), who, in addition to not being a right holder, is also the *object* of the exercise of the right holder's property right. It does not matter whether the property is a human slave or an animal: to the extent that the property is sentient and thereby possesses interests (whatever those interests are), those interests will necessarily and systematically be discounted relative to the interests of the property owner.[35]

If my analysis is correct, Bentham and Singer are guilty of the same faulty reasoning of which they accused other theorists who claimed that animals had no moral significance at all and that humans could have no direct moral obligations to animals. The Bentham/Singer position ends up being no different from the position of those, like Kant or Locke, who maintained that animals have no morally significant interests and that we have no direct obligations to them, but that we ought not to impose "gratuitous" harm on animals because such conduct will make us more likely to act in an unkind way toward other humans and thereby violate our moral obligations to those humans. Either way, animals are ultimately excluded from the moral community.

If Bentham and Singer really did apply the principle of equal consideration to animal interests, they would have to treat similar cases in a similar way and accord those interests a similar rights-type protection. Such a position would require that we abolish the institution of animal property. Otherwise, as in the case of human slavery, animals will *always* and *necessarily* count as less than "one," and the application of the principle of equal consideration to animals will be rendered impossible.[36]

A Remaining Nagging Question

The question remains: even if Bentham and Singer got it wrong, is there not some *other* position that would allow us to treat animal interests seriously but deny them a basic right not to be treated as resources, and thereby obviate our need to abolish animal exploitation? I have argued throughout that we could, of course, treat animals "better" but that, apart from the economic realities that militate against such improved treatment, to improve animal treatment would be no different from enacting a rule that it is better to beat slaves less often. We would still be treating animals as things because we would be denying the application of the principle of equal consideration to animal interests. In this final section, we will consider an approach similar to Singer's that purports to accord moral significance to animal interests but denies that there is a link between moral significance and the basic right not to be treated as a thing.

Some feminist writers known as "ecofeminists" argue that we should abandon the concept of rights because it is a patriarchal concept.[37] They claim that rights theory establishes hierarchies between those who have rights and those who do not, and thus reinforces sexism, racism, speciesism, and other forms of discrimination. They maintain that rather than appeal to rights, we should use a concept of "care" that emphasizes contextual relations and the particulars of a given situation to analyze moral problems.

Various political conceptions of rights have been used at different times to create the sort of oppressive hierarchies about which ecofeminists quite correctly complain. But there is nothing inherent in the concept of a right that is patriarchal or sexist. A right is simply a way of protecting an interest: a right provides more or less "absolute" protection for an interest and prevents that interest from being traded away in order to benefit others. In this book, I have discussed using rights as a way of protecting the interest that all sentient beings have in not being treated as things.

Although ecofeminists claim to reject rights concepts for humans and animals, they, like Singer and Bentham, do in fact retain the notion of a basic right for humans. Ecofeminists do not suggest, for example, that the moral unacceptability of rape depends on the incompatibility of the act with an ethic of "care." The act of assaulting a woman is ruled out from the outset as a violation of the woman's autonomy, irrespective of the relationship between the woman and the rapist. Ecofeminists reject the instrumental treatment of women, and of humans generally, and do not regard such treatment as acceptable if done with "care." In short, ecofeminists, following Bentham and Singer, retain what is tantamount to basic rights-type protection for humans—they rule out from the outset treating humans exclusively as a means to an end—but they do not think that we ought to extend this same basic right to animals. As I argued in Chapter 4, if all humans receive rights-type protection for their interest in not being treated exclusively as a means to the ends of others, then the principle of equal consideration requires that we extend the same protection to the interests of animals in not being treated as commodities. Such equal consideration is not a matter of patriarchy; it is a matter of fundamental fairness and the recognition that animals have morally significant interests. Indeed, other feminist theorists, most notably Drucilla Cornell, have recognized that rights are essential for moral significance.[38] The ecofeminist approach merely represents another version of a "hybrid" solution to the issue of animal interests, one that perpetuates the status of animals as property.[39]

In Chapter 3, we saw how animal welfare laws, which were intended in large part to reflect Bentham's view that animals had morally significant interests, failed to provide animals with moral status. In this chapter, we have traced the root of the problem to Bentham's utilitarian moral theory as reflected in the views of his modern proponent, Peter Singer. As long as Bentham and Singer effectively reject the property status of humans but not of animals, the application of the principle of equal consideration to animals is impossible.

In Chapter 7, we will consider some issues and implications of taking animal interests seriously.

7

Animal Rights: Your Child or the Dog?

WE HAVE SEEN that our conventional wisdom about animals is shaped by two intuitions. The first is that animals have morally significant interests in not suffering and that we have an obligation directly to them not to inflict unnecessary suffering on them. But because animals are property, the prohibition on the infliction of unnecessary suffering is wholly without meaning. We have seen that in order to take animal interests seriously and to give content to our prohibition against the infliction of unnecessary suffering, it is necessary to apply the principle of equal consideration to animal interests in not suffering. This is not to say that we must regard animals and humans as the "same," any more than we regard all humans as the same. Nor is it to say that we must accord animals all the same rights that we accord to humans. But if animals have morally significant interests in not suffering, then we must abolish, and not merely regulate, the institution of animal property, and we must stop using animals in ways in which we do not use any humans.[1]

The second intuition that shapes our moral thinking about animals is that in situations of true conflict or emergency we should choose the human over the animal. If a building is burning and we have time to run in and rescue one being, a dog or a human, we should choose the human. This choice does not depend on whether the human is our child or other relative: our intuition holds even if the human

151

in question is a complete stranger, although the force of this intuition may be weakened if the human is someone of a particularly odious moral character, such as Adolf Hitler, or if the dog is a member of our family and the human is a stranger. There are some who argue that if we extend to animals the basic right not to be treated as things, we will no longer be required to save the human over the animal in these situations of true conflict or emergency. Those who take this position maintain that in order to preserve our absolute preference for the human in the burning house, we must, despite our moral qualms about animal pain and suffering, conclude that animal interests have *no* moral significance, and we must deny animals a basic right not to be treated as things.[2]

In this chapter, we will examine the soundness of this argument. Can the animal rights position accommodate both of the intuitions that constitute our conventional wisdom concerning the moral status of animals?

I Would Save My Child Over Your Child

In the years that I have spent lecturing on animal rights, my audiences have asked me one question more than any other: given my argument that humans are not justified in treating animals as resources, would I be willing to have a dog used to save the life of my sick child? This question is, in one sense, very much beside the point. Whatever choice I would make in such a situation is irrelevant to the validity of the argument that according animals moral status means that we must apply the principle of equal consideration to them and extend to them the basic right not to be treated as things. If my argument is valid, then even if my choice of my child over the dog were inconsistent with my argument, that would say something about me and my moral inconsistency but nothing about the validity of my argument.

But put aside the dog for a moment. If we were faced with a situation in which we could save our child or the child of another, almost all of us would save our own child. Imagine that your child needs a kidney. There is one kidney available, but another child has a more acute need for the kidney. The other child will die in a matter of days if she does not receive the kidney; your child will be able to survive for several months, and another kidney may or may not become available. You are asked to choose which child will get the kidney. Is there any reader who would not choose to save her own child over the other, more needy child? Indeed, most of us would sacrifice just about any number of other humans in order to save our own child. So then, the fact that we would be willing to use a dog to save our child does not tell us much of interest.

False Conflicts: Keeping the Dog Out of the Burning House

The question of the moral status of animals is concerned with how we ought to treat animals, and such issues as the burning house arise if and only if there are conflicts between humans and animals. For the most part, our "conflicts" with animals are those that *we* create. We bring billions of sentient animals into the world for the sole purpose of killing them. We then seek to understand the nature of our moral obligations to these animals. But by bringing these animals into existence for uses that we would never consider appropriate for any humans—by having a "meat" industry or an "animal entertainment" industry or a "game animal" industry—we have already decided that nonhuman animals are outside the scope of our moral community altogether. We have already decided that nonhuman animals are the sorts of beings to whom we do not extend equal consideration and to whom we can have no direct moral obligations. We have already decided that animals have no inherent moral status whatsoever—whatever we say to the contrary.

Because animals are property, we treat every issue involving the use or treatment of them as an emergency situation analogous to the burning house, with the result that we choose the human interest over the animal even in situations where animal suffering can be justified only by human convenience, amusement, or pleasure. In the overwhelming number of instances in which we evaluate our moral obligations to animals, there is no true conflict or emergency. When we are contemplating whether to eat a hamburger or buy a fur coat, or whether a rodeo or bullfight is a morally acceptable form of entertainment, we are not confronted with a burning house and the choice of whom to save.

If we recognize that animals have a basic right not to be treated as our resources, and we abolish those institutions of animal exploitation that assume that animals are nothing but our resources just as we abolished human slavery, we will stop producing animals for human purposes and thereby eliminate the overwhelming number of these false conflicts in which we must "balance" human and animal interests. *We will no longer drag animals into the burning house, and then ask whether we should save the human or the animal.*

What about those animals now living who have been brought into existence for our use? If we were to observe the principle of equal consideration, we would be under an obligation to care for those animals until they died a natural death. But whatever we did with those domestic animals (and wild animals bred for zoos or circuses) now in existence, we would certainly be under an obligation to bring no more animals into existence for our use. A related concern is whether, if we accord to animals a basic right not to be treated as things, would we have to acknowledge the right of animals to sue in courts of law. This question misses the point of according animals a basic right not to be a thing, which is to eliminate human/animal conflicts as much as possible, and not to continue those conflicts through formalizing them within the legal system. Consider the problem in a different context. Assume that in our brave new world of genetic engineering, we start to produce in the laboratory severely retarded human beings whom we raise on "farms" until adulthood for use as a source of organ transplants for "normal" humans. Suppose that it eventually dawns on us that even if we treat such beings in a "humane" fashion, we are still treating them as our resources and that this use is immoral. We would presumably decide to discontinue the practice, care for those beings whom we had created for this purpose, and produce no more. We would eliminate the supposed conflict that existed between our interests and the interests of the organ donors, which presented a moral dilemma in the first place only because *we* created the conflict by treating these human organ donors as our resources. We dragged them, as we do animals, into the burning house, and we then asked whose interests we should prefer in a "conflict" that *we* fabricated. Would we give those engineered organ donors legal rights to sue while those currently in existence were still alive? We might very well do so, but only as a "stopgap" measure along the way to the abolition of this unethical practice. The point of recognizing that it is wrong to create these conflicts is to stop creating the conflicts, not to perpetuate them through making them legal conflicts instead of moral ones.[3]

Remaining Conflicts[4]

If we stop creating the conflicts that result from institutionalized animal exploitation and stop producing animal resources for human use, the primary potential conflicts that remain will be between humans and non-domesticated animals. But if we take animal interests seriously, most of these potential conflicts will not present us with burning-house scenarios that require that we choose between human life and animal life. Let us assume, for example, that particular animals—deer, for instance—begin to overproliferate in an area. This is a somewhat unrealistic assumption, since most deer overpopulation is caused by us, either directly by our "management" of deer populations or indirectly through the continued proliferation of suburbs. Can we maintain that we take animal interests seriously and that we accord moral status to animals while at the same time we propose to kill the deer as a solution to the problem?

The answer is clearly no. We do not regard a lethal solution to be a morally appropriate answer to the problem of human overpopulation, and unless there is some morally relevant difference between humans and animals, we cannot support a lethal solution to the deer overpopulation. To solve the deer problem using a method that we would never use to solve a similar human problem violates the principle of equal consideration. Through our acceptance of the humane treatment principle, we claim to believe that animals have morally significant interests, yet many of us also think it is acceptable to kill deer because they nibble on our ornamental shrubs. How can we claim to reject the notion that animals are things and yet maintain that the shrubs, which are not sentient and have no interests, have a value that trumps the basic right of the deer not to be treated as things? The only reason we think there is a conflict between the deer and our property rights is that we have already violated the principle of equal consideration in the way that we conceive of the participants. We do not think it appropriate to kill humans who damage our shrubs; that we do think it appropriate to kill deer in these circumstances indicates that we have already constructed the issue in a way that ensures that the deer lose out in any supposed balance of interests.

What if the deer have become so plentiful that they are running out in front of cars and threatening human life? Again, this is a rather unrealistic assumption since deer do not generally jump in front of cars for no reason; indeed, the primary reason that deer wander into roads is that they are being pursued by hunters or are otherwise frightened by human activity. In any event, if we take animal interests seriously, there are a variety of actions we could take short of killing the deer. In addition to contraception, fences and other barriers and devices, including sound devices, have been shown to be effective in keeping deer out of roads. In an extreme situation, it might be necessary to relocate the deer to another habitat.

Is Vivisection a "Burning House" Issue?

What about the use of animals in biomedical experiments that are intended to cure human diseases? If we really "need" to use animals in order to help humans, does that need constitute a true conflict or emergency similar to the situation of the burning house? In the first place, as we saw in Chapter 2, there is a serious question as to whether there is a causal relationship between animal use and benefits for humans, or whether animal use is the most efficacious way in which to address human health problems. We also saw that a great deal of animal use by vivisectors cannot make even a plausible claim to being relevant to improving the health of anything other than the bottom lines of corporations and grant-hungry universities.

But even if there are some uses of animals that provide benefit for humans, the supposed conflict between humans and animals in this context is no more real than a conflict between humans suffering from a disease and other humans we might use in experiments in order to find a cure for that disease. Data gained from experiments with animals require extrapolation to humans in order to be useful at all, and extrapolation is a most inexact science under the best of circumstances. If we want data that will be useful in finding cures for human diseases, we would be better advised to use humans. We do not, however, use unconsenting humans in experiments and we do not consider that there is any sort of conflict between those who are afflicted (or who may become afflicted) with a disease and those unconsenting humans whose use might help find a cure for that disease. Any of us could be afflicted with cancer and we would get better data relevant to cancer, and we would get it faster, if we could use unconsenting humans in cancer experiments. But we do not do so, and we do not regard this as a conflict situation. We want all humans to be part of the moral community, and although we may not treat all humans in the same way, we recognize that membership in the moral community requires at a bare minimum that we not treat any humans as "laboratory tools." Animals have no "defect" that justifies our use of them in experiments that is not shared by some group of humans, whom we would never use in experiments. Because we declare some animals "laboratory tools" yet regard it as inappropriate to treat any humans in this way, we once again create the conflict by ignoring the principle of equal consideration and treating similar cases in a different way.

In short, if we recognize that animals have a basic right not to be things, then we must stop thinking about them as our property, our resources. We must stop manufacturing conflicts in which *we* place animals in our hypothetical burning house *because* we regard them as our property, and then pretend to ask seriously whose interests we should prefer. Such an exercise is empty; it may make us feel as though we are behaving morally because we are going through the exercise of "balancing" interests, but the result was preordained.

What about True Emergencies or Conflicts?

What if we really *do* find ourselves in the unlikely situation of passing by a burning house containing a dog and a child, with time to save only one? What if we *do* find ourselves in the unlikely situation of being confronted by an angry mountain lion that is about to kill us, or a rat infected with plague that is about to bite us? What if we really *do* find ourselves in the unlikely situation of being stranded somewhere, threatened with starvation, and not a vegetable in sight? To the extent that we would favor the human over the animal in these situations, would our decision be inconsistent with our recognition that animals have moral value and that we ought not to use animals as resources?

No, of course not. We have to make difficult choices all the time, and there is nothing inconsistent in maintaining that all sentient beings have a right not to be treated as things and yet preferring certain beings over others in situations of true emergency. Consider the following example. A physician in an emergency room is confronted with a choice between two patients who have just been brought in—both victims of car accidents—and who both need a transfusion of blood. The hospital has only enough blood for one patient. If the doctor gives half of the blood to one and half to the other, both will die. The doctor must decide who lives and who dies. One patient, Simon, has a terminal illness unrelated to the accident. If Simon is given the transfusion, he will recover and live for a week before dying of his preexisting illness. The other patient, Jane, is a normal twenty-three-year-old adult who, apart from injuries sustained in the accident, is in excellent health. Assume that the doctor decides to give Jane the transfusion based simply on her better prospects for a longer life following the procedure. Assume further that every time the doctor finds herself in an emergency situation in which she must decide between allocating resources to a terminally ill patient and a healthy patient, she decides in favor of the healthy patient.

Does this mean that the doctor can now start performing painful experiments on Simon or other terminally ill humans without their consent? Does the doctor's decision to favor Jane mean that the doctor can now kill Simon or other terminally ill humans and remove their organs for transplant into other patients, thus saving multiple lives? No, of course not. True, humans will reap great benefits if Simon or other humans are used for these purposes. But that does not matter; we would reject such actions as morally repugnant. The fact that the doctor prefers the healthy young human over the terminally ill human in a situation of true conflict not of her own making does not justify her violating the basic right of Simon not to be treated exclusively as a resource for others. Similarly, even though I might always choose to save the human from the burning house rather than the dog, that does not mean that in other situations I may treat dogs (or any other sentient beings) exclusively as means to my ends.

What about the situation of self-defense? I was once asked whether I would kill a rat carrying plague that was about to bite me. I responded to the questioner that I would kill *him* or anyone else who was carrying a fatal illness and was about to bite me. We are, under the law and most moral theories, permitted to defend ourselves from imminent harm presented by other humans. If I reasonably believe that you are about to use deadly force against me without any justification—I am minding my own business, and you approach me pointing a gun and threaten to shoot me—I am justified as a matter of both law and morality in using deadly force if it is necessary to repel your attack. The fact that I am able to use deadly force in such circumstances does not mean that I may enslave you, use you as an unconsenting subject in a biomedical experiment, or remove your kidney to transplant into my sick child.

What about the situation in which we have no choice but to eat an animal or starve? Assume that Simon is stranded on a remote, snow-covered mountain after a plane crash. He is starving and there is neither a reasonable hope of rescue nor any vegetables available. When a rabbit happens by, Simon is confronted with the choice of killing the rabbit or starving. Just as we would be inclined to excuse Simon if, under these extreme circumstances, he killed and ate a human—which has in fact happened more than once—his killing the rabbit would also be excusable and completely consistent with the animal rights position.[5] If, however, Simon were eventually rescued, he would have no moral justification for continuing to eat rabbits any more than he would have a justification for continuing to eat humans.

Such emergency situations require what are in the end decisions that are arbitrary and not particularly amenable to satisfying general principles of conduct. If we prefer the human over the animal in all such situations, are we not guilty of being speciesist in that our choice represents a morally unjustifiable prejudice against animals? No, no more than the physician who would always choose to give the one available pint of blood to the healthy human over the terminally ill one is guilty of prejudice against the terminally ill. In such cases, no decision will be completely satisfactory in a moral sense and we simply must do the best we can.

Similarly, in the case of animals, we may well decide that although animals are similar to us in that they are sentient—the only characteristic that is relevant for the purpose of having a right not to be treated as a resource—there may be other characteristics of humans that cause us to tip the balance in their favor in these extreme and unusual cases. For example, I have absolutely no doubt that dogs are self-aware, intelligent beings who have a sense of the future and an interest in continuing life. Although I am certain that death is a harm for the dog, I do not know exactly what goes on in the mind of the dog and, therefore, I cannot fully appreciate what is at stake for a dog were she to die. I also lack direct access to the minds of other humans, but I am more confident that I understand better the harm of death to humans and what is at stake for them. I may, then, in these true emergency situations, in which I am forced to choose between a human and a dog, choose the human simply because I better understand what is at stake for the human than I do for the dog. But this is a matter of my own cognitive limitation and how that plays out in these extreme circumstances in which my decision will necessarily be arbitrary to some degree and in which no decision will be perfectly satisfactory. I do not think that death is a greater harm to the human than it is to the dog, but I understand (or think I do) the harm to the human in a clearer sense than I understand the harm to the dog; it is on this admittedly arbitrary and unsatisfactory basis that I break the tie between two beings, both of whom hold a basic right not to be treated as resources. But my decision to favor the human does not mean that I am morally justified in using dogs in experiments or otherwise treating dogs exclusively as means to my ends.

There may be other non-speciesist reasons why we might prefer the human over the animal in situations of true emergency consistent with our accepting that animals have the basic right not to be treated as our resources. Assume that I am passing by our perpetually burning house and there are two human occupants—Simon, a friend of mine, and Jane, a stranger. I may decide to save Simon not because I regard Jane as being worth less than Simon, but because I know Simon and his family and I know that they will suffer great grief that I would like to prevent. Jane may have family as well, but her family's grief will simply not matter to me as much because I do not know her or her family. Again, my choice is somewhat arbitrary, and not morally satisfactory: I would prefer to save both Simon and Jane. Now assume that my choice is between Jane, a stranger, and a dog. I may assume that Jane has some family and that Jane's loss will cause them grief—a grief that I certainly would understand were Jane my mother, sister, wife, or child. I may not know what relationships the dog has with other animals or with humans, or I may be unable to judge whether those affected will be more devastated than will Jane's human family. Indeed, I may legitimately assume that it is likely that human relationships will be more adversely affected by the loss of a human family member than by the loss of the dog (although this may not be true in all cases). Again, I am in a difficult, no-win situation in which I am unable to make satisfactory comparisons. If, in trying to do the best that I can, I decide to favor Jane over the dog, this decision would no more entitle me to use dogs in experiments than would my choice of Simon over Jane entitle me to use Jane in such experiments.

Religion and Animal Rights

We saw in Chapter 5 that although one of the purported justifications for treating animals as our property is linked to Judeo-Christian religious beliefs, there is no necessary inconsistency between a religious belief that God created humans in God's image and that animals are spiritual "inferiors," and according animals a basic right not to be treated as our resources. Although the creation story of the Old Testament clearly gives humans a special place in creation, passages in Genesis make it at least arguable that humans were initially stewards of nonhuman animals and did not use them for food or otherwise kill them until after Adam and Eve breached their covenant with God and fell from grace.

There is no reason why religious people who believe, for example, that only humans have souls, could not maintain both that in any situation in which there was a true emergency or conflict between a human and an animal we ought to prefer the human because only the human is ensouled *and* that animals have moral value and that we should not treat them as our resources or violate the principle of equal consideration in creating those conflicts in the first place.[6] This position is not entirely satisfactory, because the possession of a soul is a matter that depends only on species membership and reflects the prejudice of speciesism. My point is simply that those who subscribe to religious beliefs that see humans as spiritually superior to animals are not necessarily committed to the view that it is morally acceptable to use animals as resources. Those with religious beliefs may use some spiritual value, such as a soul, in the same way that the emergency physician decides to give the pint of blood to the healthy human rather than to the terminally ill one, but does not conclude that it is acceptable to use terminally ill humans as unconsenting experimental subjects or forced organ donors.

Preferring Animals over Humans?

Although we may be justified in or excused for preferring the human over the nonhuman in a situation of true emergency or conflict, this does not mean that we should not choose the animal in some circumstances. Indeed, even though our preference for the human over the animal is a compelling one, most of us already recognize that there can be situations in which the intuitive preference does not hold. If the choice is between saving an odious human or a dog, most of us would probably choose the dog. If the choice is between an animal we know and love and a human who is a stranger, the intuition to favor the human may also be weaker. There may be other circumstances as well in which our intuition to favor humans is less compelling. Assume that I am passing by the burning house and there are two occupants inside—a terminally ill human who would otherwise die of the disease in less than a week and a healthy chimpanzee. Again, this is a situation in which any choice I make will be somewhat arbitrary and no choice will be completely satisfactory from a moral point of view. I may choose to save the human, but I may also choose to save the chimpanzee. Although I may not understand fully what is at stake for the chimpanzee as a result of my own cognitive limitations, the chimpanzee shares 98.5 percent of our genetic material, and I can sensibly decide that what is at stake for the chimpanzee is very similar to what is at stake for the human. Other things being equal, I may decide to favor the chimpanzee, whose life will be longer. But then, I think that the same argument could be made if the animal in question were a healthy young dog. Even though I may not understand fully what is at stake for the dog, I understand that death is a harm to both the dog and the human and in this highly unusual and extreme situation, I may base my decision on the fact that the dog has a longer time to live.

We must keep in mind that if we took animal interests seriously, we would not be domesticating animals as "pets" and we would not have the dog in the burning house in the first place. Part of our difficulty in seeing the moral legitimacy of the decision to save the dog over the terminally ill human is based on the fact that however much we may love dogs or cats, they are still our property and we cannot help but conceptualize them as such in any hypothetical situation. As we have seen, there are parallels between the status of humans as property and the status of animals as property. Through the institution of human slavery, we created conflicts between slaves and slave owners and required a "balancing" of interests that the slaves were bound to lose. If we had a time machine and could travel back to 1850 to ask a slave owner whether he would choose to save another white person or a person of color from the burning house, we know what the answer would be. As far as the slave owner was concerned, persons of color were things that were owned. The question of whom to save simply could not make sense as long as one of the choices had the status of property and the other did not. Similarly, when we are asked whether we would choose a dog over a human, we must conceptualize that question as asking whether we would choose a piece of property over a person.

Animal Rights and Our Conventional Wisdom: A Good Fit

We saw in the Introduction that we cannot "prove" moral matters in the same way that we can "prove" that two plus two equals four. But we can see whether a moral theory explains and unifies our common sense and conventional wisdom on a particular topic. The animal rights theory for which I have argued represents a position that allows us to retain both of the intuitions that constitute our conventional wisdom about animals: that animals have morally significant interests and we have direct moral obligations to them, and that in situations of true conflict or emergency—where the conflict is not itself created through a violation of the principle of equal consideration at the outset—we may choose to prefer humans. That is, the animal rights theory allows us to achieve a reflective equilibrium or a "fit" between these intuitions.

The theory of animal rights does require that we give up the idea that it is morally acceptable to treat other sentient beings as means to our ends. Although we may be able to justify or excuse our favoring humans in situations of true conflict, we cannot manufacture those conflicts and then pretend to take animal interests seriously. If we can use animals for all sorts of unnecessary purposes for which we would never use any human beings, then a prohibition on imposing unnecessary suffering on those beings will be meaningless. If the life of a sentient being has value only as a means to human ends, then the interests of that being will, as a practical matter, have only instrumental value as well.

The alternative to the rights view is to lapse back into the pre-nineteenth-century view that animals have no morally significant interests and that humans have no direct obligations to them. We could, of course, maintain that we ought to be "kind" to animals, or treat them better than we currently do, because that will make us kinder people or more caring people, but not because we have any direct obligations to animals. There is, however, little realistic hope that such moral concerns alone will result in any significant improvement in animal care and treatment as long as animals remain economic commodities. Indeed, it is far more likely that concerns about human health and the environment will lead to changes in animal use and treatment.[7] In any event, were we to take the pre-nineteenth-century view, we would be able to argue that Simon should not torture animals if it will make him act less kindly to other humans, but we would have nothing more to say to him with regard to his treatment of animals. Our standard for animal treatment would be based solely on the consequences for humans. In addition to clashing with our view that animals do have morally significant interests, such a position only endorses the status quo or traditional views about animal use and treatment. If most people in a society eat meat, they are unlikely to believe that eating meat makes people more likely to be unkind to each other. Since most of us are naturally inclined to think of ourselves as morally decent, we are not likely to be very critical of our meat eating, or of any other widely accepted animal use.

For the most part, the only animal uses that we are likely to view as increasing the chances that the practitioners will behave to the detriment of others are those that are not traditional or those practiced by disfavored or small groups of humans. For example, in the United States, animal fighting, which is generally associated with the "lower" classes, is specifically prohibited by law in most states and is generally regarded as barbaric. But cockfighting is surely no different from many other recreational uses of animals that are considered perfectly appropriate, such as that popular American pastime, the rodeo. In both of these events, animals are subjected to treatment that would be characterized as "torture" if humans were involved, but the rodeo is a more "traditional" form of entertainment. And there is something almost surrealistically bizarre about banning cockfighting in a nation that slaughters almost 8 billion chickens annually for no reason other than that we like the taste of their flesh. There has been aggressive prosecution and social criticism of the ceremonial sacrifice of animals by those (mostly immigrants from Caribbean nations) who practice a religion known as Santeria. Although these animal sacrifices are quite brutal and often involve the exsanguination of animals such as goats, sheep, and pigs through severing of carotid arteries, or ripping off the heads of birds, these actions are no different from what goes on in American slaughterhouses every day. Nevertheless, most of us see no inconsistency in calling animal sacrifice barbaric as we sit and enjoy our lamb chops and hamburgers.[8]

Similarly, working-class amusements, such as the baiting of bears and bulls, cockfighting, and dogfighting, were all outlawed in Britain in the nineteenth century, but hunting, hare coursing, and other completely recreational animal uses are still permitted. The difference between hunting and fighting animals is not a difference in animal mistreatment. Rather, the difference is between amusements historically associated with the lower socioeconomic classes (bear baiting and animal fighting) and those associated with middle and upper classes (hunting and hare coursing).[9]

In any event, almost every society prohibits some animal uses, but such prohibitions should not be understood as recognizing that animals have morally significant interests. Rather, these prohibitions concern animal uses that are simply not part of the traditions of a particular culture, or not part of the traditions of the dominant group in a society, and therefore are not part of the institutionalized exploitation of animals in that culture. For example, Americans are often critical of bullfights, which are generally illegal in the United States, but not of rodeos or bow hunting, which are legal. Similarly, many in the United States and Great Britain are critical of Korea, China, and other countries in which it is the practice to eat cats and dogs. But eating a dog or cat is no different from eating a pig or cow except that in certain Western nations dogs and cats are the more favored form of animal property.

Finally, the view that we ought to treat animals humanely because it will make us more likely to treat one another humanely leads to the rather bizarre conclusion that because animal use may contribute to the welfare of humankind, it is not only permitted but morally *required*. It is such reasoning that leads some who support sport hunting to claim that by taking out their aggression by shooting animals, they are less likely to be aggressive toward other human beings. According to such looking-glass logic, the more animals hunters shoot, the more docile the hunters become. The hunter, who has a moral obligation only to other humans, is then morally *obligated* to be a hunter. We even regard killing animals as a way of building character. For example, in *State v. Bogardus*, a Missouri case, the court found that shooting captive pigeons purely for amusement could be justified because it was a "manly" sport and because "services which the citizen is called upon to render to the State, in exigencies, may largely depend on the qualities acquired in manly sports, and from some of the most attractive of these a certain amount of injury to dumb animals seems inseparable."[10]

If animals have no moral value and if violence toward them leads humans to be less violent to one another, or makes us better citizens, then we should all consider ourselves morally obligated to be violent in our treatment of animals. Such a position represents moral madness.

We already purport to accept, through our endorsement of the humane treatment principle, that animals are persons and not merely things. That is, we reject the views of those who denied that we cannot have any direct moral obligations to animals, and we maintain that animals have morally significant interests. If we *really* believe that, however, then we are obligated to apply the principle of equal consideration to animals and to reject their status as property. We must abolish and not merely regulate our institutionalized exploitation of animals, and no longer use or produce animals for food, entertainment, sport, clothing, experiments, or product testing. The vast majority of human/animal conflicts will evaporate because they were false conflicts that we fabricated from the outset by treating animals as economic commodities.

We may still have conflicts with, for instance, wildlife who nibble our ornamental shrubs. In such situations, we should try our best to apply the principle of equal consideration and to treat similar interests in a similar way. That will generally require at the very least a good-faith effort to avoid the intentional killing of animals to resolve these conflicts, where lethal means would be prohibited if the conflicts involved only humans. I am, however, not suggesting that the recognition that animal interests have moral significance requires that a motorist who unintentionally strikes an animal with a car be prosecuted for an animal equivalent of manslaughter; nor am I suggesting that we have a moral obligation to police disputes between mongooses and cobras.

Of course, our acceptance of the moral significance of animal interests would imply a profound change in the human condition. It is likely that we could accept that animals have moral value and abolish institutionalized exploitation only in a context in which we generally rejected the moral legitimacy of much of the violence that is routinely inflicted on humans by other humans. Similarly, it is likely that we could reject speciesism only in a context in which we generally rejected the moral legitimacy of the racist, sexist, and homophobic attitudes and behavior that still affect our culture and deny other humans full membership in the moral community.

Our abolition of animal exploitation might be the most effective thing to do to save the planet from the unquestioned environmental devastation caused by animal agriculture, as well as to improve our own health. And even if we care nothing for animals and accord moral value only to humans, we should abolish animal agriculture because it condemns a good many of our fellow humans to starvation.

We would surely pay a price for such a different world. We would have to forgo the unnecessary pleasure of eating animals and having their fat clog our arteries, the fun of watching them being tormented in rodeos or circuses, the excitement of walking in the woods and blowing them apart or wounding them with arrows, and the very questionable science involved in making them addicted to drugs that they would never use except in laboratories. We would finally have to confront our moral schizophrenia about animals, which leads us to love some animals, treat them as members of our family, and never once doubt their sentience, emotional capacity, self-awareness, or personhood, while at the same time we stick dinner forks into other animals who are indistinguishable in any relevant sense from our animal companions.

In many ways, our prevailing ways of thinking about animals should make us skeptical of our claim that it is our rationality that distinguishes *us* from *them*.

Appendix: Twenty Questions (and Answers)

IN THIS APPENDIX, I want to consider a number of questions about animal rights that I have confronted over the years. These are questions that have come up repeatedly, and they seem to appear whether the forum is in the United States or abroad, in Western nations or in non-Western nations, or whether the audience is composed of faculty and students from law schools, medical schools, veterinary schools, high schools, members of the general public who call in to a radio talk show, journalists, or neighbors at a holiday party. An examination of these questions will also help to demonstrate how the theory of animal rights that I have presented in this book is applied in concrete contexts.

1. Question: Domestic animals, such as cows and pigs, and laboratory rats would not exist were it not for our bringing them into existence in the first place for our purposes. So is it not the case that we are free to treat them as our resources?

Answer: No. The fact that we are in some sense responsible for the existence of a being does not give us the right to treat that being as our resource. Were that so, then we could treat our children as resources. After all, they would not exist were it not for our actions—from decisions to conceive to decisions not to abort. And although we are granted a certain amount of discretion as to how we treat our children, there are limits: we cannot treat them as we do animals. We cannot enslave them, sell them into prostitution, or sell their organs. We cannot kill them. Indeed, it is a cultural norm that bringing a child into existence creates moral obligations on the part of the parents to care for the child and not exploit her.

It should be noted that one of the purported justifications for human slavery in the United States was that many of those who were enslaved would not have existed in the first place had it not been for the institution of slavery. The original slaves who were brought to the United States were forced to procreate and their children were considered property. Although such an argument appears ludicrous to us now, it demonstrates that we cannot assume the legitimacy of the institution of property—of humans or animals—and then ask whether it is acceptable to treat property as property. The answer will be predetermined. Rather, we must first ask whether the institution of animal (or human) property can be morally justified.

2. Question: Rights were devised by humans. How can they even be applicable to animals?

Answer: Just as the moral status of a human or animal is not determined by who caused the human or the animal to come into existence, the application of a moral concept is not determined by who devised it. If moral benefits went only to the devisers of moral concepts, then most of humankind would still be outside the moral community. Rights concepts as we currently understand them were actually devised as a way of protecting the interests of wealthy white male landowners; indeed, most moral concepts were historically devised by privileged males to benefit other privileged males. As time went on, we recognized that the principle of equal consideration required that we treat similar cases in a similar way and we subsequently extended rights (and other moral benefits) to other humans. In particular, the principle of equal consideration required that we regard as morally odious the ownership of some humans by other humans. If we are going to apply the principle of equal consideration to animals, then we must extend to animals the right not be treated as a resource.

It is irrelevant whether animals devised rights or can even understand the concept of rights. We do not require that humans be potential devisers of rights or understand the concept of rights in order to be beneficiaries of rights. For example, a severely retarded human being might not have the ability to understand what a right is, but that does not mean that we should not accord her the protection of at least the basic right not be treated as a resource of others.

3. Question: Does the institution of pet ownership violate animals' basic right not to be regarded as things?

Answer: Yes. Pets are our property. Dogs, cats, hamsters, rabbits, and other animals are mass produced like bolts in a factory or, in the case of birds and exotic animals, are captured in the wild and transported long distances, during which journey many of them die. Pets are marketed in exactly the same way as other commodities. Although some of us may treat our companion animals well, more of us treat them poorly. In America, most dogs spend less than two years in a home before they are dumped at a pound or otherwise transferred to a new owner; more than 70 percent of people who adopt animals give them away, take them to shelters, or abandon them. We are all aware of horror stories about neighborhood dogs on short chains who spend most of their lives alone. Our cities are full of stray cats and dogs who live miserable lives and starve or freeze, succumb to disease, or are tormented by humans. Some people who claim to love their companion animals mutilate them sense-lessly by having their ears cropped, their tails docked, or their claws ripped out so that they will not scratch the furniture.

You may treat your animal companion as a member of your family and effectively accord her or him inherent value or the basic right not to be treated as your resource. But your treatment of your animal really means that you regard your animal property as having higher than market value; should you change your mind and administer daily and severe beatings to your dog for disciplinary purposes, or not feed your cat so that she will be more motivated to catch the mice in the basement of your store, or kill your animal because you no longer want the financial expense, your decision will be protected by the law. You are free to value your property as you see fit. You may decide to polish your car often or you may let the finish erode. The choice is yours. As long as you pro-vide the minimal maintenance for your car so that it can pass inspection, any other decision you make with respect to the vehicle, including your decision to give it to a scrap dealer, is your business. As long as you pro-vide minimal food, water, and shelter to your pet, any other decision you make, apart from torturing the animal for no purpose whatsoever, is your business, including your decision to dump your pet at the local shelter (where many animals are either killed or sold into research), or have your pet killed by a willing veterinarian.

Many years ago, I adopted a hamster from a law school classmate. The hamster became ill one night, and I called an emergency veterinary service. The veterinarian said that the minimum amount for an emergency visit was $50 and asked me why I would want to spend that amount when I could get a "new" hamster from any pet shop for about $3. I took the hamster to the veterinarian anyway, but that event was one of the first times my consciousness was raised about the status of animals as economic commodities.

As someone who lives with seven rescued canine companions whom I love dearly, I do not treat this matter lightly. Although I regard my companions as family members, they are still my property and I could decide tomorrow to have them all killed. As much as I enjoy living with dogs, were there only two dogs remaining in the world, I would not be in favor of breeding them so that we could have more "pets" and thus perpetuate their property status. Indeed, anyone who truly cares about dogs should visit a "puppy mill"—a place where dogs are bred in the hundreds or thousands and are treated as nothing more than commodities. Female dogs are bred repeatedly until they are "spent" and are either killed or sold into research. We should, of course, care for all those domestic animals that are presently alive, but we should not continue to bring more animals into existence so that we may own them as pets.

4. Question: If you are in favor of abolishing the use of animals as human resources, don't you care more about animals than you do about those humans with illnesses who might possibly be cured through animal research?

Answer: No, of course not. This question is logically and morally indistinguishable from that which asks whether those who advocated the abolition of human slavery cared less about the well-being of southerners who faced economic ruin if slavery were abolished than they did about the slaves.

The issue is not whom we care about or value most; the question is whether it is morally justifiable to treat sentient beings—human or nonhuman—as commodities or exclusively as means to the ends of others. For example, we generally do not think that we should use any humans as unconsenting subjects in biomedical experiments, even though we would get much better data about human illness if we used humans rather than animals in experiments. After all, the application to the human context of data from animal experiments—assuming that the animal data are relevant at all—requires often difficult and always imprecise extrapolation. We could avoid these difficulties by using humans, which would eliminate the need for extrapolation. But we do not do so because even though we may disagree about many moral issues, most of us are in agreement that the use of humans as unwilling experimental subjects is ruled out as an option from the beginning. No one suggests that we care more about those we are unwilling to use as experimental subjects than we do about the others who would benefit from that use.

5. Question: Isn't human use of animals a "tradition," or "natural," and therefore morally justified?

Answer: Every form of discrimination in the history of humankind has been defended as "traditional." Sexism is routinely justified on the ground that it is traditional for women to be subservient to men: "A woman's place is in the home." Human slavery has been a tradition in most cultures at some times. The fact that some behavior can be described as traditional has nothing to do with whether the behavior is or is not morally acceptable.

In addition to relying on tradition, some characterize our use of animals as "natural" and then declare it to be morally acceptable. Again, to describe something as natural does not in itself say anything about the morality of the practice. In the first place, just about every form of discrimination ever practiced has been described as natural as well as traditional. The two notions are often used interchangeably. We have justified human slavery as representing a natural hierarchy of slave owners and slaves. We have justified sexism as representing the natural superiority of men over women. Moreover, it is a bit strange to describe our modern commodification of animals as natural in any sense of the word. We have created completely *un*natural environments and agricultural procedures in order to maximize profits. We do bizarre experiments in which we transplant genes and organs from animals into humans and vice versa. We are now cloning animals. None of this can be described as natural. Labels such as "natural" and "traditional" are just that: labels. They are not reasons. If people defend the imposition of pain and suffering on an animal based on what is natural or traditional, it usually means that they cannot otherwise justify their conduct.

A variant of this question focuses on the traditions of particular groups. For example, in May 1999 the Makah tribe from Washington State killed its first gray whale in over seventy years. The killing, which was done with steel harpoons, antitank guns, armor-piercing ammunition, motorized chase boats, and a $310,000 grant from the federal government, was defended on the grounds that whaling was a Makah tradition. But the same argument could be (and is) made to defend clitoral mutilations in Africa and bride-burning in India. The issue is not whether conduct is part of a culture; *all* conduct is part of some culture. The issue is whether the conduct can be morally justified.

Finally, some argue that since nonhuman animals eat other nonhumans in the wild, our use of animals is natural. There are four responses to this position. First, although some animals eat each other in the wild, many do not. Many animals are vegetarians. Moreover, there is far more cooperation in nature than our imagined "cruelty of nature" would have us believe. Second, whether animals eat other animals is beside the point. How is it relevant whether animals eat other animals? Some animals are carnivorous and cannot exist without eating meat. We do not fall into that category; we can get along fine without eating meat, and more and more people are taking the position that our health and environment would both benefit from a shift away from a diet of animal products. Third, animals do all sorts of things that humans do not regard as morally appropriate. For example, dogs copulate and defecate in the street. Does that mean that we should follow their example? Fourth, it is interesting that when it is convenient for us to do so, we attempt to justify our exploitation of animals by resting on our supposed "superiority." And when our supposed "superiority" gets in the way of what we want to do, we suddenly portray ourselves as nothing more than another species of wild animal, as entitled as foxes to eat chickens.

6. Question: If we did not exploit animals, we would not have society as we now know it. Does this fact not prove that animal use by humans is morally justified?

Answer: No. In the first place, the question assumes that we would not have devised alternatives to animal use if that were necessary either because nonhuman animals were not available or because we made a moral decision not to exploit them as resources. Second, even if animal use were necessary for society as we presently know it, the same argument could be made with respect to any human activity. For example, without wars, patriarchy, and other forms of violence and exploitation, we would not have society as we now know it. The fact that a given activity was a necessary means to what some of us regard as a desirable end does not prove that the means were morally justified. Present-day Americans would not enjoy the level of prosperity that they now enjoy were it not for human slavery; that does not mean that slavery was a morally acceptable practice. Third, there is at least an argument that our present-day society, with its violence, pollution, inequitable distribution of resources, and various forms of injustice is less desirable an end than some think, and that we ought not be so eager to endorse the means that got us where we are today.

7. Question: By equating speciesism with racism and sexism, don't you equate animals, people of color, and women?

Answer: No. Racism, sexism, speciesism, and other forms of discrimination are all analogous in that all share the faulty notion that some morally irrelevant characteristic (race, sex, species) may be used to exclude beings with interests from the moral community or to undervalue interests in explicit violation of the principle of equal consideration. For example, speciesism and human slavery are similar in that in all cases animals and enslaved humans have a basic interest in not being treated as things and yet are treated as things on the basis of morally irrelevant criteria. To deny animals this basic right simply because they are animals is like saying that we should not abolish race-based slavery because of the perceived inferiority of the slaves' race. The argument used to support slavery and the argument used to support animal exploitation are structurally similar: we exclude beings with interests from the moral community because there is some supposed difference between "them" and "us" that has nothing to do with the inclusion of these beings in the moral community. The animal rights position maintains that if we believe that animals have moral significance, the principle of equal consideration requires that we stop treating them as things.

A related question that often arises in this context is whether speciesism is "as bad" as racism or sexism or other forms of discrimination. As a general matter, it is not useful to rank evils. Was it "worse" that Hitler killed Jews than that he killed Catholics or Romanies? Is slavery "worse" than genocide? Is non-race-based slavery "worse" than race-based slavery? Is sexism "worse" than slavery and genocide, or is it "worse" than slavery but not worse than genocide? Frankly, I am not even sure what these questions mean, but I suspect that persons considering them assume implicitly that one group is "better" than another. In any event, these forms of discrimination are all terrible, and they are terrible in different ways. But they all share one thing in common: they all treat humans as things without protectable interests. In this sense, all of these forms of discrimination—as different as they are—are similar to speciesism, which results in our treating animals as things.[1]

Finally, there are some who argue that in saying that some animals have greater cognitive ability than some humans, such as the severely retarded or the extremely senile, we are equating those humans with animals and characterizing them in a disrespectful way. Again, this misses the point of the argument for animal rights. For centuries, we have justified our treatment of animals as resources because they supposedly lack some characteristic that we have. But some animals have such a "special" characteristic to a greater degree than do some of us and some humans do not have that characteristic at all. The point is that although a particular characteristic may be useful for some purposes, the only characteristic that is required for moral significance is sentience. We do not and should not treat those humans who are impaired as resources for other humans. And if we really believe that animals have morally significant interests, then we ought to apply the principle of equal consideration and not treat them as resources as well. The argument for animal rights does not decrease respect for human life; it increases respect for all life.

8. Question: Hitler was a vegetarian; what does that say about vegetarians?

Answer: It says nothing more than that some evil people may also be vegetarians. The question itself is based on an invalid syllogism: Hitler was a vegetarian; Hitler was evil; therefore vegetarians are evil. Stalin ate meat and was himself no angel. He was responsible for the deaths of millions of innocent people. What does that say about meat eaters? Just as we cannot conclude that all meat eaters have anything in common with Stalin beyond meat eating, we cannot conclude that all vegetarians have anything in common with Hitler beyond vegetarianism. Furthermore, it is not certain that Hitler actually was a vegetarian. And in any event, the Nazi interest in reducing meat consumption was not a matter of the moral status of animals but reflected a concern with organic health and healing and avoidance of artificial ingredients in food and pharmaceutical products that was linked to the broader Nazi goals of "racial hygiene."[2]

Another version of this question is that since the Nazis also favored animal rights, does this mean that animal rights as a moral theory is bankrupt and attempts to devalue humans? Once again, the question is absurd. In the first place, the question is based on a factual error. The Nazis were not in favor of animal rights. Animal welfare laws in Germany restricted vivisection to some degree, but they hardly reflected any societal preference for abolishing the property status of animals. After all, the Nazis casually murdered millions of humans and animals in the course of the Second World War, behavior not compatible with a rights position, human or otherwise. It is no more accurate to say that the Nazis supported animal rights than it is to say that Americans support animal rights because we have a federal Animal Welfare Act.

But what if, contrary to fact, the Nazis did advocate the abolition of all animal exploitation? What would that say about the idea of animal rights? The answer is absolutely clear: it would say nothing about whether the animal rights position is right or wrong. That question can be settled only by whether the moral arguments in favor of animal rights are valid or not. The Nazis also strongly favored marriage. Does that mean marriage is an inherently immoral institution? The Nazis also believed that sports were essential to the development of strong character. Does this mean that competitive sports are inherently immoral? Jesus Christ preached a gospel of sharing resources on an equitable basis. Gandhi promoted a similar message, as did Stalin. But Stalin also devalued human beings. Can we conclude that the idea of more equitable resource distribution has some inherent moral flaw that taints Jesus or Gandhi? No, of course not. We no more devalue human life if we accord moral significance to animal interests than we devalue the lives of "normal" humans when we accord value to certain humans, such as the severely retarded, and prohibit their use in experiments.

9. Question: Where do you draw the line on who can have rights? Do insects have rights?

Answer: I draw the line at sentience because, as I have argued, sentient beings have interests and the possession of interests is the necessary and sufficient condition for membership in the moral community. Are insects sentient? Are they conscious beings with minds that experience pain and pleasure? I do not know. But the fact that I do not know exactly where to draw the line, or perhaps find drawing the line difficult, does not relieve me of the obligation to draw the line somewhere or allow me to use animals as I please. Although I may not know whether insects are sentient, I do know that cows, pigs, chickens, chimpanzees, horses, deer, dogs, cats, and mice are sentient. Indeed, it is now widely accepted that fish are sentient. So the fact that I do not know on what side of the line to place insects does not relieve me of my moral obligation to the animals whom I do know are sentient.

As a general matter, this question is intended to demonstrate that if we do not know where to draw the line in a matter of morality, or if line drawing is difficult, then we ought not to draw the line anywhere. This form of reasoning is invalid. Consider the following example. There is a great deal of disagreement about the scope and extent of human rights. Some people argue that health care and education are fundamental rights that a civilized government should provide to everyone; some people argue that health care and education are commodities like any other, not the subject of rights, and that people ought to pay for them. But we would, I suspect, all agree that whatever our disagreements about human rights—however unsure we are of where to draw the line—we most certainly agree, for instance, that genocide is morally wrong. We do not say that it is morally acceptable to kill off entire populations because we may disagree over whether humans are entitled to health care. Similarly, our uncertainty or disagreement regarding the sentience of ants is no license to ignore the interests of chimpanzees, cows, pigs, chickens, and other animals whom we do know are sentient.

10. Question: Do nonsentient humans, such as those who are irreversibly brain dead, have a right not to be treated as things?

Answer: If a human is really nonsentient—not conscious or aware of anything at all and will not regain consciousness or awareness of anything—then, by definition, the human cannot have an interest in not suffering (or in anything else). In such a situation, a compelling argument could be made that it is morally acceptable to use the organs of such a human to save others—and it is common practice to do so if the human has previously agreed to donate her organs or if the family consents.

We should, of course, be concerned about whether an ostensibly brain-dead human really does lack all cognitive activity. We ought also to be sensitive to the concerns of those related to the comatose human; they may oppose the instrumental use of the human for various reasons, such as religious opposition to organ transplantation. But humans who are really irreversibly brain dead are really no different from plants; they are alive but they are not conscious and have no interests to protect. According such humans a basic right not to be treated as the resources of others makes no sense.

11. Question: If we want to treat similar interests similarly, does our recognition that animals have a basic right not to be property mean that abortion should also be prohibited?

Answer: Abortion raises a number of difficult issues, particularly because of the religious dimension of the controversy. Many who oppose abortion believe that ensoulment occurs at the moment of conception. This belief leads some abortion opponents to oppose any measure that will interfere with the subsequent development of the fetus, including the use of intrauterine devices or drugs that prevent the implantation of the fertilized ovum on the uterus wall. As far as these abortion opponents are concerned, the fact that a fetus or fertilized ovum is not sentient is irrelevant; the fetus has spiritual "interests" and is considered a full and complete moral being in the eyes of God as soon as it possesses a soul.

Another complicating factor in the abortion debate is that as a cultural matter the status of a pregnant woman as a "mother" and of a fetus as a "baby" tends to kick in immediately after the woman learns that she is pregnant, particularly in cases in which the woman wants to have a child. That is, from the moment of conception, or learning of conception, we tend to think of the fetus as the human person—the baby—that it will become. But that characterization does not alter the biological fact that a fertilized ovum does not have interests in the way that the baby does.

If we approach the abortion question outside the framework of religion and souls, and outside social conventions that characterize a pregnant woman as a "mother" and a fetus as a "baby" from the moment of conception, it becomes much more difficult to understand how fetuses—particularly early-term fetuses—may be said to have interests. Although it is not certain that any fetuses are sentient, it is clear that early-term fetuses are not, and therefore they do not have interests in not suffering—they *cannot* suffer. Moreover, it is not clear how non-sentient fetuses can have an interest in continued existence. Although a normal fetus will continue to term and result in the birth of a human person, the nonsentient fetus cannot itself have an interest in continued existence.

Sentient beings are those who are conscious of pain and pleasure; those with some sort of mind and some sense of self. The harm of death to a sentient being is that she or he will no longer be able to have conscious experiences. If you kill me painlessly while I am asleep, you have harmed me because you have deprived me of having further experiences as a sentient being that I, by virtue of the fact that I have not chosen to commit suicide, wish to have. And our experience of sentient beings other than humans reasonably supports the position that *all* sentient beings share in common an interest in continuing to live—sentience is merely a means to the continued existence of organisms who are able to have mental experiences of pleasure and pain. We cannot analogize a fetus and a sleeping person; the fetus has never been sentient and therefore has never possessed the interests that are characteristic of all sentient beings.

If we claim that a nonsentient fertilized ovum has an interest in continued existence simply because there is a high degree of probability that in nine months it will become a child with interests, then we are committed to the view that a fertilized ovum has an interest in continued existence immediately upon conception. And if we can say that a fertilized ovum has an interest in continued existence immediately upon conception, it becomes difficult to understand why we would not also say that a sperm and an egg have interests in conception before their union occurs. The primary difference between the fertilized ovum, and the sperm and egg, concerns probability (it is more probable that a fertilized ovum will eventually become a human baby than it is that any particular sperm will fertilize an egg), and nothing more.

To the extent that we might say, for instance, that it is in the "interest" of the fetus that the pregnant woman not smoke cigarettes during pregnancy, such an assertion is no different from saying that it is in the "interest" of an engine to be properly lubricated or of a plant to be watered. Although it may be prudent for the pregnant woman not to smoke if *she* has an interest in having a healthy baby (just as it is prudent for us to put oil in our cars or to water our plants), the nonsentient fetus does not yet have an experiential welfare and does not prefer or want

or desire *anything*. In the absence of a religious belief about the ensoulment of fetuses, it is difficult to understand why the abortion of an early-
term fetus is morally objectionable or how abortion can be considered
a harm to a nonsentient fetus. If the abortion of a nonsentient fetus is
morally objectionable, then so would be the use of intrauterine devices
or drugs, such as RU 486, that prevent the attachment to the uterine
wall of a fertilized ovum. And we may be committed to the view that a
sperm and an egg have an interest in being united so that the use of contraception violates the interests of the sperm and the egg. Again, in the
absence of a religious framework, such views appear quite untenable.

What if we determine that some fetuses are sentient? Certainly, late-
term fetuses react to certain stimuli. It may be the case that such fetuses
are sentient and have an experiential welfare. In this case, it would make
sense to say that such fetuses have interests. But even if we assume that
sentient fetuses have a basic right that prevents their wholly instrumental
treatment, abortion presents a most unusual conflict of rights. One right
holder exists within the body of another right holder and is dependent
upon her for the very existence that serves as the predicate for the fetus
having interests in the first place. Such a conflict is unique, and protection
of fetal interests risks state intrusion on the woman's body and privacy interests in a way that no other protection of the basic right of another requires. If a parent is abusing her three-year-old, the state may remove the
child in order to protect the child's interests. The state cannot protect fetal interests without intruding on the bodily autonomy of the woman and
forcing her to continue an unwanted pregnancy. But it may be the case
that the sentience of fetuses militates in favor of abortion methods that are
equally safe for the woman but that preserve the life of the fetus.[3]

*12. Question: If we become vegetarians, animals will inevitably be harmed
when we plant vegetables, and what is the difference between raising and
killing animals for food and unintentionally killing them as part of a plant-
based agriculture?*

Answer: If we shift from a meat-based agriculture to a plant-based agriculture, we will inevitably displace and possibly kill sentient animals
when we plant vegetables. Surely, however, there is a significant difference between raising and killing animals for food and unintentionally
doing them harm in the course of planting vegetables, an activity that is
itself intended to prevent the killing of sentient beings.

In order to understand this point, consider the following example. We build roads. We allow people to drive automobiles. We know as a statistical matter that when we build a road, some humans—we do not know who they are beforehand—will be harmed as the result of automobile accidents. Yet there is a fundamental moral difference between activity that has human harm as an inevitable but unintended consequence and the intentional killing of particular humans. Similarly, the fact that animals may be harmed as an unintended consequence of planting vegetables, even if we do not use toxic chemicals and even if we exercise great care to avoid harming animals, does not mean that it is morally acceptable to kill animals intentionally.

A related question is: why don't plants have rights given that they are alive? This is the question that every vegetarian gets in the company of meat eaters. These meat eaters may be otherwise rational and intelligent beings, but when confronted with a vegetarian, their discomfort with their diet often rises to the surface in the form of defensiveness.

No one really thinks that plants are the same as sentient nonhumans. If I ate your tomato and your dog, you would not regard those as similar acts. As far as we know, plants are not sentient. They are not conscious and able to experience pain. Plants do not have central nervous systems, endorphins, receptors for benzodiazepines, or any of the other indicia of sentience. Plants do not have interests; animals do.

13. Question: Isn't taking advantage of medications or procedures developed through the use of animals inconsistent with taking an animal rights position?

Answer: No, it is not. Those who support animal exploitation often argue that accepting the "benefits" of animal use is inconsistent with criticizing the use of animals.

This position, of course, makes no sense. Most of us are opposed to racial discrimination, and yet we live in a society in which white middle-class people enjoy the benefits of past racial discrimination; that is, the majority enjoys a standard of living that it would not have had there been a nondiscriminatory, equitable distribution of resources, including educational and job opportunities. Many of us support measures, such as affirmative action, that are intended to correct past discrimination. But those who oppose racial discrimination are not obligated to leave the United States or to commit suicide because we cannot avoid the fact that white people are beneficiaries of past discrimination against people of color.

Consider another example: assume that we find that the local water company employs child labor and we object to child labor. Are we obligated to die of dehydration because the water company has chosen to violate the rights of children? No, of course not. We would be obligated to support the abolition of this use of children, but we would not be obligated to die. Similarly, we should join together collectively and demand an end to animal exploitation, but we are not obligated to accept animal exploitation or forego any benefits that it may provide.

We certainly could develop drugs and surgical procedures without the use of animals, and many would prefer we do so. Those who object to animal use for these purposes, however, have no control as individuals over government regulations or corporate policies concerning animals. To say that they cannot consistently criticize the actions of government or industry while they derive benefits from these actions, over which they have no control, is absurd as a matter of logic. And as a matter of political ideology, it is a most disturbing endorsement of unquestioned obeisance to the policies of the corporate state. Indeed, the notion that we must either embrace animal exploitation or reject anything that involves animal use is eerily like the reactionary slogan "love it or leave it," uttered by the pseudo-patriots who criticized opponents of American involvement in the Vietnam War.

Moreover, humans have so commodified animals that it is virtually impossible to avoid animal exploitation completely. Animal by-products are used in a wide variety of things, including the asphalt on roads and synthetic fabrics. But the impossibility of avoiding all contact with animal exploitation does not mean that we cannot avoid the most obvious and serious forms of exploitation. The individual who is not stranded in a lifeboat or on a mountaintop always has it within her power to avoid eating meat and dairy products, products that could not be produced without the use of animals, unlike drugs and medical procedures, which could be developed without animal testing.

14. Question: Is it likely that the pursuit of more "humane" animal treatment will eventually lead to the recognition that animals have the basic right not to be treated as things, and the consequent abolition of institutionalized animal use?

Answer: No, it is not likely. Anticruelty laws requiring the humane treatment of animals have been popular in the United States and Great Britain for well over a hundred years, and we are using more animals in more horrific ways than ever before. Sure, there have been some changes. In some places, like Britain, veal calves get more space and some social interaction before they are slaughtered; in some American states, the leghold trap is prohibited and animals used for fur products are caught in "padded" traps or raised in small wire cages before they are gassed or electrocuted. Under the federal Animal Welfare Act, primates are supposed to receive some psychological stimulation while we use them in horrendous experiments in which we infect them with diseases or try to ascertain how much radiation they can endure before they become dysfunctional. Some practices, such as animal fighting, have been outlawed, but, as I have argued, such prohibitions tell us more about class hierarchy and prejudice than they do about our moral concern for animals. All in all, the changes we have witnessed as the result of animal welfare laws are nothing more than window dressing.

This should not surprise us. Anticruelty laws assume that animals are the property of humans, and it is in this context that the supposed balance of human and animal interests occurs. But as we saw, we cannot really balance the interests of property owners against their property because property cannot have interests that are protectable against the property owner. The humane treatment principle, as applied through animal welfare laws, does nothing more than require that the owners of animal property accord that level of care, and no more, that is necessary to the particular purpose. If we are using animals in experiments, they should receive that level of care, and no more, that is required to produce valid data. If we are using purpose-bred animals to make fur coats, they should receive the level of care, and no more, that is required to produce coats that are soft and shiny. If we are raising animals for food, those animals should receive that level of care, and no more, that is required to produce meat that can be sold at a particular price level to meet a particular demand. If we are using dogs to guard our property, we should provide the level of care that is required to sustain the dog for that purpose. As long as we give the dog the minimal food and water and shelter—a dead dog will not serve the purpose—we can tie that dog on a three-foot leash and we can beat him, even excessively, for "disciplinary" purposes.

We claim to acknowledge that the interest of animals in not suffering is morally significant, but our animal practices belie that claim. If we are really to honor the moral interests of animals, then we must abolish institutionalized animal exploitation and not merely regulate animal use through animal welfare measures that assume the legitimacy of the status of animals as property.[4]

15. Question: Don't laws like the Endangered Species Act,[5] which prohibits the killing of certain species of animals facing extinction, effectively change the property status of animals?

Answer: No. The Endangered Species Act and similar measures protect only certain species that are valued by humans for human purposes; such laws do not recognize that animals have value other than that which humans bestow. Some people have argued—erroneously, in my view—that these laws actually provide "rights" for animals. In reality, these laws are no different from those that protect a rainforest, a stream, a mountain, or any other nonsentient thing that humans, for whatever reason, decide to value for human purposes. Such measures imply no recognition that the protected species has value of the sort that we attribute to every human being as a minimal condition of membership in the moral community.

Under economic pressure, governments are now seeking to withdraw some species from endangered-species protection and to readmit them as hunters' prey, so that the fees generated by hunting licenses and the trade in animal parts can help to pay for maintenance of the remaining animals. Moratoriums on killing particular species are almost always eliminated as soon as populations increase beyond bare extinction levels, thus inviting the "harvesting" of excess animals. We do not, however, treat any humans in the same way. We do not regard it appropriate to use homeless people as forced organ donors in order to subsidize the social welfare costs of other homeless people. We do not condone the "harvesting" of humans.

In any event, laws like the Endangered Species Act do not recognize that animals, because they are sentient, have moral value beyond what humans give them. Such laws regard animals as no different from any other resource that we wish to preserve for the benefit of future generations. We temporarily protect animals like elephants so that future generations of humans will have elephants to use, but elephants are, in the end, only economic commodities, and as long as there are enough elephants, we ultimately value ivory bracelets more than we value the interests of the elephant.[6]

Finally, it should be understood that it is unlikely that any significant change in the status of animals as property will come about as the result of legislation or court cases until there is a significant social change in our attitude about animals. That is, it is not the law that will alter our moral thinking about animals; it must be the other way around. It was not the law that abolished slavery; indeed, the law protected slave ownership and the institution of slavery was not abolished by the law but by the Civil War. The present-day world economy is far more dependent on animal exploitation than were the southern United States on human slavery. Animal exploitation is not going to be ended by a pronouncement of the Supreme Court or an act of Congress—at least not until a majority of us accept the position that the institution of animal property is morally unacceptable.

16. Question: If animals have rights, does that not mean that we would have to punish the killing of animals in the same way we do the killing of humans?

Answer: No, of course not. It is certainly true that if we as a society ever really accorded moral significance to animal interests and recognized our obligation to abolish and not merely regulate animal exploitation, we would very probably incorporate such a view in criminal laws that formally prohibit and punish the treatment of animals as resources. But that would not mean that we must punish the killing of an animal by a human in exactly the same way that we punish the killing of a human by another human. For example, our recognizing that animals have moral value does not require that we prosecute for manslaughter someone who, while driving recklessly, hits a raccoon. The prosecution of humans who kill other humans serves many purposes that are not relevant to animals. For example, criminal prosecutions allow the families of crime victims to experience some form of closure, and although there is ethological evidence that many nonhuman animals experience grief at the loss of family or pack members, a criminal trial would not be meaningful to them.

17. Question: If animals have rights, doesn't that mean we have to intervene to stop animals from killing other animals, or that we must otherwise act affirmatively to prevent harm from coming to animals from any source?

Answer: No. The basic right not to be treated as a thing means that we cannot treat animals exclusively as means to human ends—just as we cannot treat other humans exclusively as means to the ends of other humans. Even though we have laws that prevent people from owning other humans, or using them as unconsenting biomedical subjects, we generally do not require that humans prevent harm to other humans in all situations. No law requires that Jane prevent Simon from inflicting harm on John, as long as Jane and Simon are not conspirators in a crime against John or otherwise acting in concert, and as long as Jane has no relationship with John that would give rise to such an obligation.

Moreover, in the United States at least, the law generally imposes on humans no "duty to aid" even when other humans are involved. If I am walking down the street and see a person lying passed out, face down in a small puddle of water and drowning, the law imposes no obligation on me to assist that person even if all I need to do is roll her over, something I can do without risk or serious inconvenience to myself.

The point is that the basic right of humans not to be treated as things does not guarantee that humans will aid other humans, or that we are obligated to intervene to prevent harm from coming to humans from animals or from other humans. Similarly, the basic right of animals not to be treated as things means that we cannot treat animals as our resources. It does not necessarily mean that we have moral or legal obligations to render them aid or to intervene to prevent harm from coming to them.

18. Question: Isn't the matter of whether animals ought to be accorded the basic right not to be treated as our resources a matter of opinion? What right does anyone have to say that another should not eat meat or other animal products, or how they should otherwise use or treat animals?

Answer: Animal rights are no more a matter of opinion than is any other moral matter. This question is logically and morally indistinguishable from asking whether the morality of human slavery is a matter of opinion. We have decided that slavery is morally reprehensible not as a matter of mere opinion, but because slavery treats humans exclusively as the resources of others and degrades humans to the status of things, thus depriving them of moral significance.

The notion that animal rights are a matter of opinion is directly related to the status of animals as human property; this question, like most others examined here, assumes the legitimacy of regarding animals as things that exist solely as means to human ends. Because we regard animals as our property, we believe that we have the right to value animals in the ways that we think appropriate. If, however, we are not morally justified in treating animals as our property, then whether we ought to eat meat or use animals in experiments or impose pain and suffering on them for sport or entertainment is no more a matter of opinion than is the moral status of human slavery.

Moreover, as long as animals are treated as property, then we will continue to think that what constitutes "humane" treatment for your animal property really *is* a matter of opinion because you get to decide how much your property is worth. Just as we have opinions about the value of other things that we own, we can have opinions about the value of our animal property. Although our valuation of our property may be too high or too low relative to its market value, this is not generally considered a moral question. So when Jane criticizes Simon because he beats his dog regularly in order to make sure that his dog is a vicious and effective guard dog, Simon is perfectly justified in responding to Jane that her valuation of his property is not a moral matter up for grabs, but a matter of his property rights.

On another level, this question relates to a subject discussed in the Introduction, the position that all morality is relative, a matter of convention or convenience or tradition, with no valid claim to objective truth. If this were the case, then the morality of genocide or human slavery or child molestation would be no more than matters of opinion. Although it is certainly true that moral propositions cannot be proved in the way that mathematical propositions can, this does not mean that "anything goes." Some moral views are supported by better reasons than others, and some moral views have a better "fit" with other views that we hold. The view that we can treat animals as things simply because we are human and they are not is speciesism pure and simple. The view that we ought not to treat animals as things is consistent with our general notion that animals have morally significant interests. We do not treat any humans exclusively as the resources of others; we have abolished the institution of human property. We have seen that there is no morally sound reason to treat animals differently for purposes of the one right not to be treated as a thing, and that the animal rights position does not mean that we cannot prefer the human over the animal in situations of true emergency or conflict where we have not manufactured that conflict in the first place by violating the principle of equal consideration.

19. Question: Doesn't the animal rights position represent a "religious" view?

Answer: No, not necessarily, although the idea that we should not treat animals as things is certainly present in some primarily non-Western religious systems, such as Jainism, Buddhism, and Hinduism. The irony is that the notion of human superiority used to justify animal agriculture, vivisection, and other practices often does represent a religious position. For the most part, not only has the Judeo-Christian tradition endorsed the view of animals as things, it has been a primary support of the notion of human superiority to animals and of humans' right to use animals as resources. We saw, for instance, that the modern Western notion of animals as property can be traced directly to a particular interpretation of the Old Testament, according to which God created animals as resources for human use. Arguments for qualitative distinctions between humans and animals have often rested on nothing more than humans' supposed God-given superiority, which in turn rests on humans' good fortune in having been made "in God's image."

The animal rights position articulated in this book does not rely on any theological beliefs; it requires only a simple application of the principle of equal consideration. Humans exclusively possess no special characteristic, nor are they free of any defect that they attribute to animals.

20. Question: Of course the amount of animal suffering incidental to our use of animals is horrendous, and we should not be using animals for "frivolous" purposes, such as entertainment, but how can you expect people to give up eating meat?

Answer: In many ways this is an appropriate question with which to conclude our discussion because the question itself reveals more about the history of the human/animal relationship than any theory, and it demonstrates our confusion about moral matters in general.

Many humans like to eat meat. They enjoy eating meat so much that they find it hard to be detached when they consider moral questions about animals. But moral analysis requires at the very least that we leave our obvious biases at the door. Animal agriculture is the most significant source of animal suffering in the world today, and there is absolutely no need for it. Indeed, animal agriculture has devastating environmental effects, and a growing number of health care professionals claim that meat and animal products are detrimental to human health. We could live without killing animals and could feed more of the world's humans—the beings we always claim to care about when we seek to justify animal exploitation—if we abandoned animal agriculture altogether.

The desire to eat meat has clouded some of the greatest minds in human history. Charles Darwin recognized that animals were not qualitatively different from humans and possessed many of the characteristics that were once thought to be uniquely human—but he continued to eat them. Jeremy Bentham argued that animals had morally significant interests because they could suffer, but he also continued to eat them.

Old habits die hard, but that does not mean they are morally justified. It is precisely in situations where both moral issues and strong personal preferences come into play that we should be most careful to think clearly. As the case of meat eating shows, however, sometimes our brute preferences determine our moral thinking, rather than the other way around. Many people have said to me, "Yes, I know it's morally wrong to eat meat, but I just love hamburgers."

Regrettably for those who like to eat meat, this is no argument, and a taste for meat in no way justifies the violation of a moral principle. Our conduct merely demonstrates that despite what we say about the moral significance of animal interests, we are willing to ignore those interests whenever we benefit from doing so—even when the benefit is nothing more than our pleasure or convenience.[7]

If we take morality seriously, then we must confront what it dictates: if it is wrong for Simon to torture dogs for pleasure, then it is morally wrong for us to eat meat.

Notes

Introduction

1. David Foster, "Animal Rights Activists Getting Message Across: New Poll Findings Show Americans More in Tune with 'Radical' Views," *Chicago Tribune*, January 25, 1996, at C8.

2. John Balzar, "Creatures Great and—Equal?" *Los Angeles Times*, December 25, 1993, at A1.

3. Alec Gallup, "Gallup Poll: Dog and Cat Owners See Pets As Part of Family," *Star Tribune*, October 28, 1996, at E10.

4. Jeanne Malmgren, "Poll Proves It: We're Nuts about Pets," *Star Tribune*, June 26, 1994, at E1.

5. Melinda Wilson, "Canine Blood Bank Is Looking for Doggie Donors," *Detroit News*, November 29, 1996, at A1.

6. American Pet Manufacturers Association, cited in Ranny Green, "Here's Some New, Bizarre Gifts for Pets and Owners," *Seattle Times*, December 15, 1996, at G4.

7. Julie Kirkbride, "Peers Use Delays to Foil Hedgehog Cruelty Measure," *Daily Telegraph*, November 3, 1995, at 12.

8. Edward Gorman, "Woman's Goring Fails to Halt Death in the Afternoon," *The Times* (London), June 30, 1995, Home News Section.

9. Malcolm Eames, "Four Legs Very Good," *The Guardian*, August 25, 1995, at 17.

10. *See* Richard Mauer, "Unlikely Allies Rush to Free 3 Whales," *New York Times*, October 18, 1988, at A18; Sherry Simpson, "Whales Linger Near Freedom: Soviet Icebreaker Makes Final Pass," *Washington Post*, October 28, 1988, at A1.

11. U.S. Department of Agriculture, National Agricultural Statistics Service, *Agricultural Statistics 1999* (Washington, D.C.: U.S. Government Printing Office, 1999).

12. This number comes from the website of the Food and Agriculture Organization of the United Nations.

13. James A. Swan, *In Defense of Hunting* (New York: Harper Collins, 1995), at 7–8.

14. *See* Adrian Benke, *The Bowhunting Alternative* (San Antonio, Tex.: B. Todd Press, 1989), at 7–10, 85–90.

15. My definition of sentience as the consciousness of pain would distinguish sentient beings from beings that have nothing more than nociceptive neural reactions in whom tissue damage may cause reflex actions but where there is no perception that it is the "self" who is in pain.

16. *See generally* Gary L. Francione, *Animals, Property, and the Law* (Philadelphia: Temple University Press, 1995).

17. Bernard E. Rollin, "The Legal and Moral Bases of Animal Rights," in Harlan B. Miller and William H. Williams, eds., *Ethics and Animals* (Clifton, N.J.: Humana Press, 1983), at 106. For a general discussion of the concept of rights and rights theory in the context of laws concerning animals, see Francione, *Animals, Property, and the Law, supra* note 16, at 91–114. One of the reasons why the concept of rights is complicated is that not all rights have the *same* type of protective wall built around them. With respect to some rights, we protect individual interests from being assessed on a case-by-case basis but we do permit considerations about the general welfare to result in the forfeiture of rights protections. Assume, for example, that the legislature determines that high tax rates are inhibiting investment and that the general welfare will be served by a reduction in the tax rates. We might say that as a result of the legislative action, the taxpayers have a right to the benefit represented by the tax reduction. During the time that the reduced tax rates are in effect, the right is protected from being ignored or abrogated; the tax collector is under an obligation or duty to respect the legislative decision and to tax at the rates determined by the legislature. (We usually associate rights with claims and correlative duties, but there are other normative components of rights. *See id.* at 42–43, 95–104.) The tax collector is not permitted to tax individual taxpayers at a higher rate because he thinks this will have better overall consequences for all concerned. But just as the legislature reduced the tax rates in order to serve the general welfare, the legislature may at some future time decide to eliminate this tax benefit for everyone based on a different assessment of what is in the general welfare. It may determine that more tax revenues are needed to fund other programs and may therefore decide to eliminate the wall of protection—the right—that protected the interest of taxpayers in paying a lower tax bill.

We might think of a right to a tax reduction, or a right to drive sixty-five miles per hour rather than fifty-five miles per hour, or similar sorts of rights, as "policy-based" rights. *See id.* at 109–10. Policy-based rights are still rights in that we generally do not allow them to be abrogated based on an assessment of consequences in particular cases. But we do allow policy-based rights to be abrogated if we determine that the consequences as a general matter (not on a case-by-case basis) militate in favor of abrogation. We do not, however, regard policy-based rights, such as a right to a tax reduction, as protecting interests that are essential to us as human beings. We would all like to pay lower taxes, but the world will not come to an end if we have to pay higher taxes.

Contrasted with these policy-based rights are what we might call "respect-based" rights, which we believe are fundamental to our political system. *See id.* Respect-based rights protect interests that we believe must be protected irrespective of the general consequences. In the United States and most liberal democracies, the right of free expression is seen as protecting an interest that must be protected even if the general consequences of doing so are undesirable or problematic.

Both policy-based rights and respect-based rights protect whatever interests are involved against abrogation simply on the basis of consequences. Some would argue that policy-based rights are not really rights because the interest protected by the so-called right can ultimately be compromised by considerations of consequences. *See* Chapter 6, note 6 *infra*. Respect-based rights protect against abrogation based on both case-by-case assessments of consequences *and* general assessments of overall societal consequences. Respect-based rights are what define a political system and identify what moral beliefs are important in that culture.

Different political systems identify different rights as respect-based rights. For example, although rights to free expression and to own property may be considered essential in a liberal democracy, rights to education and health care may be considered essential as well, and may be considered more important than free expression and property in some political systems.

18. The basic right not to be treated as a thing without protectable interests is a respect-based right. *See supra* note 17. However, this basic right is a special type of respect-based right in that it is necessary in order to have any rights or moral significance at all, irrespective of the political system and whatever other respect-based rights are protected. The basic right not to be treated as a thing recognizes that the right holder is a *person. See* Chapter 4 *infra*.

19. The term "speciesism" was coined originally by Richard Ryder. *See* Richard D. Ryder, *Victims of Science: The Use of Animals in Research* (London: Davis-Poynter, 1975).

20. *See generally* Gary L. Francione, *Rain Without Thunder: The Ideology of the Animal Rights Movement* (Philadelphia: Temple University Press, 1996).

21. *See, e.g.*, Ted Benton, *Natural Relations: Ecology, Animal Rights and Social Justice* (London: Verso, 1993); Marc Bekoff and Carron A. Meaney, eds., *Encyclopedia of Animal Rights and Animal Welfare* (Westport, Conn.: Greenwood Press, 1998); Peter Carruthers, *The Animals Issue: Moral Theory in Practice* (Cambridge: Cambridge University Press, 1992); Stephen R. L. Clark, *The Moral Status of Animals* (Oxford: Clarendon Press, 1977); David DeGrazia, *Taking Animals Seriously: Mental Life and Moral Status* (Cambridge: Cambridge University Press, 1996); Gail A. Eisnitz, *Slaughterhouse: The Shocking Story of Greed, Neglect, and Inhumane Treatment Inside the U.S. Meat Industry* (Amherst, N.Y.: Prometheus Press, 1997); Lawrence Finsen and Susan Finsen, *The Animal Rights Movement in America: From Compassion to Respect* (New York: Twayne Publishers, 1994); Michael Allen Fox, *Deep Vegetarianism* (Philadelphia: Temple University Press, 1999); Francione, *Rain Without Thunder, supra* note 20; Francione, *Animals, Property, and the Law, supra* note 16; R. G. Frey, *Rights, Killing, and Suffering: Moral Vegetarianism and Applied Ethics* (Oxford: Basil Blackwell, 1983); R. G. Frey, *Interests and Rights: The Case Against Animals* (Oxford: Clarendon Press, 1980); Robert Garner, *Animals, Politics and Morality* (Manchester: Manchester University Press, 1993); Stanley Godlovitch, Roslind Godlovitch, and John Harris, eds., *Animals, Men and Morals* (New York: Grove Press, 1971); James M. Jasper and Dorothy Nelkin, *The Animal Rights Crusade: The Growth of a Moral Protest* (New York: Free Press, 1992); Michael P. T. Leahy, *Against Liberation: Putting Animals in Perspective* (London: Routledge, 1991); Andrew Linzey, *Christianity and the Rights of Animals* (New York: Crossroad, 1987);

Jim Mason, *An Unnatural Order: Uncovering the Roots of Our Domination of Nature and Each Other* (New York: Simon & Schuster, 1993); Mary Midgley, *Animals and Why They Matter* (Athens: University of Georgia Press, 1984); Barbara Noske, *Beyond Boundaries: Humans and Animals* (Montreal: Black Rose Books, 1997); Evelyn B. Pluhar, *Beyond Prejudice: The Moral Significance of Human and Nonhuman Animals* (Durham, N.C.: Duke University Press, 1995); James Rachels, *Created From Animals: The Moral Implications of Darwinism* (Oxford: Oxford University Press, 1990); Bernard E. Rollin, *Animal Rights and Human Morality*, rev. ed. (Buffalo: Prometheus Press, 1992); Rosemary Rodd, *Biology, Ethics, and Animals* (Oxford: Clarendon Press, 1990); Richard D. Ryder, *Animal Revolution: Changing Attitudes Towards Speciesism* (Oxford: Basil Blackwell, 1989); Ryder, *Victims of Science, supra* note 19; S. F. Sapontzis, *Morals, Reason, and Animals* (Philadelphia: Temple University Press, 1987); James Serpell, *In the Company of Animals: A Study of Human-Animal Relationships* (Oxford: Basil Blackwell, 1986); Richard Sorabji, *Animal Minds and Human Morals: The Origins of the Western Debate* (Ithaca: Cornell University Press, 1993).

22. Peter Singer, *Animal Liberation*, 2d ed. (New York: New York Review of Books, 1990).

23. Tom Regan, *The Case for Animal Rights* (Berkeley and Los Angeles: University of California Press, 1983).

24. *Id.* at 243.

25. *Id.* at 78.

26. F. J. Verheijen and W.F.G. Flight, "Decapitation and Brining: Experimental Tests Show That After These Commercial Methods for Slaughtering Eel *Anguilla anguilla* (L.), Death Is Not Instantaneous," in 28 *Aquaculture Research* 361, 362 (1997). *See also* Michael W. Fox, *Inhumane Society: The American Way of Exploiting Animals* (New York: St. Martin's Press, 1990), at 119–20. Support among the scientific community for the sentience of fish was bolstered by a 1979 report by the British zoologist Lord Medway. *See* Ryder, *Animal Revolution, supra* note 21, at 197, 222.

27. Regan, *The Case for Animal Rights, supra* note 23, at 324–25.

28. *See* Chapter 5, note 61 and accompanying text *infra*.

29. The notion of reflective equilibrium as an alternative to foundationalism (or the idea that moral principles can have the certainty of mathematical principles) in moral theory was first discussed by John Rawls in *A Theory of Justice* (Cambridge, Mass.: Belknap Press, 1971).

30. U.S. Department of Health and Human Services, National Institutes of Health, "Public Health Service Policy and Government Principles Regarding the Care and Use of Animals," in Institute of Laboratory Animal Resources, *Guide for the Care and Use of Laboratory Animals* (Washington, D.C.: National Academy Press, 1996), at 117.

31. Committee on Pain and Distress in Laboratory Animals, Institute of Laboratory Animal Resources, Commission on Life Sciences, National Research Council, *Recognition and Alleviation of Pain and Distress in Laboratory Animals* (Washington, D.C.: National Academy Press, 1992), at ix.

32. Some still maintain that animals are not conscious of pain. For a discussion of those who deny that animals used in experiments suffer, see Bernard E. Rollin,

The Unheeded Cry: Animal Consciousness, Animal Pain and Science (Oxford: Oxford University Press, 1990). *See also* Chapter 2 and Chapter 5 *infra*.

33. Michel E. de Montaigne, "Apology for Raymond Sebond" [c. 1592], *reprinted in* Paul A. B. Clarke and Andrew Linzey, eds., *Political Theory and Animal Rights* (London: Pluto Press, 1990), at 64.

34. *See generally* Sorabji, *Animal Minds and Human Morals, supra* note 21. *See also* Chapter 5 *infra*.

Chapter 1

1. René Descartes, *Discourse on the Method*, Part V [1637], in John Cottingham, Robert Stoothoff, and Dugald Murdoch, trans., *The Philosophical Writings of Descartes*, vol. 1 (Cambridge: Cambridge University Press, 1985), at 139.

2. Some scholars have argued that Descartes did recognize animal consciousness in certain respects and that traditional interpretations of Descartes as rejecting animal consciousness are incorrect. *See, e.g.*, Daisie Radner and Michael Radner, *Animal Consciousness* (Buffalo: Prometheus Books, 1989).

3. For a further discussion of Descartes and duties that can only concern, but are not owed to, animals, see Chapter 5 *infra*.

4. Immanuel Kant, *Lectures on Ethics*, trans. Louis Infield (New York: Harper Torchbooks, 1963), at 240. For a discussion of Kant's views about basic rights for humans, see Chapter 4 *infra*. For a discussion of Kant's views on supposed differences between humans and animals, see Chapter 5 *infra*.

5. *Id.* at 239.

6. For a discussion of the law concerning animals before the widespread enactment of anticruelty laws, see Gary L. Francione, *Animals, Property, and the Law* (Philadelphia: Temple University Press, 1995), at 121–33.

7. Jeremy Bentham, *The Principles of Morals and Legislation*, chap. XVII, § I para. 4 [1781] (Amherst, N.Y.: Prometheus Books, 1988), at 310 (footnote omitted).

8. *Id.* at 310–11, note 1. Although it is clear that Bentham argued that animal interests deserved moral consideration and that we should apply the principle of equal consideration (*see* Chapter 4 *infra*) to assess animal interests, it is not clear that Bentham thought animals and humans had any similar interests or that the moral status of animals required anything more than not inflicting "gratuitous" suffering on them. Rather, he seems to have thought that their respective interests in not suffering were dissimilar because animals had no interest in their lives and no interest in not suffering in certain circumstances in which all, or virtually all, humans had an interest in not suffering. *See* Chapter 6 *infra*.

9. N.Y. Agric. & Mkts. Law § 353 (Consol. 1999). In 1999, New York made it a felony to engage in "aggravated cruelty," which occurs when an actor without "justifiable purpose . . . intentionally kills or intentionally causes serious physical injury to a companion animal" with intent "to cause extreme physical pain" or engages in such conduct "in an especially depraved or sadistic manner." *Id.* at § 353-a(1) (Consol. 1999).

10. Del. Code. Ann. tit. 11, §§ 1325(a)(1) & (4) (1998). Delaware also provides for felony punishment if the actor "intentionally kills or causes serious injury to any animal."

11. Protection of Animals Act, 1911, ch. 27 § 1(1)(a) (Eng.).

12. 7 U.S.C. §§ 2131–2159 (1999).

13. Cruelty to Animals Act, 1876 (Eng.).

14. Animals (Scientific Procedures) Act, 1986 (Eng).

15. 7 U.S.C. §§ 1901–1906 (1999).

16. For a discussion of how anticruelty laws were intended to impose direct duties on humans based on the moral significance of animal interests (as opposed to merely indirect duties based on a concern for how the treatment of animals affected the treatment of humans), see Francione, *Animals, Property, and the Law, supra* note 6, at 122–23. In Chapter 3, we will see how anticruelty laws were never really interpreted to impose legal obligations owed directly to animals, but were concerned exclusively with human interests. It is interesting to note that Kant believed that any duties we ostensibly owed directly to animals were really owed indirectly to other humans because we could owe no direct duties to animals. *See supra* note 4. Kant's analysis leaves open the question to whom we might owe a direct duty in the case of a duty owed indirectly to humans, given that all real duties are direct and can be owed only to humans. I think that a less confusing approach is to regard duties imposed on humans that concern animals but that are owed ultimately to humans to be direct duties as far as humans are concerned and indirect as far as animals are concerned.

17. *State v. Prater*, 109 S.W. 1047, 1049 (Mo. Ct. App. 1908).

18. *Stephens v. State*, 65 Miss. 329, 331 (1887).

19. *Hunt v. State*, 29 N.E. 933, 933 (Ind. Ct. App. 1892).

20. *Grise v. State*, 37 Ark. 456, 458 (1881).

21. *Oglesby v. State*, 37 S.E.2d 837, 838 (Ga. App. 1946); *People v. Brunell*, 48 How. Pr. 435, 437 (N.Y. City Ct. 1874).

22. Animals (Scientific Procedures) Act, 1986, ch. 14, § 5(4) (Eng.).

23. Ray V. Herren and Roy L. Donahue, *The Agricultural Dictionary* (New York: Delmar Publishers, 1991), at 167. For general descriptions and discussion of the treatment of farm animals, see C. David Coats, *Old MacDonald's Factory Farm: The Myth of the Traditional Farm and the Shocking Truth About Animal Suffering in Today's Agribusiness* (New York: Continuum, 1989); Michael W. Fox, *Farm Animals: Husbandry, Behavior, and Veterinary Practice* (Baltimore: University Park Press, 1984); Andrew Fraser and D. M. Broom, *Farm Animal Behaviour and Welfare*, 3d ed. (London: Bailliere Tindall, 1990); Jim Mason and Peter Singer, *Animal Factories*, rev. ed. (New York: Harmony Books, 1990); Jeremy Rifkin, *Beyond Beef: The Rise and Fall of the Cattle Culture* (New York: Plume, 1992); Bernard E. Rollin, *Farm Animal Welfare: Social, Bioethical, and Research Issues* (Ames: Iowa State University Press, 1995). For a description and discussion of the slaughtering process, see Gail A. Eisnitz, *Slaughterhouse: The Shocking Story of Greed, Neglect, and Inhumane Treatment Inside the U.S. Meat Industry* (Amherst, N.Y.: Prometheus Press, 1997).

24. National Animal Health Monitoring System, U.S. Department of Agriculture, *Swine Slaughter Surveillance Project* (Fort Collins, Colo.: USDA, 1991); John Robbins, *Diet for a New America* (Walpole, N.H.: Stillpoint Publishing, 1987).

25. A number of books deal with the detrimental health effects of a meat-based diet and the advantages of a plant-based diet. *See, e.g.,* Gill Langley, *Vegan Nutrition: A Survey of Research* (Oxford: Vegan Society, 1988); Craig Winston, *Eating for the Health of*

It (Eau Claire, Mich.: Golden Harvest Books, 1993). *See also* Virginia Messina and Mark Messina, *The Vegetarian Way* (New York: Three Rivers Press, 1996). The health advantages of a vegetarian diet are now recognized even by popular publications produced by mainstream medical organizations. *See, e.g.,* Donna Arbogast, "Vegetarian to the Core" and "Vegetarian Diets for Kids," *Digestive Health and Nutrition,* September/October 1999. *Digestive Health and Nutrition* is a publication of the American Gastroenterological Association, a society of physicians and scientists.

26. *See, e.g.,* David Pimentel, "Livestock Production: Energy Inputs and the Environment," in Shannon L. Scott and Xin Zhao, eds., *Proceedings of the Canadian Society of Animal Science: 47th Annual Meeting* (Montreal: Canadian Society of Animal Science, 1997), at 16. Professor Pimentel's work is based on his own original research and on data from sources such as the U.S. Department of Agriculture, the World Health Organization, and the work of other scholars.

27. The actual amount of plant protein required to produce meat—the conversion ratio—differs by type of animal or animal product. It takes approximately 16.4 kilograms of grain or 30 kilograms of forage to produce 1 kilogram of lamb; 13.3 kilograms of grain to produce 1 kilogram of beef cattle; 4.3 kilograms of grain to produce 1 kilogram of turkey; 8.3 kilograms of grain to produce 1 kilogram of eggs; 6.3 kilograms of grain to produce 1 kilogram of pig; and 2.6 kilograms of grain to produce 1 kilogram of chicken. *See id.* at 19.

28. *See id.* at 22–23.

29. For example, it takes 54 kilocalories of fossil energy to produce 1 kilocalorie of beef protein; 50 kilocalories of fossil energy to produce 1 kilocalorie of lamb protein; 26 kilocalories of fossil energy to produce 1 kilocalorie of egg protein; 17 kilocalories of fossil energy to produce 1 kilocalorie of pork protein; 13 kilocalories of fossil energy to produce 1 kilocalorie of turkey protein; and 4 kilocalories of fossil energy to produce 1 kilocalorie of broiler protein. *See id.* at 18–20.

30. Quoted in Arbogast, "Vegetarian to the Core," *supra* note 25, at 29.

31. James Rachels, *Created From Animals: The Moral Implications of Darwinism* (Oxford: Oxford University Press, 1990), at 212.

32. James A. Swan, *In Defense of Hunting* (New York: Harper Collins 1995), at 3.

33. *See, e.g.,* U.S. Department of the Interior, Bureau of Land Management, *Big Game Habitat Management* (Washington, D.C.: BLM 1993), at 1, 9. BLM states that the public lands in western states annually provide "5.4 big game hunting recreational days" and that "big game hunting contributes an estimated $152.8 million in annual revenues." BLM also says that its overall goal for big game management is to "[e]nsure sufficient quantity and quality to maintain and enhance viable big game populations, and to sustain identifiable economic and social contributions to the American people." Similarly, the U.S. Fish and Wildlife Service has the goal of improving "the ability of managers to provide maximum hunting opportunities consistent with long-term resource maintenance." U.S. Department of the Interior, Fish and Wildlife Service, *Adaptive Harvest Management: Considerations for the 1996 Duck Season* (Washington, D.C.: FWS, 1996), at 2. The New Jersey Division of Fish, Game, and Wildlife states that "the deer resource . . . has been managed primarily for the purpose of sport hunting." New Jersey Division of Fish, Game, and Wildlife, *An Assessment of Deer Hunting in New Jersey* (Trenton: FGW, 1990), at 8.

34. Tom Beck, "A Failure of the Spirit," in David Peterson, ed., *A Hunter's Heart: Honest Essays on Blood Sport* (New York: Henry Holt, 1996), at 200–201.

35. Contraception has already proved to be an effective method of population control. It has been adopted by the U.S. government as a wildlife management tool and is being used in pilot studies in many other countries. *See* Priscilla N. Cohn, Edward D. Plotka, and Ulysses S. Seal, eds., *Contraception in Wildlife, Book 1* (Lewiston, N.Y.: Edwin Mellen Press, 1996).

36. "1997 Hunting Season Outlook," *Connecticut Wildlife*, September/October 1997, at 7.

37. For descriptions of canned hunts, see Ted Williams, "Canned Hunts," *Audubon*, January 1992, at 12.

38. Pennsylvania law forbids cruelty to animals, but despite numerous attempts by animal advocates, the Pennsylvania courts have refused to find that the Hegins pigeon shoot is a violation of the law. Indeed, in 1891, a Pennsylvania court held that there was nothing inherently cruel about a pigeon shoot, and that is still the law in Pennsylvania. *See Commonwealth v. Lewis*, 21 A.2d 396 (Pa. 1891). The legislature of Pennsylvania has on several occasions considered a bill that would prohibit the event, but it has passed no law to date. In February 2000, the organizers of the shoot canceled it voluntarily to avoid yet another legal challenge from protesters, but pigeon shoots go on across Pennsylvania on a regular basis.

39. *See* Michael Clayton, *The Chase: A Modern Guide to Foxhunting* (London: Stanley Paul, 1987), at 89.

40. Patrick Bateson, *The Behavioural and Physiological Effects of Culling Red Deer: Report to the Council of the National Trust* (1997), at 19. In order to measure muscle stress and other variables, Bateson analyzed and compared blood samples taken from deer killed in different contexts.

41. *Id.* at 69.

42. *See* Introduction, note 26 *supra*.

43. *See* Andrew N. Rowan, *Of Mice, Models, and Men: A Critical Evaluation of Animal Research* (Albany: State University of New York Press, 1984), at 83.

44. *See* Michael W. Fox, *Inhumane Society: The American Way of Exploiting Animals* (New York: St. Martin's Press, 1990), at 119–20.

45. *See* Michael Strauss, "Fish Catch Hits a New High," in Worldwatch Institute, *Vital Signs 1998: The Environmental Trends That Are Shaping Our Future* (New York: W. W. Norton, 1998), at 34.

46. *See* Paula MacKay, "Fish," in Marc Bekoff and Carron A. Meaney, eds., *Encyclopedia of Animal Rights and Animal Welfare* (Westport, Conn.: Greenwood Press, 1998), at 175.

47. Many issues involving the use of animals in entertainment are discussed in a congressional hearing that dealt with federal regulation of animals used in exhibitions. *See Review of Agriculture's Enforcement of the Animal Welfare Act, Specifically of Animals Used in Exhibitions, Hearing before the Subcomm. on Dept. Operations, Research, and Foreign Agric. of the Comm. on Agric.*, House of Representatives, 102d Cong., 2d Sess. (1992). It should be noted, however, that many uses of animals for entertainment purposes are not covered under federal law.

48. There are many other uses of animals for entertainment purposes, such as "greased pig" contests, that I have not discussed.

49. For a general description and discussion of zoo animals, including the sale of "surplus" zoo animals to commercial hunting facilities, see John Grandy, "Zoos: A Critical Reevaluation," *HSUS News*, summer 1992; John Grandy, "Captive Breeding in Zoos: Destructive Programs in Need of Change," *HSUS News*, summer 1989; and Michael Winikoff, "Blowing the Lid Off of Canned Hunts," *HSUS News*, summer 1994.

50. For a description and discussion of rodeo practices, see Gail Tabor, "They Chute Horses, Don't They: Making Sense of Rodeo Rules," *Arizona Republic*, February 5, 1993, at B5; Humane Society of the United States, *Bucking the Myth: The Cruel Reality of Rodeos* (Washington, D.C.: Humane Society of the United States, 1995); Humane Society of the United States, *Fact Sheet: Rodeos* (Washington, D.C.: Humane Society of the United States, 1993).

51. *See* "Breakdowns," *Sports Illustrated*, November 1, 1993, at 80.

52. This information was provided by the Greyhound Protection League.

53. Quoted in Joel S. Newman and Neal D. Barnard, *The Military's Animal Experiments: A Report from the Physicians Committee for Responsible Medicine* (Washington, D.C.: PCRM, 1994), at 4.

54. Jill Donner, "Lassie Stay Home," *Variety*, May 2, 1989, in *Review of Agriculture's Enforcement of the Animal Welfare Act, Specifically of Animals Used in Exhibitions*, *supra* note 47, at 191 (excerpted as attachment to statement of Bob Barker).

55. Most of this material was obtained from the Humane Society of the United States, the Coalition to Abolish the Fur Trade, and World Animal Net.

Chapter 2

1. For a discussion of the concern about vivisection in England in the early 1900s, see Coral Lansbury, *The Old Brown Dog: Women, Workers, and Vivisection in Edwardian England* (Madison: University of Wisconsin Press, 1985). For a discussion of the concern about vivisection in the modern American animal rights movement, see Susan Sperling, *Animal Liberators* (Berkeley and Los Angeles: University of California Press, 1988).

2. *See generally* Gary L. Francione, *Rain Without Thunder: The Ideology of the Animal Rights Movement* (Philadelphia: Temple University Press, 1996).

3. Foundation for Biomedical Research, *Understanding the Use of Animals in Biomedical Research* (Washington, D.C.: Foundation for Biomedical Research, 1992), at 5–6, 12; Foundation for Biomedical Research, *Caring for Laboratory Animals* (Washington, D.C.: Foundation for Biomedical Research, 1996), at 1.

4. The "three R's" were formulated by W.M.S. Russell and R. L. Burch in *The Principles of Humane Experimental Technique* (Springfield, Ill.: Charles C. Thomas Publishers, 1959).

5. *See* Bernard E. Rollin, *The Unheeded Cry: Animal Consciousness, Animal Pain and Science* (Oxford: Oxford University Press, 1990).

6. U.S. Congress, Office of Technology Assessment, Rep. No. OTA–BA–274, *Alternatives to Animal Use in Research, Testing, and Education* (Washington, D.C.: U.S. Government Printing Office, 1986), at 10.

7. The branch of the USDA responsible for enforcement of the Act is the Animal and Plant Health Inspection Service (APHIS).

8. Andrew Rowan, who is a moderate critic of animal experimentation, claims that more than 70 million animals are used annually. Andrew N. Rowan, *Of Mice, Models, and Men: A Critical Evaluation of Animal Research* (Albany: State University of New York Press, 1984), at 67–70.

9. This statement is taken from the Charles River website.

10. Quoted in Judith Reitman, *Stolen for Profit: How the Medical Establishment Is Funding a National Pet-Theft Conspiracy* (New York: Pharos Books, 1992), at 167.

11. *See generally id.* It was the theft of pets for medical research that motivated and was the focus of the original Laboratory Animal Welfare Act of 1966, which became known as the federal Animal Welfare Act. Pet theft has continued to be a focus of the Act. *See* Gary L. Francione, *Animals, Property, and the Law* (Philadelphia: Temple University Press, 1995), at 190–200.

12. For a general discussion of legal regulations concerning the use of animals in experiments, see Francione, *Animals, Property, and the Law, supra* note 11, at 165–250. *See also* Chapter 3 *infra.*

13. Dani P. Bolognesi, "A Live-Virus AIDS Vaccine?" 6 *Journal of NIH Research* (1994), at 55, 59–62.

14. E. Northrup, "Men, Mice, and Smoking," in *Science Looks at Smoking* (New York: Coward-McCann, 1957), at 133.

15. *See* P. E. Enterline, "Asbestos and Cancer," in Leon Gordis, ed., *Epidemiology and Health Risk Assessments* (New York: Oxford University Press, 1988).

16. Quoted in Robert Sharpe, *The Cruel Deception: The Use of Animals in Medical Research* (London: Thorsons Publishing Group, 1988), at 77.

17. U.S. General Accounting Office, *Cancer Patient Survival: What Progress Has Been Made?* (Washington, D.C.: General Accounting Office, 1987), at 25.

18. Jerome Leavitt, "The Case for Understanding the Molecular Nature of Cancer: Some Recent Findings and Their Implications," *Medical News,* September 9, 1985, at 89.

19. *See generally* John R. Paul, *A History of Poliomyelitis* (New Haven: Yale University Press, 1971).

20. R. T. Domingo, C. Fries, P. Sawyer, and S. Wesolowski, "Peripheral Arterial Reconstruction: Transplantation of Autologous Veins," 9 *Transactions of the American Society of Artificial Internal Organs* 305 (1963).

21. A number of organizations composed of physicians, scientists, and other health care professionals are questioning the scientific efficacy of animal experiments. One such organization is the Medical Research Modernization Committee, which regularly publishes volumes of essays in which scientists and other health professionals critique animal use from a scientific point of view. *See, e.g.,* Medical Research Modernization Committee, *Perspectives on Medical Research,* vol. 3 (New York: Medical Research Modernization Committee, 1990) (essays concerning animal use and muscular dystrophy, degenerative neurological diseases, psychological research, animal cognition, vaccine production and control, cold injury, and basic research).

22. Frank A. Beach, "Conceptual Issues in Behavioral Endocrinology," in Ronald Gandelman, ed., *Autobiographies in Experimental Psychology* (London: Lawrence Erlbaum Associates, 1985), at 5.

23. Kenneth M. Rosenberg, "Effects of Pre- and Postpubertal Castration and Testosterone on Pup-Killing Behavior in the Male Rat," 13 *Physiology & Behavior* 159 (1974).

24. Michael B. Fortuna, "Elicitation of Aggression by Food Deprivation in Olfactory Bulbectomized Male Mice," 5 *Physiological Psychology* 327 (1977).

25. Klaus A. Miczek, James T. Winslow, and Joseph. F. DeBold, "Heightened Aggressive Behavior by Animals Interacting with Alcohol-Treated Conspecifics: Studies with Mice, Rats, and Squirrel Monkeys," 20 (3) *Pharmacology Biochemistry & Behavior* 349 (1984).

26. Gary P. Moberg and Valeria A. Wood, "Neonatal Stress in Lambs: Behavioral and Physiological Responses," 14 *Developmental Psychobiology* 155 (1981).

27. Michael N. Guile and N. Bruce McCutcheon, "Prepared Responses and Gastric Lesions in Rats," 8 *Physiological Psychology* 480 (1980).

28. Peter D. Spear, Lillian Tong, and Carol Sawyer, "Effects of Binocular Deprivation on Responses of Cells in Cats' Lateral Suprasylvian Visual Cortex," 49 *Journal of Neurophysiology* 366 (1983).

29. Michael M. Merzenich et al., "Somatosensory Cortical Map Changes Following Digit Amputation in Adult Monkeys," 224 *Journal of Comparative Neurology* 591 (1984).

30. Charles V. Voorhees, "Long-Term Effects of Developmental Exposure to Cocaine on Learned and Unlearned Behaviors," in Cora Lee Wetherington, Vincent L. Smeriglio, and Loretta P. Finnegan, eds., *Behavioral Studies of Drug-Exposed Offspring: Methodological Issues in Human and Animal Research* (Washington, D.C.: U.S. Department of Health and Human Services, National Institutes of Health, 1996), at 3–52.

31. Vincent P. Dole, "On the Relevance of Animal Models to Alcoholism in Humans," 10 *Alcoholism Clinical and Experimental Research* 361 (1986).

32. For a review, discussion, and bibliography of maternal-deprivation experiments, including Harlow's, see Murry J. Cohen, *A Critique of Maternal Deprivation Monkey Experiments at the State University of New York Health Science Center* (New York: Medical Research Modernization Committee, 1996); Martin L. Stephens, *Maternal Deprivation Experiments in Psychology: A Critique of Animal Models* (Jenkintown, Pa.: The American Anti-Vivisection Society, 1986).

33. For a review of learned helplessness experiments, including those of Seligman, see Kathryn Hahner, "Learned Helplessness: A Critique of Research and Theory," in Stephen R. Kaufman and Betsy Todd, eds., *Perspectives on Animal Research*, vol. 1 (New York: Medical Research Modernization Committee, 1989), at 1.

34. *See* U.S. General Accounting Office, *Army Biomedical Research: Concerns About Performance of Brain-Wound Research* (Washington, D.C.: General Accounting Office, 1990).

35. For a description and discussion of some of the uses of animals in military experiments, see Joel S. Newman and Neal D. Barnard, *The Military's Animal Experiments: A Report from the Physicians Committee for Responsible Medicine* (Washington, D.C.: PCRM, 1994).

36. *See, e.g.,* Animal Welfare Institute, *Beyond the Laboratory Door* (Washington, D.C.: Animal Welfare Institute, 1985); Dallas Pratt, *Alternatives to Pain in Experiments on Animals* (New York: Argus Archives, 1980); Sharpe, *The Cruel Deception, supra* note 16, at 271–77.

37. Foundation for Biomedical Research, *Understanding the Use of Animals in Biomedical Research, supra* note 3, at 12, 13.

38. For a discussion of these and similar cases, see Francione, *Animals, Property, and the Law, supra* note 11, at 222–24. For a discussion of animal care standards at various universities and corporations, see Animal Welfare Institute, *Beyond the Laboratory Door, supra* note 36, at 1–93.

39. Mary T. Phillips, "Savages, Drunks and Lab Animals: The Researcher's Perception of Pain," 1 *Society and Animals* 61, 76 (1993).

40. For a description and discussion of "routine" laboratory procedures, see A. A. Tuffery, ed., *Laboratory Animals: An Introduction for New Experimenters* (New York: Wiley-Interscience, 1987).

41. For a more detailed discussion of the University of Pennsylvania case, see Francione, *Animals, Property, and the Law, supra* note 11, at 178–83.

42. *See generally* Alix Fano, *Lethal Laws: Animal Testing, Human Health and Environmental Policy* (London: Zed Books Ltd., 1997); Sharpe, *The Cruel Deception, supra* note 16.

43. Sharpe, *The Cruel Deception, supra* note 16, at 101.

44. *See* Fano, *Lethal Laws, supra* note 42, at 75.

45. F. E. Freeberg, D. T. Hooker, and J. F. Griffith, "Correlation of Animal Eye Test Data with Human Experience for Household Products: An Update," 5 *Journal of Toxicology—Cutaneous and Ocular Toxicology* 115 (1986).

46. *See* L. B. Lave, F. K. Ennever, H. S. Rosenkranz, and G. S. Omenn, "Information Value of the Rodent Bioassay," 336 *Nature* 631 (1988).

47. D. Salsburg, "The Lifetime Feeding Study of Mice and Rats: An Examination of Its Validity as a Bioassay for Human Carcinogens," 3 *Fundamental and Applied Toxicology* 63 (1983).

48. Gillette Company, *1994 Report on Research with Laboratory Animals.*

49. Madhusree Mukerjee, "Trends in Animal Research," *Scientific American,* February 1997, at 93. The figure of 5.7 million animals used for educational purposes comes from Mukerjee's article.

50. The right of a student to object to vivisection or dissection in the classroom is protected by a variety of doctrines under federal and state law. *See* Gary L. Francione and Anna E. Charlton, *Vivisection and Dissection in the Classroom: A Guide to Conscientious Objection* (Jenkintown, Pa: The American Anti-Vivisection Society, 1992).

Chapter 3

1. For a discussion of how the status of animals as property determines the application of animal welfare laws, see Gary L. Francione, *Animals, Property, and the Law* (Philadelphia: Temple University Press, 1995). *See also* Gary L. Francione, *Rain Without Thunder: The Ideology of the Animal Rights Movement* (Philadelphia: Temple University Press, 1996).

2. Jeremy Rifkin, *Beyond Beef: The Rise and Fall of the Cattle Culture* (New York: Dutton Books, 1992), at 28.

3. U.S. Const. Amend. V. *See* Francione, *Animals, Property, and the Law, supra* note 1, at 46–48.

4. *See* Francione, *Animals, Property, and the Law, supra* note 1, at 38–40. *See also* Chapter 5 *infra*.

5. *See* John Locke, *Two Treatises of Government*, ed. Peter Laslett (Cambridge: Cambridge University Press, 1988). For more discussion of Locke's theory of property rights and its application to animals, see Francione, *Animals, Property, and the Law, supra* note 1, at 38–42. For a general discussion of Locke's theory of rights, see A. John Simmons, *The Lockean Theory of Rights* (Princeton: Princeton University Press, 1992).

6. Genesis 1:26 (New King James Version).

7. Locke's notion of a natural right is to be distinguished from the concept of a basic right as discussed in the Introduction *supra* and in Chapter 4 *infra*.

8. It is certainly questionable whether Locke was correct to interpret God's grant of dominion over animals as a license to dominate and exploit animals. *See* Chapter 5 *infra*.

9. John Locke, *An Essay Concerning the True Original, Extent, and End of Civil Government* ("Second Treatise"), § 26, lines 10–12, in Locke, *Two Treatises of Government, supra* note 5, at 286–87 (emphasis omitted).

10. *Id.* at § 30, lines 16–18, at 290 (emphasis omitted).

11. *Id.* at lines 1–4, at 289 (emphasis omitted).

12. *Id.* at § 6, line 18, at 271.

13. John Locke, "Some Thoughts Concerning Education" [1693], *reprinted in* Paul A. B. Clarke and Andrew Linzey, eds., *Political Theory and Animal Rights* (London: Pluto Press, 1990), at 119–20.

14. John Locke, *The False Principles and Foundation of Sir Robert Filmer, and his Followers, are Detected and Overthrown* ("First Treatise"), § 92, lines 1–5, in Locke, *Two Treatises of Government, supra* note 5, at 209.

15. 2 William Blackstone, *Commentaries on the Laws of England*, *2 (Chicago: Callaghan, 1872), at 329.

16. *Id.*, *2–3 (quoting Genesis), at 330.

17. 1 William Blackstone, *Commentaries on the Laws of England*, *139 (Chicago: Callaghan, 1872), at 89.

18. Godfrey Sandys-Winsch, *Animal Law* (London: Shaw & Sons, 1978), at 1. It should be noted that the view that animals are things without moral status is certainly not restricted to Western liberal political thought or other traditions that are particularly concerned with private property. For example, Marx, who was critical of private property, rejected the notion that animals had any significance beyond use for humans. *See* Chapter 5 *infra*. This is not to say, however, that those who accept a Marxist or leftist perspective on economic and political matters necessarily reject the moral significance of animals. *See, e.g.*, Ted Benton, *Natural Relations: Ecology, Animal Rights and Social Justice* (London: Verso, 1993); Barbara Noske, *Beyond Boundaries: Humans and Animals* (Montreal: Black Rose Books, 1997).

19. T. G. Field-Fisher, *Animals and the Law* (London: Universities Federation for Animal Welfare, 1964), at 19.

20. Jeremy Waldron, *The Right to Private Property* (Oxford: Clarendon Press, 1988), at 27 (footnote omitted).

21. For a further discussion of specific exemptions to anticruelty laws, see Francione, *Animals, Property, and the Law, supra* note 1, at 139–42. It should be noted that many states have laws that concern animals apart from general anticruelty statutes, such as laws regulating animal slaughter.

22. Cal. Penal Code § 599c (Deering 1999).

23. Del. Code Ann. tit. 11, § 1325(b)(4) (1998).

24. Ky. Rev. Stat. Ann. § 525.130(1)(c) (Baldwin 1998).

25. *Id.* at §§ 525.130(2)(a-d) & (3).

26. Md. Code Ann., Cruelty to Animals § 59(c) (1999).

27. Neb. Rev. Stat. § 28–1013 (1999).

28. Or. Rev. Stat. § 167.335(4) & 167.310(2) (1997). The Oregon statute also exempts rodeos, hunting, trapping, and other activities, subject to there not being gross negligence on the part of the defendant. This would suggest that if a defendant followed "accepted practice" but did so negligently, there can be no criminal liability. *See* note 56 *infra*.

29. 18 Pa. Cons. Stat. Ann. §§ 5511(Q) (1999).

30. *See, e.g.,* Del. Code Ann. tit. 11, § 1325(a) (1998).

31. 7 U.S.C. §§ 2121–2159 (1999). For a discussion of the regulation of the Animal Welfare Act, see Francione, *Animals, Property, and the Law, supra* note 1, at 165–249; Francione, *Rain Without Thunder, supra* note 1, at 87–95. *See also* Chapter 2 *supra*.

32. 7 U.S.C. §§ 2143 (6)(A)(i) & (6)(A)(iii) (1999). Defenders of the Animal Welfare Act often argue that the act was improved in 1985 when the law was amended to require that each research facility have an animal care committee to approve animal experiments conducted at the facility. The problem is that these committees were explicitly prohibited from undertaking any ethical merit review of experiments. Indeed, the committee may take no action unless the experimenter is violating basic rules of animal husbandry or is inflicting pain and suffering under circumstances that threaten the production of reliable scientific data. *See* Francione, *Animals, Property, and the Law, supra* note 1, at 203–6.

33. For a further discussion of instances in which courts exempt institutional exploitation from the scope of anticruelty statutes even in the absence of explicit statutory exemptions, see Francione, *Animals, Property, and the Law, supra* note 1, at 142–56.

34. *Cinadr v. State*, 300 S.W. 64, 64–65 (Tex. Crim. App. 1927).

35. *Murphy v. Manning*, 2 Ex. D. 307, 313–14 (1877) (Cleasby, B.).

36. *Lewis v. Fermor*, 18 Q.B.D. 532, 534 (1887) (Day, J.).

37. *Murphy v. Manning*, 2 Ex. D. 307, 314 (1877) (Cleasby, B.). It should be noted that in *Manning* the court held that cutting the combs of cocks, a painful procedure, violated the anticruelty law. The court noted, however, that the primary reason for cutting the combs was to use the animals for cockfighting, which was illegal.

38. *People ex. rel. Freel v. Downs*, 136 N.Y.S. 440, 445 (City Magis. Ct. 1911).

39. *Bowyer v. Morgan*, 95 L.T.R. 27 (K.B. 1906). In *Humane Society v. Lyng*, 633 F.Supp. 480 (W.D.N.Y. 1986), the court found that branding an animal on the face with a hot iron was not acceptable, but this practice was not part of accepted animal husbandry.

40. *Lewis v. Fermor*, 18 Q.B.D. 532, 532 (1887).

41. *Id.* at 534 (Day, J.).

42. *Id.* at 537 (Willis, J.).

43. *Callaghan v. Society for Prevention of Cruelty to Animals*, 16 L.R. Ir. 325, 330 (C.P.D. 1885) (Morris, C. J) (quoting *Murphy v. Manning*, 2 Ex. D. 307, 314 [1877]).

44. *Id.* at 332–33 (Harrison, J.).

45. *Id.* at 334 (Murphy, J.).

46. *Ford v. Wiley*, 23 Q.B.D. 203, 209 (1889) (Coleridge, C. J.).

47. *Id.* at 215.

48. *Id.* at 219 (Hawkins, J.).

49. The court in *Ford* interpreted *Fermor* as supporting the proposition that an honest but unreasonable belief that the infliction of suffering on an animal is justified constitutes a defense to a charge of cruelty. *See id.* at 224 (1889). The court in *Ford* maintained that at the very least the defendant must have an honest belief based on reasonable grounds; that is, his conduct must be reasonable under the circumstances. Such an interpretation of *Fermor* as not requiring an honest belief to be objectively reasonable as well is unsound for two reasons. First, whether a belief is considered to be reasonable depends on the prevailing practice with respect to the conduct that is the subject of the belief. The practice at issue in *Fermor* was explicitly recognized by the court to be widespread in the region at the time. The widespread nature of the practice supported the view that Fermor had a reasonable belief that the procedure was necessary to render the animal fit for the purposes of the owner. Second, *Fermor* explicitly stated that a bona fide belief that the suffering was necessary had to be a reasonable belief and "[t]here was no evidence here to shew that the question whether or not the operation is beneficial is removed from the category of legitimate doubt." *Fermor*, 18 Q.B.D. at 536 (Willis, J.).

The problem in any event is that a requirement that conduct toward animals be "reasonable" in an "objective" sense does not provide much protection for animals. Indeed, an objective standard does nothing more than establish the "industry" standard as an external measure against which the defendant's conduct is measured. *See, e.g., Hall v. RSPCA*, unreported, Queen's Bench Division (CO/2876/92), November 11, 1993. And the industry standard may allow for the infliction of terrible suffering, as is the case in modern intensive agriculture. The British lawyer and animal welfare advocate Mike Radford claims that "the test of 'unnecessary suffering'. . . has much to commend it," even though he admits that "animals may be disadvantaged, particularly in commercial situations, where the accepted standard applied to an activity (what the reasonable person would regard as acceptable) falls below that of best practice." Mike Radford, "'Unnecessary Suffering': The Cornerstone of Animal Protection Legislation Considered," [1999] *Criminal Law Review* 702, 712. Putting aside the fact that Radford fails to appreciate that the common law has always regarded the accepted standard to be "best practice," even defenders of the "unnecessary suffering" standard such as himself seem on some level to appreciate that the standard is without meaningful content when applied to the use of animals as economic commodities.

50. *Roberts v. Ruggiero*, unreported, Queen's Bench Division, April 3, 1985.

51. *State v. Crichton*, 4 Ohio Dec. 481 (Police Ct. 1892).

52. *Id.* at 482.

53. *Commonwealth v. Anspach*, 188 A. 98 (Pa. Super. Ct. 1936).

54. *Taub v. State*, 463 A.2d 819, 821 (Md. 1983). At the time, the Maryland statute provided that "no person shall be liable for criminal prosecution for normal human activities to which the infliction of pain to an animal is purely incidental and unavoidable." Shortly after the *Taub* decision, the Maryland legislature amended the state anticruelty statute to cover all animals, including animals used in experiments. Nevertheless, the *Taub* decision demonstrates how far a court will go in reading in an exemption not explicitly contained in the statute. For a further discussion of the *Taub* case, including further litigation involving the animals involved in Taub's experiments, see Francione, *Animals, Property, and the Law, supra* note 1, at 72–90, 150, 179, 230.

55. For further discussion of the requirement of a culpable mental state, see Francione, *Animals, Property, and the Law, supra* note 1, at 135–39.

56. If an anticruelty statute does not require one of these mental states, then the statute may be said to impose strict liability, or liability without fault. *See id.* at 135. Such a characterization would be inaccurate, however, since even if the statute does not specify a particular mental state, it usually prohibits only "unreasonable" or "unnecessary" suffering and this usually involves some inquiry into the actor's motivation, in order to ascertain whether the animal suffering was wholly gratuitous or whether it was inflicted as part of an institutionalized use of animals. Moreover, many argue that mere negligence is not sufficient for criminal liability, which requires at least criminal negligence, or a "gross deviation" from the conduct of a reasonable person.

57. *Regalado v. United States*, 572 A.2d 416, 420 (D.C. 1990).

58. *Id.* at 421.

59. *State v. Fowler*, 205 S.E. 2d 749, 751 (N.C. Ct. App. 1974). It is interesting to note in passing that the dog in question was a male with a name, Ike; nevertheless, the court held that we could ignore Ike's interest in humane treatment as long as Fowler administered the punishment in order to train *it* and not merely to torture *it*. On the one hand, we explicitly acknowledge that Ike has characteristics that distinguish him from a *thing*, an *it*. On the other hand, we refer to *him* as *it*. Our moral confusion about animals manifests itself even in our language.

Fowler represents a view long accepted in the interpretation of anticruelty cases. The beating of an animal if "solely for the purpose of training, however severe it might be . . . would not be malicious, within the meaning of the statute, and therefore it would be no offense." *State v. Avery*, 44 N.H. 392, 397 (1862).

60. *Callaghan v. Society for Prevention of Cruelty to Animals*, 16 L.R. Ir. 325, 335 (C.P.D. 1885).

61. *Ford v. Wiley*, 23 Q.B.D. 203, 221–22 (1889) (Hawkins, J.).

62. *Commonwealth v. Barr*, 44 Pa. C. 284, 288 (Lancaster County Ct. 1916).

63. *Commonwealth v. Vonderheid*, 28 Pa. D. & C.2d 101, 106 (Columbia County

Ct. 1962). For further discussion of the relationship between human slavery and the institution of animal property, see Chapter 4 *infra*.

64. For further discussion of penalty and enforcement difficulties, including standing, see Francione, *Animals, Property, and the Law, supra* note 1, at 65–90, 156–58.

65. *See, e.g.,* "2 Teens Convicted, But Not of Felony, for Killing Cats," *Chicago Tribune*, November 8, 1997, at 3; "2 Guilty of Misdemeanors in Cat Slayings," *Washington Post*, November 8, 1997, at A16.

66. For an argument that animal welfare laws do not establish rights for animals, see Francione, *Animals, Property, and the Law, supra* note 1, at 91–114.

67. In Britain, private prosecutions, or criminal prosecutions brought by private parties rather than the state, are more common.

68. *See* Francione, *Animals, Property, and the Law, supra* note 1, at 65–90. In a 1998 decision, a federal court found that a visitor to a zoo who objected to what he regarded as the inhumane confinement of primates could challenge government regulations for failing to implement congressional directives requiring that primates be provided with an environment that promoted their psychological well-being. *See Animal Legal Defense Fund v. Glickman*, 154 F.3d 426 (D.C. Cir. 1998) (en banc), *cert. denied*, 119 S. Ct. 1454 (1999). A later proceeding affirmed the zoo visitor's standing to challenge the regulations, but upheld the validity of the regulations themselves as establishing the minimum standards required by statute while leaving flexibility for the professional judgment of veterinarians. *See Animal Legal Defense Fund v. Glickman*, 204 F.3d 229 (D.C. Cir. 2000). It is as yet unclear as to what effect this decision will have on the ability of humans to challenge federal regulations concerning animals used in experiments and for other purposes. Moreover, it is important to understand that standing to sue was predicated on a human's having an "aesthetic interest" in the animals, who, as property, can have no independent standing to assert their interests in court.

69. *Commonwealth v. Lufkin*, 89 Mass. (7 Allen) 579, 581 (1863). For a discussion of situations in which courts find or uphold violations of anticruelty laws, see Francione, *Animals, Property, and the Law, supra* note 1, at 137, 153–56.

70. *State v. Tweedie*, 444 A.2d 855 (R.I. 1982).

71. *In re William G.*, 447 A.2d 493 (Md. Ct. Spec. App. 1982).

72. *Motes v. State*, 375 S.E.2d 893 (Ga. Ct. App. 1988).

73. *Tuck v. United States*, 477 A.2d 1115 (D.C. 1984).

74. *People v. Voelker*, 172 Misc.2d 564 (N.Y. Crim. Ct. 1997).

75. *LaRue v. State*, 478 So.2d 13 (Ala. Crim. App. 1985).

76. *State v. Schott*, 384 N.W.2d 620 (Neb. 1986).

77. *See* Francione, *Animals, Property, and the Law, supra* note 1, at 211–13. As I mentioned in note 68, the regulations promulgated by the USDA were upheld with respect to primates exhibited at a zoo. *See Animal Legal Defense Fund v. Glickman*, 204 F.3d 229 (D.C. Cir. 2000).

78. Robert Garner, *Animals, Politics and Morality* (Manchester: Manchester University Press, 1993), at 103.

79. *Humane Methods of Slaughter Act of 1977: Hearing on H.R. 1464 Before the Subcomm. on Livestock and Grains of the Comm. on Agric.*, 95th Cong., 2d Sess. 35 (1978) (statement of Emily Gleockler). For an excellent description of the slaughtering process, see Gail A. Eisnitz, *Slaughterhouse: The Shocking Story of Greed, Neglect, and*

Inhumane Treatment Inside the U.S. Meat Industry (Amherst, N.Y.: Prometheus Press, 1997). For a discussion of animal welfare laws concerning humane slaughter, see Francione, *Rain Without Thunder, supra* note 1, at 95–102. It should be noted that if we did not accept that animals were conscious of pain, we would have no need of laws that require that animals be rendered unconscious before being killed.

80. Garner, *Animals, Politics and Morality, supra* note 78, at 234. *See generally* Francione, *Rain Without Thunder, supra* note 1.

81. *See* Francione, *Rain Without Thunder, supra* note 1, at 190–219.

82. *Miller v. State*, 63 S.E.571, 573 (Ga. Ct. App. 1909).

83. *Richardson v. Fairbanks N. Star Borough*, 705 P.2d 454, 456 (Alaska 1985).

84. *See, e.g., Knowles Animal Hosp., Inc. v. Wills*, 360 So.2d 37 (Fla. Dist. Ct. App. 1978) (a dog placed on a heating pad and kept there for a day and a half died of severe burns). *See* Francione, *Animals, Property, and the Law, supra* note 1, at 57–63.

85. *See, e.g., Jankoski v. Preiser Animal Hosp., Ltd.*, 510 N.E.2d 1084 (Ill. App. Ct. 1987). *See also* Francione, *Animals, Property, and the Law, supra* note 1, at 57–63.

86. *Farmer and Stockbreeder*, January 30, 1962, quoted in Jim Mason and Peter Singer, *Animal Factories*, rev. ed. (New York: Harmony Books, 1990), at 1.

87. J. Byrnes, "Raising Pigs by the Calendar at Maplewood Farm," *Hog Farm Management*, September 1976, at 30, quoted in *id.*

88. "Farm Animals of the Future," *Agricultural Research* (Washington, D.C.: U.S. Department of Agriculture), April 1989, at 4, quoted in *id.*

Chapter 4

1. The requirement that moral theories incorporate the principle of equal consideration and reflect universal judgments rather than self-interest or the interests of "special" or elite groups has a long history, from the Golden Rule attributed to Moses to the commandment of Jesus to "love thy neighbor as thyself" to modern ethical theory, whether utilitarian, deontological, or existential. Indeed, it is generally agreed that equal consideration and the universal applicability of moral judgments are inseparable from the very concept of moral theory. *See* Peter Singer, *Practical Ethics*, 2d ed. (Cambridge: Cambridge University Press, 1993), at 10–15.

2. It is, however, difficult for Caucasians, and particularly for Caucasian males, to argue that they have not benefited from past discrimination against people of color and women.

3. Peter Singer, *Animal Liberation*, 2d ed. (New York: New York Review of Books, 1990), at 5. As we will see in Chapter 6, Bentham's theory, which is adopted by Singer, is somewhat confused in its application of the principle of equal consideration.

4. There may be disagreements about the exact meaning of "slavery," or how slavery differs from other conditions, such as serfdom, indentured servitude, or conscription. *See* R. M. Hare, "What Is Wrong with Slavery," 8 *Philosophy and Public Affairs* 103 (1979). For purposes of applying the principle of equal consideration to animal interests, it is sufficient to acknowledge that animals have interests in not being used in the ways that we use them, and that we do not use humans for such purposes.

5. For a discussion concerning the status of slaves as property, see Gary L. Francione, *Animals, Property, and the Law* (Philadelphia: Temple University Press, 1995), at 110–12.

6. Daniel J. Flanigan, "Criminal Procedure in Slave Trials in the Antebellum South," in Kermit L. Hall, ed., *The Law of American Slavery* (New York: Garland Publishing, 1987), at 191.

7. Chancellor Harper, "Slavery in the Light of Social Ethics," in E. N. Elliott, ed., *Cotton Is King, and Pro-Slavery Arguments* (Augusta, Ga.: Pritchard, Abbott & Loomis, 1860), at 559.

8. Stanley Elkins and Eric McKitrick, "Institutions and the Law of Slavery: Slavery in Capitalist and Non-Capitalist Cultures," in Hall, *The Law of American Slavery, supra* note 6, at 115 (quoting William Goodell, *The American Slave Code in Theory and Practice* [New York, 1853], 180).

9. *State v. Mann*, 13 N.C. (2 Dev.) 263, 267 (1829).

10. Elkins and McKitrick, "Institutions and the Law of Slavery," *supra* note 8, at 115 (quoting Thomas R. R. Cobb, *An Inquiry into the Law of Slavery in the United States of America* [Philadelphia, 1858], 98).

11. A. Leon Higginbotham, Jr., *In the Matter of Color* (New York: Oxford University Press, 1978), at 36.

12. Alan Watson, *Slave Law in the Americas* (Athens: University of Georgia Press, 1989), at xiv and 31 (quoting Justinian's *Institutes*).

13. *State v. Hale*, 9 N.C. (2 Hawks) 582, 585–86 (1823).

14. David Brion Davis, *The Problem of Slavery in Western Culture* (Ithaca: Cornell University Press, 1966), at 58.

15. Richard A. Posner, *The Problems of Jurisprudence* (Cambridge: Harvard University Press, 1990), at 379–80 (footnote omitted).

16. Indeed, a recent book argues that despite the universal moral condemnation of slavery, it persists throughout the world. *See* Kevin Bales, *Disposable People: New Slavery in the Global Economy* (Berkeley and Los Angeles: University of California Press, 1999). Whether Bales' claims are accurate or not, the fact remains that the universal community condemns slavery as a violation of the basic right of all humans to be treated as persons.

17. Many people also object to the supposedly consensual sale of organs by their "owners," as well as the supposedly voluntary participation in biomedical experiments, because the objectors view these as actions compelled by economic deprivation. Irrespective of the merits of these objections, it is clear that there is general opposition to chattel slavery or the property status of humans.

18. The concern about the instrumental use of human beings is so great that at least some are concerned about the use of fetal tissue for scientific purposes even though no one maintains that fertilized ova and early-term fetuses are sentient. *See* Nicholas Wade, "Scientist at Work: Brigid Hogan; In the Ethics Storm on Human Embryo Research," *New York Times*, September 28, 1999, at F1.

19. *See* Alison Mitchell, "Clinton Regrets 'Clearly Racist' U.S. Study," *New York Times*, May 17, 1997, § 1, at 10.

20. Michael D'Antonio, "Atomic Guinea Pigs," *New York Times*, August 31, 1997, § 6, at 38.

21. *See* Introduction, and particularly notes 17–18 *supra*.

22. Although most Marxist theorists reject rights theory as representing protection of individual interests to the detriment of communal values, Marxist theory abhors slavery and implicitly accepts that humans have the right not to be

treated exclusively as means to the ends of others. Although Marxists may reject as bourgeois certain rights, such as the right to own private property, or rights schemes, such as one that accords humans a right to vote but that denies them a right to health care or education, they must recognize some limits on the interests of the individual that may be sacrificed for the common good. A failure to respect those limits is precisely what led to Stalin's massacre of millions of peasants in the collectivization of Russia in the 1930s. For Marx's views about animals, see Chapter 5 *infra*.

23. Immanuel Kant, *The Metaphysics of Morals*, §§ 6:237–38, trans. and ed. Mary Gregor (Cambridge: Cambridge University Press, 1996), at 30–31. Kant also referred to this pre-political or pre-legal right as a "natural" right.

24. Roger J. Sullivan, *Immanuel Kant's Moral Theory* (Cambridge: Cambridge University Press, 1989), at 248.

25. Henry Shue, *Basic Rights*, 2d ed. (Princeton: Princeton University Press, 1996). Regan uses the concept of basic rights, in *The Case for Animal Rights*, as a right that does not depend on voluntary acts or social institutions, and that is possessed equally by all relevantly similar individuals. *See* Tom Regan, *The Case for Animal Rights* (Berkeley and Los Angeles: University of California Press, 1983), at 266–329. Regan's use of basic rights is not restricted to the basic right not to be treated as a thing, but I believe that his theory of animal rights can be understood as proposing an idea close to the notion of the basic right that Shue uses in the context of human rights and that I use in the context of animal rights. *See* Gary L. Francione, *Rain Without Thunder: The Ideology of the Animal Rights Movement* (Philadelphia: Temple University Press, 1996), at 152–55. Regan does not, however, acknowledge that this basic right may be derived solely from the principle of equal consideration.

26. Shue, *Basic Rights*, *supra* note 25, at 20.

27. *Id.* at 19.

28. *Id.* at 20.

29. *Id.* at 21.

30. For a discussion of the basic right (or equal inherent value) as concerning *inclusion* within the moral community, and as different from the *scope* of rights that a particular human may have, see Gary L. Francione, "Ecofeminism and Animal Rights: A Review of *Beyond Animal Rights: A Feminist Caring Ethic for the Treatment of Animals*," 18 *Women's Rights Law Reporter* 95 (1996). For example, the United States abolished human slavery in 1865, and although the abolition of slavery was tantamount to giving slaves a right not to be treated exclusively as economic commodities (and inclusion in the moral community), abolition did not itself establish the scope of rights that those former slaves would have.

In the context of feminist theory, Drucilla Cornell has made similar arguments about the importance of minimal conditions for the membership of women in the moral community. Cornell argues that it is necessary to provide to women the "minimum degree of individuation" that is necessary "for the equivalent chance to transform [themselves] into individuated beings who can participate in public and political life as equal citizens." Cornell argues that only rights-type protection can provide for these minimum conditions of individuation. Drucilla Cornell, *The Imaginary Domain: Abortion, Pornography and Sexual Harassment* (New York: Routledge, 1995), at

4. Some feminist writers have rejected the concept of rights as inherently patriarchal, a view that I address later. *See* Francione, "Ecofeminism and Animal Rights," *supra*. *See also* Chapter 6, notes 37–39 and accompanying text *infra*.

31. *See* Immanuel Kant, *Grounding for the Metaphysics of Morals*, §§ 428–29, 434–35, trans. James W. Ellington, 3d ed. (Indianapolis: Hackett Publishing, 1993), at 35–36, 40–41; Kant, *The Metaphysics of Morals, supra* note 23, §§ 6:434–35, at 186–87. *See also* Sullivan, *Immanuel Kant's Moral Theory, supra* note 24, at 195–96. Kant maintained that if the interests of humans in not being things was not protected by some notion of inherent moral value, then some humans would be valued in conditional terms exclusively and would, in effect, become nothing more than economic commodities. Kant believed that the concept of the dignity or inherent value of humans was the only way to ensure that humans would be treated as ends in themselves and not merely as means to the ends of others. I do not mean to suggest that Kant was particularly egalitarian; his views about children and women were problematic in several respects, and he restricted moral protection only to rational beings, or those able to understand moral universals. And as we have seen, and will see further in Chapter 5, he excluded animals from the moral community.

32. This is a commonsensical and logical conclusion based on observation of physiological similarity and common evolution. If someone wanted to deny this assertion, the burden should be on her to explain why these humans do not have preferences or desires despite these similarities and despite the fact that we have no problem attributing preferences and desires to normal adult humans even though we have no complete or certain access to minds other than our own.

33. *See* Michael D. Kreger, "History of Zoos," in Marc Bekoff and Carron A. Meaney, eds., *Encyclopedia of Animal Rights and Animal Welfare* (Westport, Conn.: Greenwood Press, 1998), at 369.

34. *Model Penal Code* (Philadelphia: American Law Institute, 1980), § 250 cmt. 1.

35. *Commonwealth v. Turner*, 26 Va. (5 Rand.) 678, 678 (1827).

36. *Id.* at 680.

37. We might say that all sentient beings have a "welfare" that is positively or adversely affected by what happens to the sentient being. The use of this term, however, threatens some confusion given that animal "welfare" laws assume that animals are property and have no protectable interests. *See generally* Francione, *Rain Without Thunder, supra* note 25.

Chapter 5

1. The distinction between an obligation that is owed to an animal and one that merely concerns an animal was discussed in Chapter 1.

2. R. G. Frey, *Interests and Rights: The Case Against Animals* (Oxford: Clarendon Press, 1980), at 82. Frey acknowledges that the "'higher' animals can suffer unpleasant sensations." *Id.* at 170. But he still denies that an animal who can "suffer unpleasant sensations" has an interest in avoiding those unpleasant sensations. Philosopher Donald Davidson makes an argument similar to Frey's. See Donald Davidson, *Inquiries into Truth and Interpretation* (Oxford: Clarendon Press, 1984), at 155–70. This view—that lack of language in animals means that animals cannot

have beliefs or desires and possess no sort of mind whatsoever—is often linked to philosopher Ludwig Wittgenstein (1889–1951). *See, e.g.*, Peter Singer, *Animal Liberation*, 2d ed. (New York: New York Review of Books, 1990), at 14; Bernard E. Rollin, *The Unheeded Cry: Animal Consciousness, Animal Pain and Science* (Oxford: Oxford University Press, 1990), at 137–43. I am grateful to Professor Cora Diamond for pointing out to me that there is nothing in Wittgenstein that supports the view that he regarded animals as Cartesian automatons that were incapable of cognition.

Neurologist Antonio Damasio has argued that language is not required for self-consciousness, including autobiographical or representational self-consciousness. *See infra* text accompanying notes 30–32.

3. Peter Carruthers, *The Animals Issue: Moral Theory in Practice* (Cambridge: Cambridge University Press, 1992), at 171, 194.

4. I will focus only on the religious foundation of modern Western property theory and the status of animals as "inferiors" within that theory. For a discussion of animals in Eastern religious doctrine, see Tom Regan, ed., *Animal Sacrifices* (Philadelphia: Temple University Press, 1986). *See also* Michael Allen Fox, *Deep Vegetarianism* (Philadelphia: Temple University Press, 1999). For example, the doctrine of *ahimsa*, or universal nonviolence, which is reflected in a number of Eastern religions, militates against the treatment of animals as things or commodities.

5. John Locke, *An Essay Concerning the True Original, Extent, and End of Civil Government ("Second Treatise")*, § 6, lines 16–19, in John Locke, *Two Treatises of Government*, ed. Peter Laslett, (Cambridge: Cambridge University Press, 1988), at 271 (emphasis omitted).

6. John Locke, *The False Principles and Foundation of Sir Robert Filmer, and his Followers, are Detected and Overthrown ("First Treatise")*, § 92, lines 1–5, in Locke, *Two Treatises of Government*, *supra* note 5, at 209.

7. Matthew 8:28–34; Mark 5:1–20; Luke 8:26–39 (New King James Version). It must be remembered that Jews were forbidden to eat pork and the swine were, therefore, symbolic of not just animal life but a particularly unclean form of animal life. The prodigal son, during his period of profligacy, was a swineherd. Moreover, Professor Alan Watson maintains that it is probably the case that the episode never occurred because it is unlikely that Jesus was ever in the Decapolis, the Gentile area in which the story is set. Watson argues that certain aspects of the episode, illustrated most clearly in Mark, indicate that it is symbolic of the position that Jesus' mission was not to the Gentiles. For example, the evil spirits ask Jesus not to send them out of the (Gentile) area and to cast them in unclean animals. For Watson, this indicates that the Gentiles wish to remain unclean and are hostile to Jesus' ministry. The formerly possessed man, a Gentile, seeks to join Jesus but Jesus rejects the offer because he does not want a Gentile among his disciples. *See* Watson, "Jesus and the Gerasene/Gadarene Demoniac (Mark 5:1–20)" (forthcoming).

8. Saint Augustine, *City of God*, bk. 1, chap. 20, trans. Henry Bettenson (Harmondsworth: Penguin, 1984), at 32.

9. Saint Thomas Aquinas, *Summa Contra Gentiles*, bk. 3, chap. 112, in Anton C. Pegis, ed., *Basic Writings of Saint Thomas Aquinas*, vol. 2 (New York: Random House, 1944), at 222.

10. For a discussion of the equation of "dominion" with "domination," see Jim Mason, *An Unnatural Order: Uncovering the Roots of Our Domination of Nature and Each Other* (New York: Simon & Schuster, 1993).

11. *See, e.g.,* Andrew Linzey, *Christianity and the Rights of Animals* (New York: Crossroad, 1987).

12. Genesis 1:29–30 (New King James Version) (emphases omitted). Even Saint Thomas Aquinas accepted the view that humans did not eat animals in the Garden of Eden.

13. Genesis 3:17–19 (New King James Version) (emphases omitted).

14. For example, in the story of Cain and Abel, the sons of Adam and Eve, Cain was a "tiller of the ground" and Abel was a "keeper of sheep." Cain offered God a sacrifice of his fruit; Abel offered a sacrifice of his animals. God "respected Abel and his offering, but He did not respect Cain and his offering." *Id.* at 4:4–5. Cain became angry and killed his brother, and God cursed Cain, making him a "fugitive and a vagabond." We are not told that there was any difference in the personal moral integrity of the two men offering the sacrifices, yet God not only approved of animal sacrifices; he disapproved of the sacrifice of the fruit. This would indicate that God regarded the killing of an animal as something that was not only permissible, but was a desirable exercise of human dominion over animals.

Another example—and the most important portion of Genesis for our purposes—is the story of Noah. It is in this context that God made a new covenant with humans and explicitly allowed humans to eat animals. When God decided to destroy the world with a flood, he instructed Noah to build an ark and to place both clean and unclean animals on the ark. After the flood waters receded, "Noah built an altar to the Lord, and took of every clean animal and of every clean bird, and offered burnt offerings on the altar. And the Lord smelled a soothing aroma." *Id.* at 8:20–21. As part of God's covenant with Noah never again to destroy the world with a flood, God blessed Noah and his sons, enjoining them to "[b]e fruitful and multiply, and fill the earth." God added, "And the fear of you and the dread of you shall be on every beast of the earth, on every bird of the air, on all that move on the earth, and on all the fish of the sea. They are given into your hand. Every moving thing that lives shall be food for you. I have given you all things, even as the green herbs." *Id.* at 9:1–2. Note that the sacrifice of the animals is, as in the story of Cain and Abel, something that God found not only acceptable but desirable. Note also that God's blessing of Noah—"Be fruitful and multiply, and fill the earth"—was almost identical to God's initial blessing of Adam and Eve, but this time God very explicitly indicated that humankind need not limit itself to the herbs and trees that God spoke of earlier in Genesis. This suggests that the new covenant made by God with Noah is, at least in part, intended to clarify or redefine the nature of the human/animal relationship. God rewards Noah's obedience by allowing him to kill animals for food.

15. For a discussion of animal rights as consistent with religious beliefs, see Chapter 7 *infra*.

16. Deuteronomy 25:4 (New King James Version).

17. Proverbs 12:10 (New King James Version) (emphasis omitted).

18. Isaiah 1:11, 11:6, 9 (New King James Version).

19. *See e.g.*, Exodus 21 (New King James Version).

20. Genesis 9:25 (New King James Version).

21. John Rankin, "Letter IX," in William H. Peas and Jane H. Peas, eds., *The Antislavery Argument* (Indianapolis: Bobbs-Merrill, 1965), at 118–23. It should be noted that in the early church, the curse of Canaan was "regarded as an explanation of slavery, but not of blacks, simply because slavery at the time was 'colourless.' The association of the curse of Canaan with *blackness* arose only much later in medieval Talmudic texts." Jan Nederveen Pieterse, *White on Black: Images of Africa and Blacks in Western Popular Culture* (New Haven: Yale University Press, 1992), at 44.

22. Chancellor Harper, "Slavery in the Light of Social Ethics," in E. N. Elliott, ed., *Cotton Is King, and Pro-Slavery Arguments* (Augusta, Ga.: Pritchard, Abbott & Loomis, 1860), at 559–60.

23. Genesis 3:16 (New King James Version).

24. Exodus 21:22–23 (New King James Version).

25. A qualitative distinction is a distinction of *type* or *kind*, and is distinguished from a *quantitative* distinction, or one of *degree*. Although Albert Einstein was better at mathematics than I, the difference between our mathematical abilities is a matter of degree. I have *some* ability to do mathematics; Einstein had a *great* deal more. The fact that a bird can fly, however, represents a qualitative difference, or a difference of kind, between me and the bird. It is not that I cannot fly as well as the bird; I cannot fly at all.

26. John Locke, *An Essay Concerning Human Understanding*, bk. II, ch. XI, ed. John W. Yolton (London: J. M. Dent & Sons, 1961), at 126, 127 (emphasis omitted).

27. Aristotle, *Politics*, bk. 1, chap. 8, § 1256b, lines 16–17, in Richard McKeon, ed., *The Basic Works of Aristotle* (New York: Random House, 1941), at 1137. There were certainly dissenting views among the Greeks. For example, Aristotle's predecessors, Pythagoras and Empedocles, maintained that we had duties of justice toward animals, and Aristotle's own successor, Theophrastus, also maintained that animals were part of the moral community. *See generally* Richard Sorabji, *Animal Minds and Human Morals: The Origins of the Western Debate* (Ithaca: Cornell University Press, 1993).

28. Charles Darwin, *The Descent of Man* (Princeton: Princeton University Press, 1981), at 105, 76, 77. *See* James Rachels, *Created From Animals: The Moral Implications of Darwinism* (Oxford: Oxford University Press, 1990).

29. Donald R. Griffin, *Animal Minds* (Chicago: University of Chicago Press, 1992), at 248–49.

30. Antonio R. Damasio, *The Feeling of What Happens: Body and Emotion in the Making of Consciousness* (New York: Harcourt Brace, 1999), at 16.

31. *Id.*

32. *See id.* at 198, 201.

33. Colin Allen and Marc Bekoff, *Species of Mind: The Philosophy and Biology of Cognitive Ethology* (Cambridge: MIT Press, 1997); Marc Bekoff and Dale Jamieson, *Readings in Animal Cognition* (Cambridge: MIT Press, 1996); Griffin, *Animal Minds, supra* note 29; Donald R. Griffin, *Animal Thinking* (Cambridge: Harvard University Press, 1984); Carolyn A. Ristau, ed., *Cognitive Ethology: The Minds of Other An-*

imals: Essays in Honor of Donald R. Griffin (Hillsdale, N.J.: Lawrence Erlbaum Associates, 1991).

34. *See* Jonathan Leake, "Scientists Teach Chimpanzee to Speak English," *Sunday Times* (London), July 25, 1999, Foreign News Section.

35. *See* Jeffrey Moussaieff Masson and Susan McCarthy, *When Elephants Weep: The Emotional Lives of Animals* (New York: Delacorte Press, 1995). *See also* Jeffrey Moussaieff Masson, *The Emperor's Embrace: Reflections on Animal Families and Fatherhood* (New York: Pocket Books, 1999); Jeffrey Moussaieff Masson, *Dogs Never Lie About Love: Reflections on the Emotional World of Dogs* (New York: Crown Publishers, 1997).

36. Frans de Waal, *Good Natured: The Origins of Right and Wrong in Humans and Other Animals* (Cambridge: Harvard University Press, 1996), at 218.

37. *See, e.g.*, Eugene Linden, *The Parrot's Lament and Other True Tales of Animal Intrigue, Intelligence, and Ingenuity* (New York: Dutton, 1999), at 19–20.

38. *See* Carl Sagan and Ann Druyan, *Shadows of Forgotten Ancestors* (New York: Ballantine Books, 1992), 117–18.

39. *See* de Waal, *Good Natured, supra* note 36, at 160.

40. *See* A. Whiten, J. Goodall, et al., "Cultures in Chimpanzees," 399 *Nature* 682 (1999). There has for some years been an international effort designated as "The Great Ape Project" that aims to secure certain rights for the great apes (other than human beings, who are also great apes). This project was started by the publication of a book entitled *The Great Ape Project* (New York: St. Martin's Press, 1994), edited by Paola Cavalieri and Peter Singer, which sought "the extension of the community of equals to include all great apes: human beings, chimpanzees, gorillas and orang-utans." *Id.* at 4. The author was a contributor to *The Great Ape Project. See* Gary L. Francione, "Personhood, Property, and Legal Competence," *id.* at 248–57. New Zealand prohibits the use of the great apes—chimpanzees, gorillas, bonobos, and orangutans—in research, testing, or teaching, unless such use is "in the best interest" of the ape, or "is in the interest of the species" to which the ape belongs. The use of great apes in experiments is also generally prohibited in Britain.

41. William Mullen, "Image of the Bird Brain May Be Dispelled," *Philadelphia Inquirer*, November 28, 1997, at A35.

42. This is the danger of an enterprise like The Great Ape Project; it facilitates the creation of new hierarchies where some nonhumans are considered more deserving of the basic right not to a be treated as a resource than others because of their similarity to humans. In my essay in *The Great Ape Project*, I stressed the view the sentience alone should determine membership in the moral community. Frans de Waal argues that if the moral status of some animals depends on their similarity to humans, then it is difficult to avoid "ranking" humans as above other species. *See* de Waal, *Good Natured, supra* note 36, at 215. I agree with de Waal's observation insofar as he identifies the problem of linking moral status with similarity to humans (beyond sentience).

43. Sorabji, *Animal Minds and Human Morals, supra* note 27, at 2.

44. Thomas Nagel, "What Is It Like to Be a Bat?" 83 *Philosophical Review* 435 (1974).

45. The notable exception to this view is Peter Singer, who has argued that in

certain circumstances, we may use some humans as resources for the benefit of other humans. *See* Chapter 6 *infra.*

46. Carruthers, *The Animals Issue, supra* note 3, at 181.

47. Karl Marx, *Economic and Philosophic Manuscripts* [1844], in Robert C. Tucker, ed., *The Marx-Engels Reader,* 2d ed. (New York: W. W. Norton, 1978), at 75.

48. For an excellent and definitive discussion of the Greek and Roman views of animal minds, and the relationship between those views and theories about the moral status of animals, see generally Sorabji, *Animal Minds and Human Morals, supra* note 27.

49. John Rawls, *A Theory of Justice* (Cambridge, Mass.: Belknap Press, 1971), at 505, 512.

50. Carl Cohen, "The Case for the Use of Animals in Biomedical Research," 315 *New England Journal of Medicine* 865, 866 (1986).

51. Thomas Hobbes, "De Homine" [1658], *reprinted in* Paul A. B. Clarke and Andrew Linzey, eds., *Political Theory and Animal Rights* (London: Pluto Press, 1990), at 17–21.

52. Rawls, *A Theory of Justice, supra* note 49, at 512. As Sorabji correctly points out, Rawls' theory is either arbitrary or inadequate with respect to animals. If the human contractors do not consider the possibility that they might occupy the position of animals in the society, then Rawls is simply arbitrary in excluding that possibility. If the human contractors do not consider that possibility because rational contractors could not occupy the position of animals in the society, then Rawls' theory is not competent to assess what duties of justice are owed to animals. *See* Sorabji, *Animal Minds and Human Morals, supra* note 27, at 165.

53. A variant of the reciprocity argument is that what distinguishes humans from animals is that humans are able to extend moral consideration across species boundaries and animals are not able to do so. This is merely a restatement of the view that humans can respond to moral claims and animals cannot. Putting aside that there have historically been many instances in which animals have ostensibly extended moral concern to humans, there are humans who are unable to extend moral concern to members of their own species, let alone cross species boundaries, but we do not treat such humans as resources. Psychopaths engage in aggressive and sometimes violent behavior against other humans and animals with little or no feeling of guilt or remorse. We may not wish to employ such people as school teachers or as animal care workers in humane societies, and we imprison them if they commit crimes, but we do not use them as forced organ donors. There is, however, an even more peculiar aspect of this argument. The fact that we are able to extend moral significance to the interests of animals, just as we extend moral significance to humans who lack whatever characteristic it is that we believe establishes a qualitative difference between humans and animals, militates in favor of extending that concern to animals and not merely restricting it to other humans. A claim to take morality seriously implies a rejection of arbitrary refusals to apply the principle of equal consideration.

54. Carruthers, *The Animals Issue, supra* note 3, at 114.

55. *Id.* at 114–15.

56. *Id.* at 117.

57. Cohen, "The Case for the Use of Animals in Biomedical Research," *supra* note 50, at 866.

58. S. A. Cartright, M.D., "Slavery in the Light of Ethnology," in Elliott, *Cotton is King, supra* note 22, at 700–701.

59. *See* Edward H. Clarke, M.D., *Sex in Education, or a Fair Chance for the Girls* (Boston: James R. Osgood, 1873; reprinted by Arno Press, New York, 1972). For a discussion on supposed biological differences between men and women that have been used to justify discrimination against women, see Ruth Hubbard, Mary Sue Henifin, and Barbara Fried, eds., *Biological Woman: The Convenient Myth* (Cambridge, Mass.: Schenkman Publishing, 1982); Barbara Ehrenreich and Deirdre English, *For Her Own Good: 150 Years of Experts' Advice to Women* (New York: Doubleday, 1978).

60. *Bradwell v. Illinois*, 83 U.S. 130, 141 (1873) (Bradley, J., concurring) (footnote omitted).

61. For example, Richard Sorabji argues that inherent value can admit of degrees, which effectively results in reestablishing the moral importance of some cognitive characteristic, such as possession of belief, as the minimum criterion for membership in the moral community. *See* Sorabji, *Animal Minds and Human Morals, supra* note 27, at 216. Sorabji states that even rights theorist Regan maintains that certain cognitive characteristics may be relevant to inherent value. Sorabji's position is based on what is admittedly a confused argument made by Tom Regan in *The Case for Animal Rights* (Berkeley and Los Angeles: University of California Press, 1983). The problem is best illustrated by Regan's use of the following hypothetical. Five survivors—four normal adults and one normal dog—are on a lifeboat. There is room in the boat for four only, and one of the occupants must be thrown overboard. Regan maintains that his rights theory provides an answer to the problem. Although death is a harm to the dog, Regan argues, death would be a qualitatively greater loss, and, accordingly, a greater harm, to any of the humans: "To throw any one of the humans overboard, to face certain death, would be to make that individual worse-off (i.e., would cause *that* individual a greater harm) than the harm that would be done to the dog if the animal was thrown overboard." *Id.* at 324. It would, in Regan's view, be morally obligatory to kill the dog. Further, Regan claims that even if the choice were between a million dogs and one person, it would still be obligatory under rights theory to throw the dogs overboard.

To the extent that Regan's point is that the theory of animal rights is consistent with preferring humans in truly exceptional circumstances that do not include institutionalized exploitation, I agree with his position. *See* Chapter 7 *infra*. To the extent that in such situations Regan would *require* choosing the human interest over the animal interest based on a difference in inherent value, or to the extent that Regan regards cognitive differences as having any relevance to the basic right not to be treated as a resource, as is indicated by his view that we ought to choose to save one human over a million dogs, then his resolution of the lifeboat matter is problematic and relies on "perfectionist" theories that he purports to reject. *See* Gary L. Francione, "Comparable Harm and Equal Inherent Value: The Problem of the Dog in the Lifeboat," 11 *Between the Species* 81 (1995).

Frans de Waal also appears to maintain that animals have "inherent beauty and dignity," but that we may use them as human resources in ways that we never use any humans. I understand de Waal's position to be an example of the view that animals have lesser inherent value than do humans, all of whom have equal inherent value. *See* de Waal, *Good Natured, supra* note 36, at 215.

Chapter 6

1. Jeremy Bentham, *The Principles of Morals and Legislation*, chap. XVII, § I para. 4 [1781] (Amherst, N.Y.: Prometheus Books, 1988), at 310 (footnote omitted).

2. *Id.* at 310–11, note 1 (footnote within footnote omitted).

3. *Id.*

4. *See generally* Gary L. Francione, *Animals, Property, and the Law* (Philadelphia: Temple University Press, 1995).

5. J.J.C. Smart, "An Outline of a System of Utilitarian Ethics," in J.J.C. Smart and Bernard Williams, *Utilitarianism: For and Against* (Cambridge: Cambridge University Press, 1973), at 9. For a general discussion of act- and rule-utilitarianism, see William K. Frankena, *Ethics*, 2d ed. (Englewood Cliffs, N.J.: Prentice-Hall, 1973), 34–60; Amartya Sen and Bernard Williams, eds., *Utilitarianism and Beyond* (Cambridge: Cambridge University Press, 1982). Some theorists argue that the distinction between act- and rule-utilitarianism collapses. *See, e.g.,* David Lyons, *Forms and Limits of Utilitarianism* (Oxford: Clarendon Press, 1965).

6. Many policy-based legal rights may be said to reflect rights as the rule-utilitarian understands that concept. Policy-based rights provide protection against violating the protected interest in particular situations, but may be abrogated in light of overall social consequences. The rule-utilitarian would also view respect-based rights as prescribing a rule to be followed as long as doing so will maximize the best overall consequences. *See* Introduction, note 17 *supra.*

7. Utilitarians may disagree about what consequences are relevant. For example, classical utilitarians such as Jeremy Bentham and John Stuart Mill (who was more of a rule-utilitarian) argued that for the most part pleasure alone was the nonmoral value that utilitarians should seek to maximize. Other utilitarians, such as Peter Singer, maintain that the morally correct act is that which furthers the preferences or interests of those affected. *See infra* text accompanying note 17.

8. Bentham maintained that there could be legal rights but that there could be no nonlegal rights. " 'Rights are the fruits of the law and of the law alone; there are no rights without law—no rights contrary to law—no rights anterior to the law.'" H.L.A. Hart, *Essays on Bentham* (Oxford: Oxford University Press, 1982), at 82 (quoting Bentham). The basic right not to be a thing is obviously a pre-legal or pre-political right of the sort that Bentham would ostensibly reject, but, as noted in the text, Bentham seemed to accept such a right in the context of his opposition to human slavery.

9. *Id.* at 72–73, 97. Most Bentham scholars argue that Bentham's opposition to slavery was based more on the consequences of slavery than on the principle of equal consideration. It would, however, appear to be difficult to base opposition to human slavery exclusively on consequences. After all, it may very well be that certain very "humane" forms of slavery—even if institutionalized and practiced widely—

would increase aggregate social welfare in that the overall suffering of slaves would be less than the overall benefits enjoyed by the slave owners and the rest of society. And it may very well be that certain humans might be more productive as slaves than as free laborers. Bentham's opposition to slavery must therefore be viewed as some mixture of his acceptance of the principle of equality and his recognition that all humans had a similar interest in not being treated as things, together with his view that slavery, as an institution, would not as a factual matter advance net aggregate welfare.

There is ostensibly a tension in utilitarian theory. If there is no limitation (other than consequential reasons) on how we can treat humans, then some humans will be valued at "zero." Their interests may be ignored completely, and they will be excluded from the moral community. If the purpose of utilitarian theory is to ensure that all human interests are accorded moral significance, to allow any humans to be "degraded into the class of *things*" would seem to be inconsistent with that purpose. This would suggest that utilitarian theory requires that slavery be rejected by utilitarians irrespective of consequences if the principle of equal consideration is to be meaningful within utilitarian theory. *See infra* note 36 and accompanying text.

10. Bentham, *The Principles of Morals and Legislation, supra* note 1, at 310–11, note 1. Bentham claimed that "[t]he death they suffer in our hands commonly is, and always may be, a speedier, and by that means a less painful one, than that which would await them in the inevitable course of nature." *Id.* Bentham ignored the fact that the domestic animals that we raise for food would not have a death "in the inevitable course of nature," because they are only brought into existence as our resources in the first place. It is, therefore, problematic to defend the killing of domestic animals by comparing their deaths with those of wild animals, saying that the infliction of unnecessary pain on domestic animals that we do not need to eat is less than the pain that may necessarily be suffered by wild animals.

11. Peter Singer, *Animal Liberation*, 2d ed. (New York: New York Review of Books, 1990).

12. It is one of the great ironies of modern animal ethics that Singer is regarded by many as the "father of the Animal Rights Movement." *See* Gary L. Francione, *Rain Without Thunder: The Ideology of the Animal Rights Movement* (Philadelphia: Temple University Press, 1996), at 51–53.

13. This group would include all infants, but because children will in the ordinary course develop self-awareness and future desires, Singer focuses instead on severely retarded humans and the irreparably brain damaged, who do not have such potential for self-awareness. *But see infra* note 19, and note 24 and accompanying text.

14. Singer, *Animal Liberation, supra* note 11, at 228.

15. *Id.* at 229.

16. *Id.* at 20.

17. Peter Singer, *Practical Ethics*, 2d ed. (Cambridge: Cambridge University Press, 1993), at 14.

18. That Singer is not an act-utilitarian is clear in that he does not ask on a case-by-case basis whether we should use particular humans as unconsenting biomedical subjects or as forced organ donors or as slaves. He presumes against such uses as violating the principle of utility. This is not to say that the presumption may not be overcome in particular cases—if, for example, killing an innocent human would save

the entire human race. Singer acknowledges that he "would never deny that we are justified in using animals for human goals, because as a consequentialist [he] must also hold that in appropriate circumstances we are justified in using humans to achieve human goals (or the goal of assisting animals)." Peter Singer, "Ethics and Animals," 13 *Behavioral & Brain Sciences.* 45, 46 (1990). But for the most part, the presumption against treating humans as the resources of other humans functions in a way substantially similar to the basic right or inherent value discussed in Chapter 4 that Singer claims to reject. Moreover, Singer maintains that sentient beings have a "right to equal consideration," which at least arguably implies that sentient beings cannot be resources, because the principle of equal consideration could never apply to them. *See also infra* note 36 and accompanying text.

It should be noted that in Singer's discussion of the principle of equal consideration, he states that "[e]quality is a moral idea, not an assertion of fact," and that "*[t]he principle of the equality of human beings is not a description of an alleged actual equality among humans: it is a prescription of how we should treat human beings.*" Singer, *Animal Liberation, supra* note 11, at 4, 5. I disagree with Singer in that the basic right not to be treated as a thing and equal inherent value are both predicated on a *factual* similarity shared by all humans irrespective of their particular characteristics beyond sentience: all humans do have an interest in not being treated exclusively as means to the ends of others. *See* Chapter 4 and Chapter 5 *supra.* Singer seems on one level to recognize this factual similarity in that he acknowledges that at least normal humans have an interest in not being treated as replaceable resources, but his application of the principle of equality is based on equality exclusively as a normative, and not a descriptive, idea.

19. Singer has taken the position that certain nonhuman primates—chimpanzees, gorillas, and orangutans—are in a community of equals with humans, and that these great apes are relevantly similar to humans in that they are self-aware. *See* Paola Cavalieri and Peter Singer, eds., *The Great Ape Project* (New York: St. Martin's Press, 1994). *See also* Chapter 5, notes 40 and 42 and accompanying text *supra.* Singer has stated that in addition to the great apes, "[a] case can also be made, though with varying degrees of confidence, on behalf of whales, dolphins, monkeys, dogs, cats, pigs, seals, bears, cattle, sheep and so on, perhaps even to the point at which it may include all mammals—much depends on how far we are prepared to go in extending the benefit of the doubt, where a doubt exists." Singer, *Practical Ethics, supra* note 17, at 132. This represents a significant development of Singer's views as expressed in *Animal Liberation* and it should be noted that Singer only states that a case can be made for the self-awareness of animals other than great apes; he comes to no conclusion. If Singer were to acknowledge cows and pigs as self-aware, he would be faced with some interesting dilemmas. If a pig is self-aware, then we cannot treat the animal as a replaceable resource, but we can treat severely retarded or severely brain-damaged humans as replaceable. Moreover, we can treat disabled infants as replaceable. *See infra* note 24 and accompanying text. Therefore, it would be morally permissible (and perhaps morally obligatory) to sacrifice a disabled human infant or a severely retarded adult (who is conscious but, according to Singer, not self-aware) to save a pig. Moreover, in a recent interview, Singer was asked about an operation in which surgeons implanted the aorta of a cow in a thirteen-

month-old child. Singer replied "that if it was genuinely a choice between the cow and the boy they should save the boy." Michael Specter, "The Dangerous Philosopher," in *New Yorker*, September 6, 1999, at 53. If the cow is self-aware, then we are dealing with two beings neither of whom should be treated as a replaceable resource, and it becomes difficult to understand how Singer can approve of the use of the cow.

20. Singer, *Animal Liberation, supra* note 11, at 229.

21. *Id*. at 229–30.

22. *Id*. at 228–29.

23. I do not suggest that Damasio would agree with the view that animals other than apes, monkeys, and dogs possess extended consciousness. *See* Antonio R. Damasio, *The Feeling of What Happens: Body and Emotion in the Making of Consciousness* (New York: Harcourt Brace, 1999), at 198. Nevertheless, he acknowledges that "there are many levels and grades" of extended consciousness, *id*. at 16, and it becomes difficult (and somewhat arbitrary) to maintain that some dogs have extended consciousness but that most or all dogs do not, or that other mammals and birds, who do possess memory and reasoning but not language, have some form of autobiographical self.

24. Singer, *Practical Ethics, supra* note 17, at 186.

25. Singer, *Animal Liberation, supra* note 11, at 15.

26. *Id*. at 16, 15. It is simply not realistic to believe that humans—who have "superior mental powers," which according to Singer make them suffer more than animals in "certain circumstances"—will very often conclude that the suffering of animals viewed as replaceable resources will outweigh the suffering of humans.

27. That is, because Singer regards animals as replaceable resources, we may use them for purposes for which we would never use normal humans. When we do use an animal for such purposes, Singer does not require that we inflict no pain or suffering on the animal, but only that we ensure that the animal has a reasonably pleasant life and a relatively painless death. In a sense, then, humans and animals cannot be similarly situated with respect to the imposition of suffering if certain uses of humans are ruled out from the beginning.

28. *Id*. at 16.

29. *See* R. G. Frey, *Rights, Killing, and Suffering: Moral Vegetarianism and Applied Ethics* (Oxford: Basil Blackwell, 1983), at 197–203.

30. We must exercise caution when we talk about "free-range" agriculture, as there is no standard, agreed-upon definition of that term. For example, "free-range" turkeys may have larger cages than those in mass production but may still not be allowed outdoors or be raised in anything resembling our image of the "family farm." *See* Jack Brown, "The Short and Sweet Life of a Free-Range Turkey," *Philadelphia Inquirer*, November 25, 1999 at W1.

31. For a discussion of incremental changes in animal welfare that arguably go beyond the treatment of animals as economic commodities but stop short of recognizing animals' basic right not to be treated as things, see Francione, *Rain Without Thunder, supra* note 12, at 190–219.

32. Hart, *Essays on Bentham, supra* note 8, at 97 (quoting Bentham).

33. In more recent times, economists have argued that even if a society started

off with slavery, the institution would eventually be abolished because it would maximize overall social wealth to allow slaves to buy their way out of bondage and act
as free paid labor. *See* Francione, *Animals, Property, and the Law, supra* note 4, at
27–28. Obviously, the status of animals as property will not be abolished (for these
reasons) even if the economic analysis of human slavery is correct. *See id.*

34. *Callaghan v. Society for Prevention of Cruelty to Animals*, 16 L.R. Ir. 325, 335
(C.P.D. 1885) (Murphy, J.).

35. Philosopher Robert Nozick argues we have "utilitarianism for animals, Kantianism for people," in that "human beings may not be used or sacrificed for the
benefit of others; animals may be used or sacrificed for the benefit of other people
or animals *only if* those benefits are greater than the loss inflicted." Robert Nozick,
Anarchy, State, and Utopia (New York: Basic Books, 1974), at 39. A consequence of
utilitarianism for animals and of Kantianism for people is that "nothing may be inflicted upon persons for the sake of animals." *Id.* at 40–41. To the extent that we
recognize property rights in animals, we inflict harm on a property owner when we
regulate the owner's use of animal property. Moreover, if humans derive great utility from animal exploitation, the animal will almost always lose out in any "balance."
For a discussion of Nozick's version of a "hybrid" analysis that requires us to balance the interests of beings who have rights against those who do not, see Francione, *Animals, Property, and the Law, supra* note 4, at 104–10.

36. My analysis suggests that on the question of the abolition of animal exploitation, Singer ought to come out at the same place as does Tom Regan in *The
Case for Animal Rights* (Berkeley and Los Angeles: University of California Press,
1983). For a discussion of Regan's position, and a comparison of his views to those
of Singer, see Francione, *Rain Without Thunder, supra* note 12. Singer might argue
that the utilitarian protection of humans from slavery rests on a rule-utilitarian basis and is therefore distinguishable from the classical rights position articulated by
Regan. This would make Singer's position closer to what L. W. Sumner argues for
in "Animal Welfare and Animal Rights," 13 *Journal of Medicine & Philosophy* 159
(1988). In any event, as applied to animals, adoption of a strong rule-utilitarian position (similar to the position Singer holds with respect to normal humans) would
mean that Singer's position would be much closer to Regan's in that Singer would
at least have an almost irrebuttable presumption against the use of animals as resources. Moreover, although Singer rejects rights concepts, he does at times talk
about a "right to equal consideration." It may be argued that a right to equal consideration precludes any sentient being's having property status because property
cannot have interests similar to those of property owners.

Indeed, it appears as though any use of animals as resources is inconsistent
with the principle of equal consideration, which is ostensibly accepted in the utilitarian theory of both Bentham and Singer. *But see supra* note 9. For example,
David DeGrazia argues that "[w]hile equal consideration is compatible with different ethical theories, it is incompatible—if extended to animals—with all views
that see animals as essentially resources for our use." David DeGrazia, *Taking Animals Seriously: Mental Life and Moral Status* (Cambridge: Cambridge University
Press, 1996), at 47. Nevertheless, DeGrazia maintains that it may still be permissible to treat some animals as resources, but he concedes that his analysis ulti-

mately rests on "giving animals *serious*—not necessarily *equal*—consideration." *Id.* at 258.

37. *See, e.g.,* Josephine Donovan and Carol J. Adams, eds., *Beyond Animal Rights: A Feminist Caring Ethic for the Treatment of Animals* (New York: Continuum, 1996).

38. *See* Drucilla Cornell, *The Imaginary Domain: Abortion, Pornography and Sexual Harassment* (New York: Routledge, 1995). *See also* Chapter 4, note 30 *supra*.

39. For a further discussion of ecofeminist theories, see Gary L. Francione, "Ecofeminism and Animal Rights: A Review of *Beyond Animal Rights: A Feminist Caring Ethic for the Treatment of Animals*," 18 *Women's Rights Law Reporter* 95 (1996).

Chapter 7

1. Some animal rights advocates maintain that the abolition of animal exploitation may be achieved through the regulation of animal use. For a refutation of this position and a discussion of the differences between the animal rights and animal welfare positions, see Gary L. Francione, *Rain Without Thunder: The Ideology of the Animal Rights Movement* (Philadelphia: Temple University Press, 1996).

2. This is in a nutshell the argument against animal rights made by Peter Carruthers in his book *The Animals Issue: Moral Theory in Practice* (Cambridge: Cambridge University Press, 1992). Carruthers argues that there are certain moral views on which there is general agreement. One such view is that in an emergency, such as our burning house containing a human and a dog, we should save the life of a human over that of a nonhuman. Carruthers argues that this generally agreed-on moral principle should compel us to conclude that animals do not matter morally.

3. In a 1999 article in the *New York Times*, I was quoted as saying that gorillas "'should be declared to be "persons" under the Constitution,' with constitutional rights." William Glaberson, "Legal Pioneers Seek to Raise Lowly Status of Animals," *New York Times*, August 18, 1999, at A1. I made that comment in response to a question from Glaberson about what sort of lawsuit would arguably affect the property status of animals and not as a general statement in support of formalizing the human/animal conflict through lawsuits or according animals the same legal rights (constitutional or otherwise) that we accord humans. I do not share the view that chimpanzees are any different from dogs, rats, or fish insofar as their having a basic right is concerned. *See* Chapter 5, note 42 and accompanying text *supra*. It is my view that any sentient being ought to be considered a "person" in that the interests of that being ought to be considered morally significant. But I do not think that according animals constitutional rights is a particularly helpful framework in which to address the overall problem of animal exploitation; indeed, that tends to confuse the issue because it suggests that animals should have the same constitutional rights as humans.

4. For a further discussion of conflicts that would remain if we granted animals a basic right not to be treated as things, see Gary L. Francione, "Wildlife and Animal Rights," in Priscilla N. Cohn, ed., *Ethics and Wildlife* (Lewiston, N.Y.: Edwin Mellen Press, 1999).

5. Whether we would impose criminal liability on someone who ate another human in such circumstances is a separate question. In *Regina v. Dudley & Stephens*, 1881–85 All E.R. 61 (Q B D. 1884), four men were afloat in a small boat after their

sailing vessel sank. After nine days without food and seven days without water, Dudley and Stephens killed Parker, and proceeded to eat him and drink his blood. Several days later, a passing ship rescued the men and Dudley and Stephens were tried for murder. The defendants raised the defense of necessity, arguing that they reasonably believed that had they not killed Parker, all four of the men would have died (Brooks, the fourth occupant, did not approve of Parker's killing or participate in the act, but he did partake of Parker). The court rejected the claim, found Dudley and Stephens guilty of murder, and sentenced the defendants to death. Their sentence was commuted to six months' imprisonment by Queen Victoria, which indicated that the Crown appreciated the dilemma facing Dudley and Stephens. In an American case, *United States v. Holmes*, 26 F.Cas. 360 (C.C.E.D. Pa. 1842) (No. 15,383), the defendants ejected fourteen passengers from a lifeboat that had begun to leak. The court convicted the defendants of the lesser crime of manslaughter and sentenced them to six months' imprisonment even though the maximum potential penalty was three years' imprisonment. Again, there appeared to be an appreciation of the dilemma faced by the defendants.

Both *Dudley & Stephens* and *Holmes* had peculiar facts that created some doubt on the part of the respective courts as to whether the defense of necessity was appropriate. In the former, there was some question as to whether death was really imminent for Dudley and Stephens, or whether they could have waited longer before deciding to kill Parker. In the latter, those ejected from the lifeboat were passengers on a ship and the defendants were crew members who arguably should have gone down with the ship before throwing passengers out of the lifeboat. Moreover, the court expressed concern that lots should have be drawn to determine who would be sacrificed.

Such "lifeboat" cases are, like "burning house" cases, rare. Nevertheless, there are compelling arguments that killing another person in a true situation of necessity, particularly if it will save the lives of many others, is either a justifiable act (an act that would otherwise be culpable but is considered as morally acceptable under the circumstances and deserving of no criminal punishment or moral censure, such as a killing in self-defense), or an excusable act (an act that is wrong but for which the actor deserves no punishment because of the compelling circumstances in which she acted, such as a crime committed under duress). The fact that the defendants in both cases were given very light sentences suggests that such acts are viewed as very different from other instances of homicide. Our failure to prosecute doctors or others who make choices about resource allocations, such as to whom to give the last transfusion of blood, supports the view that such choices are considered justifiable or excusable but not deserving of criminal punishment in any event.

6. Indeed, unless one believes that a being must possess a soul to have any moral value whatsoever, it would seem that if only humans have souls and animals do not, that would militate in favor of greater concern for the treatment of animals. After all, if humans have souls, and if souls are immortal (as they are thought to be in traditional religious doctrine), then it would seem that what happens to humans on earth is not particularly relevant given that seventy or so years out of eternity is a rather small slice of time. If, however, animals do not possess souls and their existence is limited to their time on earth, then their treatment during that existence is of utmost importance.

7. An essay in *Time* written by the editorial director of the Worldwatch Institute predicts that "the era of mass-produced animal flesh, and its unsustainable costs to human and environmental health, should be over before the next century is out." Ed Ayres, "Will We Still Eat Meat?" *Time*, November 8, 1999, at 106–7.

8. The United States Supreme Court has held that animal use by adherents of Santeria may not be targeted for prosecution, but did not prohibit authorities from applying neutral anticruelty laws to these types of killings, considered apart from their religious context. See *Church of the Lukumi Babalu Aye, Inc. v. City of Hialeah*, 508 U.S. 520 (1993). In addition, many Santeria ceremonies occur in cities where there are laws other than anticruelty laws, such as regulations concerning animal slaughter in multi-family dwellings or interstate transportation of livestock, that can and have been used to prohibit these animal sacrifices.

9. *See* Richard D. Ryder, *Animal Revolution: Changing Attitudes towards Speciesism* (Oxford: Basil Blackwell, 1989), at 100–101.

10. *State v. Bogardus*, 4 Mo. App. 215, 217 (1877).

Appendix

1. In this respect, my views differ sharply from those of Tom Regan, who argues that slavery is less morally odious than vivisection because "being a slave owner was not a profession people prepared for by attending colleges or universities," and that vivisection, unlike slavery, is "enmeshed" in "social institutions that not only permit, [but] train people to commit evil, and then reward them for doing it." Tom Regan, "The Blackest of All the Black Crimes," *AV Magazine*, winter 1998, at 5. In the first place, many American universities in the eighteenth and nineteenth centuries supported slavery, directly or indirectly, through confirmatory scholarship and through curricula that portrayed slavery as desirable or necessary. But more important, even if there were no university courses in slave ownership, there clearly were social institutions that provided a normative context in which people were "train[ed] . . . to commit evil." That is what it means to have an "institution" of slavery. Whether this training occurred outside universities is irrelevant. Moreover, slave owners were rewarded financially and politically: several presidents of the United States and many of the wealthiest Americans were slave owners.

Regan also argues that the Nazi experiments on humans are morally less offensive than animal vivisection because the Nazi doctors, "after being trained to do good, chose to do evil. Not so in the case of vivisectors. In their case, vivisectors choose to do evil after they have been professionally trained to do it." *Id.* But if vivisectors are trained to believe that the use of animals to obtain benefits for humans is morally justifiable (and even laudable), then, as a matter of personal moral culpability, they are surely *less* culpable than those who are taught to serve the needs of all humans and then choose to exploit certain humans based on race or ethnicity.

2. *See* Robert N. Proctor, *Racial Hygiene: Medicine under the Nazis* (Cambridge: Harvard University Press, 1988), at 223–50.

3. For further discussion of the abortion issue, see Gary L. Francione, "Abortion and Animal Rights. Are They Comparable Issues?" in Carol J. Adams and

Josephine Donovan, eds., *Animals and Women: Feminist Theoretical Explorations* (Durham, N.C.: Duke University Press, 1995), at 149.

4. For more detailed discussion on the structural limitations of animal welfare laws, see Gary L. Francione, *Rain Without Thunder: The Ideology of the Animal Rights Movement* (Philadelphia: Temple University Press, 1996); Gary L. Francione, *Animals, Property, and the Law* (Philadelphia: Temple University Press, 1995).

5. 16 U.S.C.S. §§ 1531–1544 (1999).

6. It should also be noted that many environmentalists have been reluctant to see the moral status of animals as a component of environmental ethics. For a discussion of this phenomenon, see Michael Allen Fox, *Deep Vegetarianism* (Philadelphia: Temple University Press, 1999).

7. For a fascinating discussion of the inconsistent and irrational attitudes that characterize much of our thinking about vegetarianism and the use of animals as food, see *id.*

Index

This book presents a cumulative and extended argument in support of the theory that the moral significance of animals logically and morally precludes their use as our property. Certain concepts and individuals appear throughout the book, and many concepts, such as the notion of animals as property, resources, or things, overlap. The indexed citations are intended to guide the reader to salient but not all instances of the discussion of these concepts and individuals.

abortion, 100, 125, 177–79
ahimsa, 210
American Dietetic Association, 14
American Humane Association, 27
animal agriculture. *See* diet, meat-based; factory farming; food, use of animals for
Animal and Plant Health Inspection Service, 197
animal cruelty laws. *See* animal welfare laws
animal exploitation, abolition vs. regulation of, xxix, xxxi, xxxii–xxxiv, 148, 151–54, 181–82; *see also* animal rights; animal welfare; animal welfare laws
animal rights, xxviii–xxx, xxxi, xxxii–xxxiii, 98–100, 151–66, 168–69, 175–76, 184–86, 220–21; organizations, xxxi; and religion, 160–61; as religious view, 186–87; *see also* property, right not to be treated as; rights, basic
animals, attitudes toward, xix–xx, 1; *see also* animals, moral status of

animals, moral status of, xxi–xxiii, 4–9, 81–82, 98–102, 127–29, 134, 142–48, 201; before nineteenth century, 1–3; *see also* humane treatment principle
animals, use and treatment of, xx–xxi, xxiv, 9–49, 73–76; disparity between moral norms and, xxiv, 8–9, 54–56; *see also* entertainment; experiments; fishing; food; fur; humane treatment principle; hunting; pets; teaching and education; toxicity testing
animals as pets. *See* pets
animals as property. *See* property, animals as
animals as things, xxvi, 1–3; *see also* animal rights; persons; property, animals as; resources, animals as
Animals (Scientific Procedures) Act (Britain, 1986), 7, 9
animal welfare, xxxi, 181–84, 209; *see also* animal welfare laws
Animal Welfare Act (U.S., 1966), 7, 33, 42, 57–58, 68, 71, 73, 198, 202

225

animal welfare laws, xxiii, 3, 7–9, 32, 54–73, 181–84, 223; economic self-interest and, 66–67; enforcement of, 67–70; exemptions in, 56–63; "state of mind" and, 63–66, 204; *see also names of individual laws and court cases*
anticruelty laws. *See* animal welfare laws
Aquinas, Saint Thomas, 108, 112–13, 211
Aristotle, 112–13, 142
Augustine, Saint, 108
Ayres, Ed, 223

balance of human and animal interests. *See* humans vs. animals; interests, animal, balancing
Barker, Bob, 28
Bateson, Patrick, 21
Bentham, Jeremy, 5–6, 72–73, 85–86, 130–34, 146–48, 188, 193, 216–17
Binti, 116
Blackstone, William, 53–54
Bolognesi, Dani, 36–37
bow hunting, xx
Bowyer v. Morgan, 59
Bradwell v. Illinois, 127
Brooks Air Force Base, 41
Bross, Irwin, 37

Callaghan v. Society for the Prevention of Cruelty to Animals, 60–61, 66, 147–48
Carruthers, Peter, 106, 121, 123–24, 221
Chantek, 116
Charles River Laboratories, 34–35
Charlton, Anna, 49
Cinadr v. State, 58
circuses, 23
Clarke, Edward H., 126–27
cognitive abilities of animals, xxviii–xxix, xxxvi–xxxvii, 111–27; Aristotle on, 112–13; Darwin on, 113–14; Descartes on, 2; Kant on, 3, 113; Locke on, 112; *see also* self-awareness, of animals; special characteristics used to justify differential treatment of animals
Cohen, Carl, 122, 125
Commonwealth v. Anspach, 63
Commonwealth v. Barr, 66–67
Commonwealth v. Turner, 98–99
Commonwealth v. Vonderheid, 67
conflicts, moral. *See* humans vs. animals
Cornell, Drucilla, 150, 208–9

cruelty, legal definition of, 7, 54–67
Cruelty to Animals Act (Britain, 1876), 7

Damasio, Antonio, 114–15, 121, 139, 210, 219
Darwin, Charles, xxxvii, 113–14, 187–88
death penalty, 111
DeGrazia, David, 220–21
Descartes, René, 2, 73, 104–5, 193
de Waal, Frans, 116, 216
diet, meat-based: defenses of, 16–17, 187–88; environmental consequences of, xxiv, 14–16, 195; health consequences of, xxiv, 14; *see also* food, use of animals for
dog racing, 26–27
Donner, Jill, 27

ecofeminism, 149–50
economic self-interest, 66–67
education. *See* teaching and education
Einstein, Albert, 17
emergencies, choosing humans in. *See* humans vs. animals
emotions, of animals, 116, 120; Darwin on, 113–14
Empedocles, 212
Endangered Species Act (U.S., 1999), 183–84
entertainment, use of animals for, xxi, xxiv, 22–28
environment, animals' ability to transform, 121–22
environmentalism, and animal rights, 224; *see also* diet, meat-based, environmental consequences of
Epicureans, 123
equal consideration, principle of, xxv–xxvi, xxxii, xxxiv, 81–102, 127, 142–46, 165, 206, 218, 220–21; *see also* Bentham, Jeremy; Singer, Peter
equal inherent value, 93, 96–98, 127–29
experiments, use of animals for, xxi, xxiv, 32–45, 73–74, 170–71, 198; *see also* vivisection

factory farming, 9–13, 76, 144–46
family farms, 10, 17, 76
feminism, 208–9; *see also* ecofeminism; sexism
film, animals in, 27–28
fishing, 21–22

food, use of animals for, xx, xxiv, 9–17,
    109–10, 134, 136; in emergency situa-
    tions, 158; *see also* diet, meat-based;
    fishing; hunting
Ford v. Wiley, 61, 62, 66, 203
Fort Sam Houston, 41
Foundation for Biomedical Research, 32–
    33, 42
free-range agriculture, definition of, 219
free speech, right of, xxvii
Frey, R. G., 104–5, 209
fur, use of animals for, xix, xxi, xxiv, 28–30

game ranches, xx, 19–20
Gillette, 48
Great Ape Project, 213
Griffin, Donald, 114, 120, 138

Harlow, Harry, 40
Harvard University, 43
Hitler, Adolf, 174–75
Hobbes, Thomas, 123
Holocaust, xxxv
horse racing, 26
Humane Slaughter Act (U.S., 1958), 7,
    75–76
humane treatment principle, xxi–xxiii, 5–9,
    85–86; failure of, xxiv–xxv, 54–73, 85–
    86, 146–48; *see also* animal welfare laws;
    equal consideration; interests, animal,
    balancing
humans, instrumental use of. *See* resources,
    humans as; slavery
humans vs. animals, choosing between, xxi–
    xxii, xxiv–xxv, xxx–xxxi, xxxiii, xxxiv,
    151–62, 215
hunting, xix, xx, 17–21, 165, 195
"hybrid" moral or legal systems, 98, 148,
    220

inherent value. *See* equal inherent value
In re William G., 70
insects, 6, 175–76
instrumental use. *See* animals as things;
    property, animals as; resources, animals
    as; resources, humans as; slavery
interests, animal, xxiii, xxviii–xxx, 2–6, 7–8,
    100, 113, 133–34, 137–38, 146–48,
    206; balancing, vis-à-vis human inter-
    ests, xxiii, xxiv–xxv, xxix–xxx, 8–9, 55,
    85–86; 142–46, 148; *see also* equal con-
sideration; interests, generally; humane
    treatment principle; sentience; unnec-
    essary suffering
interests, generally, xxiii, xxvi–xxvii, 82–85,
    92–98, 135–36

justice, animals' sense of, 122

Kant, Immanuel, 3, 94, 113, 122, 209

language, animals and, 2, 105, 112, 115–16,
    119–20, 123, 209–10
LaRue v. State, 70
law regarding animals. *See* animal welfare
    laws; malicious mischief laws; *names of
    individual laws and court cases*
Leavitt, Jerome, 37
Lewis v. Fermor, 58, 60, 203
liberty, right of, xxvii
Little, Clarence, 37
Locke, John, 51–54, 73, 94, 106–9, 112, 201

Makah, 172
malicious mischief laws, 3, 7–8
marine-mammal shows, 27
Marx, Karl (and Marxism), 121–22, 201,
    207–8
Masson, Jeffrey, 116
means to ends. *See* animals as things; prop-
    erty, animals as; resources, animals as;
    resources, humans as; slavery
meat-eating. *See* diet, meat-based; food, use
    of animals for
Miller v. State, 78
Montaigne, Michel E. de, xxxvii
moral behavior, of animals, 116
moral conflicts between humans and ani-
    mals. *See* humans vs. animals
moral status, of animals. *See* animals, moral
    status of
moral theory, generally, xxxiv–xxxvi, 82–85,
    186, 206; *see also* equal consideration;
    humane treatment principle; *names of
    individual moral theorists*
Motes v. State, 70
Murphy v. Manning, 58, 202

Nagel, Thomas, 119–20
NASA, 41
National Research Council, xxxvii
Nazism, and animal rights, 174–75, 223

necessity, choosing humans in cases of. *See* humans vs. animals

Nozick, Robert, 220

obligations, moral and legal, concerning animals, 1–3; owed directly to animals, 4–9, 30, 54, 72–73, 85–86, 98–102, 137, 146, 194; *see also* animal welfare laws; equal consideration; humane treatment principle

Office of Technology Assessment (U.S.), 34

Ohio State University, 42–43

pain and suffering, of animals. *See* sentience; unnecessary suffering; *specific uses of animals*

Panbanisha, 115–16

People v. Voelker, 70

persons, animals as, 100–102, 221

pets, animals as, xix, 76–79, 162, 169–70

Phillips, Mary, 43–44

pigeon shoots, xx, 20, 196

plants, 6–7, 180

Posner, Richard, 89

principle of equal consideration. *See* equal consideration

product testing, use of animals for. *See* toxicity testing

property, animals as, xxiv–xxv, xxxii, xxxiii–xxxiv, 50–80, 98–100, 133–35, 146–48, 181–84; waste of, prohibited, 70–73, 98; *see also* animals as things; resources, animals as

property, humans as. *See* resources, humans as; slavery

property, right not to be treated as, xxvii–xxviii, xxix, xxxiii–xxxiv; 98–102; *see also* animal rights; rights, basic

property, right to own, xxvii, 50–54

Protection of Animals Act (Britain, 1911), 7

Pythagoras, 212

qualitative differences between humans and animals. *See* special characteristics used to justify differential treatment of animals

qualitative distinction, definition of, 111, 212

"quasi-persons," 101

Rachels, James, 17

racism, xxix, 16, 84–85, 126–27, 173–74

Radford, Mike, 203–4

Rawls, John, 113, 122–23, 214

reciprocity theory of rights, 122–23, 214; *see also* Rawls, John

reflective equilibrium, between moral theory of human/animal relationship and competing intuitions, xxxvi, 162–63, 192; *see also* Rawls, John

Regalado v. United States, 64

Regan, Tom, xxxii–xxxiv, 208, 215, 220, 223

Regina v. Dudley & Stephens, 221–22

regulation. *See* animal exploitation

religion, animals and, 106–11, 112–13, 160–61, 186–87, 222, 223; as basis for Western property law, 53, 75, 93–94; Bible on, 51, 108, 109–11, 210, 211; Locke on, 51–53, 106–8

resources, animals as, xxvi, 50–80, 98–102, 106–11, 147–48, 153, 167–68; *see also* animal rights; animals as things; entertainment; experiments; fishing; food; fur; humane treatment principle; hunting; pets; property, animals as; teaching and education; toxicity testing

resources, humans as, xxvi, xxvii–xxviii, 86–98, 207, 208; Kant on, 209; *see also* rights, basic; slavery

Richardson v. Fairbanks North Star Borough, 78–79

rights, animal. *See* animal rights

rights, generally, xxvi–xxx, 168–69, 190–91; basic, xxvi, xxvii–xxviii, 92–98, 125–26, 191, 208; ecofeminism and, 149–50, 208–9; natural, 52, 75, 93–94; utilitarianism and, 132–33, 216–17, 220–21; *see also* animal rights

Roberts v. Ruggiero, 62

rodeos, 25–26

Rutgers University, 38

self-awareness, of animals, 113–15, 120–21, 136–42; Bentham on, 134; Damasio on, 114–15, 139, 219; Griffin on, 114, 138; Kant on, 3, 113; Singer on, 136–42; *see also* sentience; special characteristics

used to justify differential treatment of animals
self-defense, killing animals in, xxx, 158
Seligman, Martin, 41
sentience, xxii–xxiii, xxvi, xxxiii, xxxvi–xxxvii, 4–7, 99, 104–6, 111, 125–26, 128, 190, 209; Descartes on, 2; difficulties in defining, 6–7, 175–77; Regan on, xxxii–xxxiii; Singer on, xxxii, 137–38; *see also* unnecessary suffering
sexism, xxix, 16, 84–85, 126–27, 173–74; in Bible, 110–11
Shue, Henry, 94–95
Singer, Peter, xxxii, 135–48, 213–14, 217–19, 220
slaughter of food animals, 12–13, 75–76
slavery, xxviii, 126, 206, 207–8, 219–20; Bentham on, 132–34, 146–48, 216–17; in Bible, 110–11, 212; and equal consideration, xxvi, xxxii, 86–90, 98–100, 101; Regan on, 223; Singer on, 135–36, 220; *see also* equal inherent value; resources, humans as; rights, basic
social contract, animals and, 122–24, 214; *see also* Rawls, John
Sorabji, Richard, 119, 215
souls, animals and, 160–61, 222; Augustine on, 108; Aquinas on, 108, 112–13; Descartes on, 2
special characteristics used to justify differential treatment of animals, 111–27, 134, 136–42
speciesism, xxix, 126–27, 161, 173–74, 191
standing, 69–70, 205
State of North Carolina v. Fowler, 64–65, 204
State University of New York at Albany, 39
State University of New York at Oswego, 38
State v. Crichton, 62
State v. Hale, 88
State v. Mann, 87–88
State v. Schott, 72
State v. Tweedie, 70
Stoics, 122

Taub v. State, 63
teaching and education, use of animals for, xxi, xxiv, 49, 200; *see also* vivisection
testing, use of animals for. *See* toxicity testing
Theophrastus, 212
"things plus," 101
toxicity testing, use of animals for, xxi, xxiv, 45–49; *see also* vivisection
tradition, as basis for animal exploitation, 16, 21, 28, 31, 171–72; *see also* religion, animals and
trapping, 28–29
Tuck v. United States, 70
Tufts University, 39

U.S. Army, 41
U.S. Department of Agriculture, xx, 14, 34, 42–43, 73–74
U.S. Public Health Service, xxxvi–xxxvii
United States v. Holmes, 222
University of California at Berkeley, 38
University of California at Davis, 39
University of California at San Francisco, 39
University of Pennsylvania, 41, 44
University of Wisconsin, 39, 40
unnecessary suffering, xxi–xxv, xxix–xxx, 1, 30, 50, 81, 163; *see also* animal welfare; animal welfare laws; humane treatment principle
utilitarianism, 131–33, 216–17; *see also* Bentham, Jeremy; Singer, Peter

vegetarianism, 14, 17, 174–75, 179–80, 187–88; *see also* diet, meat-based; food, use of animals for
vivisection, 31–49, 57–58, 156–57; Regan on, 223; *see also* experiments; teaching and education; toxicity testing

Watson, Alan, 88, 210
wildlife agencies, 18–19
Wittgenstein, Ludwig, 210

zoos, 23–25, 205